GURKHA TALES

GURKHA TALES

GURKHA TALES

From Peace and War, 1945–2011

J. P. Cross

Foreword by Field Marshal Sir John Chapple

FRONTLINE BOOKS,
LONDON

First published in 2012 by Frontline Books,
an imprint of
Pen & Sword Books Ltd.,
47 Church Street, Barnsley, S. Yorkshire, S70 2AS.

Visit us at www.frontline-books.com, email info@frontline-books.com or
write to us at the above address.

ISBN 978-1-84832-690-3

CIP data records for this title are available from the British Library.

Typeset by JCS Publishing Services Ltd, www.jcs-publishing.co.uk

Printed and Bound by CPI Group (UK) Ltd, Croydon, CR0 4YY

Contents

To my countless Gurkha comrades-in-arms between 1944 and 1982, and to my many, many other friends in the Hills since then, my life would have been less colourful, less interesting and less happy without your constant companionship.

Illustrations

Foreword
by Field Marshal Sir John Chapple
GCB CBE DL

The Gurkha Tales set out here are just that – Tales of events and incidents about Gurkhas and those who served with them over the past sixty-five years or so. They have been brought together by J. P. Cross. They illustrate his long association with Gurkhas – an association which continues today. John Cross is one of very few non-Nepalis who is permitted to live, post-retirement, in Nepal.

These Tales provide a sub-text to the history of Gurkha service over the past half-century since the final stages of the Second World War. They do not purport to be any sort of official history. Indeed, it is necessary to know something of the campaigns and service of this period in order to appreciate what these Tales illustrate. They add much to understanding the contribution made by the Gurkha soldiers – and to the involvement of John Cross in many interesting but under-recorded aspects of this history.

John's own service of thirty-nine years with Gurkhas form much of the basis for these Tales. However, his knowledge of Nepal, having walked over 16,000km in the Hills, and met and talked to so many in their home villages, has added greatly to our understanding of those who have served in the Armies of India and Nepal and in the British Brigade of Gurkhas.

The Tales are not set out in chronological order – which makes it even more important to have some knowledge of the events, actions and campaigns. They cover service on the North-West Frontier, French Indo-China and the Regimental Centres before the Partition of India; then service during the Malayan Emergency including at the Jungle Warfare School and with the aboriginal people in northern Malaya; then into the Confrontation period in Borneo, with the raising of the Border Scouts by John Cross, and again much contact with Ibans, Land Dyaks and other tribal peoples. There follows John's service in Laos in the 1970s, and then his long time living and serving in Nepal. The Tales also include memoirs of the service of Nepal Army units.

John is well known for his amazing knowledge of other people's languages. He speaks so many languages and dialects of all the 'tribes' in Nepal, as well as those in Malaysia and Laos. There is mention in one Tale of learning Temiar (Senoi in North Malaya) in five days. Then he talked to the Meo in Laos and to many of the people in Sarawak. This love of language has led him to dig deep into the origins of many words which in turn give clues to the origins of many different peoples. This may also explain John's fascination with words, indeed being mesmerised by word-play in English.

There is so much to enjoy in these Gurkha Tales, and so much to learn about these superb soldiers with whom we have been privileged to serve.

Introduction

Gurkhas, certainly the older men and especially former soldiers, love telling stories. The habit of 'capping' stories is not confined to gnarled fingers grasping pint pots of ale in English pubs: one-time Gurkha warriors also manage to cap them just as well if not better. As my father told me, 'most stories have a cocked hat and a sword'.

Stories flow naturally. Many of those in this book have their genesis more than half a century ago, some even earlier, before wireless (we did not know 'radio' in those days), television, cell phones et cetera swamped the airwaves and made people 'more receivers than givers'. In the late 1970s, at the camp where western Gurkha recruiting took place, two hundred yards from the Indian border, a film was shown once a week; otherwise the only after-dinner entertainment was conversation. Visitors from Hong Kong or Britain were taken aback at having to be 'out-going' for a change and found the cut and thrust of conversation almost foreign and certainly half-forgotten: only then came their stories.

In Gurkha villages, after dark chiefly, the menfolk would call in to others' houses to discuss the day's events. When a soldier returned on leave or pension, great excitement ensued and his house would be crowded, with the fire the only source of light and warmth – and what stories followed until sleep overtook both recounter and listeners. Fifty to sixty years ago most elderly men

1

were barely literate (one of the tests for enlistment for a pre-World War II Gurkha was to count up to fifteen); there were no books and, even if there had been any, lighting in the houses was never bright enough to read anything by, even if a person were literate; yet again life was communal to a degree seldom seen in Britain. The family 'mattered' and the village was, almost by definition, an extended family.

Half a century ago not many Gurkhas managed to achieve the desired three victories in life: to reach the age of five in robust health; to find an honourable job, especially one with a pension, rather than the back-breaking and prematurely-aging toil of ploughing and reaping; to enjoy the pension without less successful but more senior and rapacious officials wanting their erroneously perceived 'cut' and then trying to bring forced and forged lawsuits to prevent a new house from being built or a new field from being bought and other men to maintain it, to say nothing of buying a shotgun for hunting.

Service in the army took men and, when they were senior enough their family, to new places with strange names and stranger people. As for overseas service, certainly during a war, while there always was the possibility of death or capture by the enemy, there was also the lure of a bravery award and faster promotion. As for the former, it didn't matter where a person was on the day of his death or the manner of his dying – a person's fate is written inside the forehead and he would have died at that time in any case wherever he might happen to be, home or abroad.

And now I must introduce myself. I, an Englishman, was fourteen when World War II broke out. I never thought I would have to fight for my country. However, at the magic age of seventeen years, nine months and two weeks, with the war still 'in the balance', it was incumbent on all citizens not in a reserved occupation to join up. I joined the army. If I had learnt 'gas' as a recruit I would not have had to spend two extra weeks learning it later, just at the critical time when troops were being mustered to invade Europe. It was that lack of military knowledge that put me in pole position for the first batch of men drafted, as opposed to volunteering, to go to India to take part in the war against the Japanese.

I was commissioned in India and, although linguistically a dullard, I was advised to join the Indian Army as the experience would stand me in good stead but only in a regiment that spoke the *lingua franca* of the Indian Army, Urdu, 'Even though, for you, one language might be one too many,' I was told. But, without volunteering for them, Fate sent me to be an officer of Gurkhas, so beginning a wonderful, virtually non-stop involvement with these magnificent people, in its sixty-seventh year as I write these words.

My elder brother, as near a genius as any I have met, was unnecessarily killed when his orders, from an Englishman to an Englishman in English, were misunderstood. How much more difficult would it be for me to avoid unnecessary deaths in Burma against the Japanese when leading Gurkhas and speaking their language? But my brother's ability somehow infused itself into me for forty-eight hours after his death, giving my body a strange tingling feeling, and, from having been an officer whose men would only follow him out of curiosity, my Nepali language ability blossomed miraculously.

It takes time and effort to be accepted by a different group of people, speaking a different language, worshipping different gods and ruled by different mores: just one example, I from a Christian island and they from a chiefly Hindu landlocked country. But, despite all these differences, there were enough similarities for a so-far unbreakable bond of trust to be perfected and this has stood the test of time however much politics intervened – higher authority, civil and military. The regimental British officer is the nerve end between the sentient, individual soldier and amorphous and anonymous authority, known generically as 'Sarkar'. The former is 'man to man', the latter looks on soldiers as an expensive collective commodity which, by definition, lacks humanity.

I was taught the Gurkhas' language, now known as Nepali, by an exemplary language teacher. He was an elderly lieutenant-colonel whose father had raised the 2/1 Gurkha Rifles in 1886 – and it was a great talking point at our last get-together for old 1 Gorkha Rifles men in 2011, a 125-year link. Such is important in a society where age and seniority are respected.

I suppose my nearness to Gurkhas has been more than most other officers' if only because in the first thirty years of my thirty-nine plus years' service I spent the equivalent of ten years 'under the canopy' in the jungles of Burma, Malaya and Borneo with them. At the end of hard day's patrolling or an irksome ambush, whispered or low-voiced gossip after stand-down came as naturally as night follows day. Also, during three long operations of fifty-two, seventy and eighty days on the Malay-Thai border with only ten men each time, we took it in turns telling a story after dark.

So, likewise, during the more than ten thousand miles I have walked in the mountains and hills of Nepal, mostly with my 'eyes' (I have had hardly any of my own eyesight since 1981) and surrogate son, Buddhiman Gurung, sharing home and hearth with many an old friend, even more stories came to my ears.

A typical nugget, that is too short to be a story in its own right, came from Buddhiman when he told me a tale he vividly remembered hearing when he was a lad. 'Much of the time the talk was on local matters, farming, politics, village history and family affairs,' he told me, 'but I especially remember one day when the conversation was exciting. The talk had got on to the cleverness of the British. One man, recently returned to the village on pension, told the most extraordinary story about men getting to the moon.

Everybody was thrilled and then one old fellow said he knew all about it so could explain how it could happen. "These fair-skinned ones, as cunning and as hairy as the monkey god, Hanuman, used to live somewhere up in the heavens, probably on the moon. They were strictly told not to eat the flesh of cows but they did eat it. So they were punished by having to live on earth with other men. They were told that they would only get back to the moon by effort and luck. Now, thousands of years later, they've done it!" All the others slowly nodded in agreement. How else could such a marvel have happened?'

The first story I wrote, after much hesitation, was in 1949. I saw the event I described as a tiny time capsule of something more than mundane trivia that could add flesh and flavour compared to an otherwise quickly forgotten, never-to-be recorded and otherwise colourless and insipid incident, so write it I did.

The recording habit slowly grew as hearing what the 'old sweats' as well as I myself found of interest made me realise that I, too, was encountering situations that, even if they were too short to include in anything except a letter home to fill the bottom of the last page, they were worth recording even, sometimes, in memory if not on paper.

And they were useful many years later. Since 2001 I have lectured all the young men only just recruited into the Brigade of Gurkhas and the Gurkha Contingent of the Singapore Police while still in Nepal and have used some of them as examples of 'what happens, or does not happen, if . . .'. The link from the known to the unknown, Nepal to Britain, Brunei, Singapore (but Hong Kong no longer), has helped, even just a little, to bridge the culture shock in store on leaving home and well-known surroundings behind. One recruit sent me a letter, 'Dear Grandfather, I was homesick until you made me laugh after which I felt I could face the future with confidence.' Another wrote, 'Dear Grandfather, recruit training was almost too hard to bear until I remembered some of the stories you had told us about what our fathers and grandfathers had done.'

So, please accept my offerings, all either written to fill a few pages of the Brigade of Gurkhas regimental magazine, *The Kukri* (and I thank the current editor for allowing such and previous editors for printing them) or written to friends in letters. What you have here is a mixture of what I felt was worth recording from my point of view and also from the Gurkhas' point, including such stories as number 1, where I start myself, and number 4, with Gurkhas merely in the background.

I hope you enjoy reading them as much I did writing them, even if there are 'no cocked hats or swords'.

❦ *1* ❧

Thirty-Eight Years Later

Looking back over the years the wonder is not so much that I was ever allowed to start serving so much that I was allowed to continue once launched, defying all the laws of military averages, escaping all redundancies and violating all the accepted rules of career planning, the definition of which could be 'a military confidence trick designed to make a person believe he has a Field Marshal's baton lurking somewhere in the bottom of his knapsack but making him do some unappetisingly murky jobs the while'. No posting out of Asia since 1944, none of your conventional staff jobs, thank you, except one period of penance as a GSO3 (they don't come any lower) in the late 1950s, and now, on the last lap, enlisting Gurkhas who, similarly, have no idea what it's really about. Thirty-eight years ago . . .

On 2 April 1943 I went to Enfield to volunteer for service in the Army. Had I not done so, I would have been called up the very next day. I felt that my show of patriotism might enable me to join the Regiment of my Choice, which, in turn, might shield me from one of the more perplexing organs of the Modern Army. To become an embryo infantryman would not detract from any glory there might be forthcoming and would placate an inborn aversion from and a latent allergy to matters technical.

The Recruiting Centre was the local Drill Hall. I went inside and looked around. Apart from a number of others looking as lost as myself, I saw many little tables and stalls dotted about, reminiscent of a vicarage bun-fight in happier times. I was ordered to visit one and thus started a series of tests which were run by brusque and impersonal men and which included almost everything includible between head and toe. To find my way from unmarked booth to unmarked booth was a mockery of a treasure hunt for a one-way ticket. I was baffled by failing to rejoin three pieces of lavatory chain, I was chastened by failing to give correct answers to a test I had felt appropriate to half-wits, I was told to strip and was embarrassed by my proximity to shivering nudity, all trying to fill glass bottles with an air of studied detachment until the problems of time and space overtook them at the very end. I was then told to put my clothes on and, after waiting some time, was called into the office. There was Authority, the Recruiting Officer, sitting amongst stained and squalid furniture which included an overcrowded desk littered with papers. His manner betrayed an indifference bordering on the apathetic. I took a pitying dislike to him and, in the brashness of youth, felt that if I finished up my service by only being allowed to recruit people, then I could count myself a failure. I was motioned to one side whilst he looked first at my Enlistment Form, then presumably at the result of my test papers. Both were uninspiring and he remained uninspired. He sighed, shook his head, absent-mindedly picked his teeth and started asking me the questions which would make me a soldier. He mumbled and interpolated to a degree that left me confused. I thereby failed correctly to answer one question which demanded a reply other than a direct affirmative and in the ensuing verbal mix-up I was loudly and soundly castigated 'a fool, like the rest of you all'. Thus I earned my first rebuke literally before the ink on the paper was dry.

In due course I received papers complete with the railway warrant for a one-way ticket, my army number and an order to report to Colchester. A train journey to the town, a bus ride to some unlovely cavalry barracks found me furtively making contact with the sentry at the gate, shyly asking directions at the Guard Room and hesitatingly looking for an Orderly Room at which to report my arrival. I eventually got to a Company Office which I can remember were printed all the words to the bugle calls. Some were mandatory: 'You cannot have a baby in the ITC' (which I had learnt meant Infantry Training Centre). Others were cautionary: 'Pioneer, Pioneer, Pioneer, Dog shit on the square'. Yet others were defamatory, like the Quarter Dress call: 'You've got a face like a chicken's arse'. I was frankly appalled by the indelicacy of it all.

My musings on the world of depravity that I had just entered were interrupted by a gruff request from nearby asking 'What the 'ell are you doing?' Anyone wearing plain clothes in wartime was suspect and one so dressed as I, well within the barrack precincts, was an obvious target. An Orderly Sergeant, or some such lesser godling, was nonplussed by my arrival. It appeared that I was a day ahead of the rest of my draft. I reluctantly entered the barrack room I had been peremptorily shown, feeling like a condemned man. It was a large barn of a place with two-storeyed 'bedcots' neatly arranged along two walls. It all smelt strongly of carbolic soap. At one end were two normal beds and a table at which sat two men. One was a grizzled and embittered corporal, the other his mercurial underling who found me an easy target. Both of these men, to my over-charged imagination, loomed more than unusually large. In fact the whole barrack area had, to that time, given me the impression of an unhappy and vengeful void, dotted with sullen, sardonic, morose men whose only fault was that there was another batch of recruits to train. The minutes ticked by with unnatural slowness and terrifying deliberation, both in the Mess Hall where, compared with the civilian standards, the food was lavish, and in the barrack room where the comparison was merely odious. Withering silence watched me undress that night and I realised the value of protective mingling with even such a small audience as those two NCOs. It was obvious, certainly as a short-term policy, that only a chameleon-like non-description and prosaic conformity would make life bearable.

The long-term was too remote to bother with. Thick army blankets on a straw-filled paillasse and pink pyjamas coincided only for that first night. 'Lights Out' gave a blessed seclusion seldom since encountered. Sleep was fitful.

Reveille blared all too soon and I discovered that an Orderly NCO really did shout 'Wakey! Wakey! Hands off cocks, hands on socks'. Later that morning I went to the company stores to draw my uniform and saw an old soldier, to me a land-locked version of the Ancient Mariner. He wore two inverted stripes on his left sleeve.

'Excuse me, please, Corporal,' I chirruped, 'but will you explain what those inverted stripes on your arm mean?' He appraised me sourly and said in a clipped monotone, tapping them with a tobacco-stained finger, 'Five years, my boy, five years . . .' There was a reflective pause and he added, '. . . and the first five years are the worst.'

❧   ❧

Five years, five months or five days, the time passed quickly. After recruit training I graduated to corps training and found myself a fledgling Lance Corporal. I was in command of a barrack room full of thirty hardened untamables, all bar one many years senior to me. I underwent a Section Leader's cadre, driving instruction and did my full whack of guard mounting and fatigue duties. In short I was learning what it was like to be the 'toad under the harrow'. I only won the soldiers' respect after I had had to resort to bare fists. As far as Higher Authority was concerned I still had a long way to go . . . but an awareness of protective colouring came to my rescue. The Company Sergeant-Major held a practice drill parade one Friday evening, prior to a Depot parade the next morning. In my hurry I forgot to take my bayonet with me, but reckoned that a rear-rank soldier might 'get away with it'. Alas, I was ordered to be Right Marker and one of the first commands was 'Fix bayonets'. We all knew that on the command 'Fix' you don't, but even so, the second command has to come, sooner or later. My immediate and instinctive reaction was to reach for my bayonet and, having embarked on a course of deceit, I carried on by pretending to fix it. Later I pretended to unfix it and was relieved, to say the least of it, when we were dismissed with nothing said. Two weeks later I asked for a 36-hour pass and was told, succinctly by the CSM, 'Yes, but you wouldn't 'ave got it if you 'adn't been through the motions that day!'

But it was not always so easy to react successfully to the unexpected. As soon as I came back from my 36-hour holiday a draft of young officers arrived and there was to be a demonstration Guard Mounting. The guard consisted of two NCOs and four Private Soldiers. Webbing equipment was worn, heavily blancoed and with brasses highly polished. Basic pouches and haversack, complete with waterproof groundsheet, mess tins, comprised the equipment. I was detailed as the second-in-command. Interest was intense the night before when Daily Detail was pinned to the notice board. 'Who was the inspecting officer?' Pros and cons, in minutest detail, were known about all those who took it in turn to inspect the guard. Most would have been singularly unflattered had they known the opinions we held of them. For the morrow we were dealing with an enigma, reported by some as an out-and-out rotter, by others as no worse than the rest. We were excused duties from mid-morning to get ready. Debs to a Palace garden party would have paid no less attention to their straps than we did to ours. The top of the haversack had to be in line with the shoulders, hence the straps had to be exactly the right length. Half an hour from guard mounting an excited Orderly Corporal ran in to say, 'Haven't you heard? It's all been changed! It's greatcoats on!' Having delivered his bombshell he cantered off. The significance to us was that the length of both beautifully blancoed belt and straps would have to be altered. This in itself would not have mattered had there been time to re-blanco. There was no time for the wretched stuff to dry so that belt and straps were altered with as much care as if dismantling a time-bomb.

On the square we awaited the Duty Officer. There were no spectators visible. The Officers' Mess was on one side of the square and it was presumed they would watch from the warmth of a room with a fire. There was no rancour, we would have done the same had we had the chance. The Duty Officer approached and we froze into immobility. Reports were given, compliments paid and salutes answered: the inspection had begun. The inspecting officer was tall and angular, and had the cautious tread of a hunter. His eyes darted everywhere and, except for the slow crunch of footsteps on gravel, the world stood still. Out of the corner of my eye I saw him approaching. I stared to my front as he reached me, towering somewhere above my head. I heard a distant voice say, 'Corporal, your belt is dirty.' The effect was instantaneous. The Orderly Sergeant minutely examined the even minuter offending tell-tale marks where the belt had been lengthened for that blasted greatcoat and then yelled 'Orderly Corporal' at the top of his voice to that individual standing ten yards away, presumably for such an auspicious occasion. 'Sir,' he bellowed, rushing forward as he did so. His voice echoed round the barracks flanking the square and gradually faded away. At the time I wondered how he did it. I was asked my number, rank, name and initials, which I duly gave. These were written down in a dog-eared notebook and he doubled back to his position of square-leg umpire. The inspection continued.

The front of both ranks having been scrutinised, the back then claimed the attention of Eagle-Eye and his yapping satellite, Kite Hawk. The one thing I was concerned about was that I felt my haversack straps had been lengthened too much even for a greatcoat. And the one thing I noticed the Duty Officer doing was lifting up the packs to see how tight the straps were. I felt vulnerable but hit on a desperate plan. When I judged he was two away from me I filled my lungs to bursting point, inflated my chest, tightened the offending straps and raised the haversack to the correct height, in line with my shoulders. I waited, statue-like. But to no avail because he must have seen my bursting red face and bulging eyes. He waited. He had more patience than I had lung power and, containing myself no longer, exhaled long and luxuriously. He pounced and, being deflated, my straps were looser than ever.

Another pantomime ensued, from which I knew there would be no reprieve. Nemesis caught up with me a week later. Sweating it out for seven days made it a relief when I was eventually warned. As luck would have it I was Orderly Corporal and had been instructing on a weapon training period. Coming off parade, wearing denim overalls and a steel helmet, I popped into the company office to get my platoon's mail. The office was sordid, dark and small, with an even darker passage outside. It had been a soldier's married quarter pre-war. I was yelled at by the CSM that I was 'up before the Company Commander, now!' He brushed aside my remonstrations about not being dressed for the part. I was ordered to stand to attention and take my helmet off. A passing Lance Corporal had his hat pulled off by the CSM who plonked it on my head, ordering me to stand still as he did so.

I was marched inside, if not the holy of holies, the next worst thing. 'Mark time, halt, right turn.' Simple, straightforward words of command. No danger of misunderstanding them. The Major had a small piece of paper in front of him. He started to read from it, without looking up.

'14499786, Lance Corporal Cross, J P ?'

I thought the question superfluous but, as he had not bothered to set eyes on me, I presumed he was just checking up.

'Sir.' No need for prevarication.

'You are charged with an act prejudicial to good order and military discipline in that you, at Colchester, on 23 February 1944, were shabbily turned out on Guard Mounting . . . what the bloody hell have you done with your hat?' he spat out venomously.

I was uncertain what was expected of me. I dimly realised that this last question was not in the script, was unrehearsed. The seconds ticked by and I was puzzled by the unexpected turn of events. In truth I had done nothing to my hat at all, in fact it was someone else's put there in the dark passage by the CSM. What little military training I had had made me realise that movement, unordered, was a heinous offence. Even so my left hand started a journey up the side of my trousers, sneaked past my waist, crawled up my side and eventually reached the summit and grasped the offending hat, only to find that I was wearing it back to front. In one brief flurry the hat, with the Regimental Badge, was back to the position long hallowed by tradition and my hand was back just behind the seam of my trousers. After some pithily delivered histrionics we settled down to the main course on the menu and it seemed rather a come-down only to be admonished. However, I was later looked on with awe by my comrades; but not by my company commander. He called me to one side two days later and said, 'You are no good as a Lance Corporal, so I'm sending you off to try your luck as a Second Lieutenant.'

[1981]

~ *2* ~

1944

Two days after D-Day, on 8 June 1944, not yet nineteen, I
found myself with 120 others in a large draft, the first of its
kind, for training in India. While waiting for our boat we had
been given lectures to prepare us for our new existence. I can
recall only two; one on the composition of the Indian Army and
the other on health in the tropics. Once again I was shocked when
the medical officer, without a trace of a smile, warned us about
sex. 'Don't forget, a woman for children, a boy for pleasure, but for
real ecstasy, a goat.'

We embarked on the antiquated troopship SS *Maloja*, the
flagship of the convoy, and sailed into the Atlantic, escorted by
an aircraft carrier and at least two destroyers. We swung back
through the Mediterranean, passing the Gibraltar Narrows with
paravanes out, feeling slightly heroic when told that we were only
the second convoy to sail that way and wondering what would
happen after being spotted by an enemy aircraft. We reached Port
Said unscathed.

'You're going the wrong way,' the troops guarding the Suez
Canal shouted at us as we steamed through. 'Who's King back
there now?' 'Send your washing back to England? Call this overseas service?' were some of the more printable soldierly witticisms
offered in return.

The time spent in the Red Sea (with a submarine escort) was

15

a penance: crowded, stuffy mess decks; heaving, sweaty bodies; unnatural proximity; and a heat none of us had ever imagined. The boat turned round and steamed north for one hour each evening to allow some breeze to pervade below decks. It rained slightly as we stretched our legs in Aden.

We were taught 'Roman' Urdu, the *lingua franca* of the Indian Army, by an officer whose patience proved less durable than my stupidity. I just could not make sense of its arabesque, nasal cadences, its strange sounding vowels nor the intricacies of its 'soft' and 'hard' consonants. However much I chanted *yih mez hai* – this is a table; *wuh kursi hai* – that is a chair, I could not relate to real tables and chairs. In short, I was such a dunce that I was banned from classes, being given the option of working in the galley or being an officer's batman. I told the 'bloke' that I had elected the galley fatigues and the Sergeant Major that I would be batman. For two days I played hooky; for the last week of the voyage I scrubbed the mess decks every morning in addition to other expropriatory chores. We were all relieved to get off the boat at Bombay.

Bombay! The gateway to India! How romantic it had sounded from afar but how sordid it looked and how horrible it smelt from close quarters. I gazed in fascinated horror at the crowds of teeming humanity, ever milling, scantily dressed and, for the most part, volubly gesticulating, excitably demonstrative and depressingly poor. The turbans, the beards, the dhotis, the shirts outside the trousers, the pyjamas by day could become unnoticed features of the everyday landscape. What jarred then – and ever after – were the pitiful, the blind, the beggars, the wheedling children, the laden women, the scavenging dogs, the bare-ribbed horses pulling overloaded gharries, their bulb horns honking mournfully, the old and rheumy-eyed, the young prematurely shrivelled, ever eddying and swirling in kaleidoscopic patterns in the monsoon-laden, fetid air. The raucous black crows and cows wandering in the streets with an air of indifference were the only living creatures seemingly unaffected by the heat, the clamour and the squalor.

Doors on Indian railway carriages open inwards and it was fun to sit on the steps, in a cooling breeze, watching the landscape go by. The three-day rail journey north to Delhi then on up to the Indian Military Academy at Dehra Dun, merely enlarged the canvas. The beggars at the railway stations, maimed, blind, clothed in rags and underfed, the mangy, slinking curs, the skeletal cattle, the impoverished shacks, even using boiling water from the engine to brew tea, all jarred my senses. At dawn on the second morning the rails were so slippery that the wheels could get no traction and the train could not get up a gradient. We were ordered out to push it up! It was another world, one totally alien to me. Even the lightning on the horizon was taken for flashes from Japanese artillery fire!

I had a letter of introduction to the Viceroy, Field Marshal Lord Wavell, given to me by my great-uncle, a one-time classmate of the Highest in the Land. 'Give it to Archie,' had been my instructions but, even as I looked furtively at the imposing address on the envelope as we waited for our next train at Delhi station, I knew that the gap between me and the Viceroy was wider than the one between Dives and Lazarus. I never did use it and, many years later, burnt it unopened.

And so, a month after we left England, we arrived at the Indian Military Academy (the 'Sandhurst of India', with Gentlemen Cadets as opposed to the mere officer cadets at other training schools), our destination and home for the next five months. We were met by the officers who were going to teach us and who wore exciting new cap badges and shoulder titles. The expressions on their faces as they regarded us, travel-worn and pale, long-haired and badly turned-out, the first-ever course to come *en masse* from England, showed us as much enthusiasm as we had shown for the Bombay crowds. To us, used to seeing an older generation of officer in England, they struck us as incredibly young compared with their grizzled counterparts on the Home Establishment. Not one word was spoken until a gorgeously starched wonder leisurely strolled over to us but, instead of any word of welcome, it looked down its nose and drawled, 'If you want a pee, go behind that hedge there.' We had arrived.

The camp was superb, set in spacious grounds made wonderfully green by the monsoon rain. After the cramped conditions on board ship, our accommodation – and being looked after by a bearer – was palatial. Here we could be, and were, happy.

Once our training had started, we found what the old lags had said was true, 'the scene changes, but the music never'. For elementary subjects we were taken in hand by gnarled British warrant officers and sergeants who told us that 'when in Rome you do as India does. Get it?' And get it we did. As we progressed with our training, the officers taught us tactics and jungle warfare. Only now did those earlier lectures on the Indian Army penetrate my insular mind and begin to make sense. It was only when these different peoples were produced in the flesh that I could equate a name with a type. I don't think it ever occurred to me that by no means did all Indians speak Urdu as their first language. The majority of India's millions speak their own. I found I could get on with the local people I came into contact with. I tried out my smattering of Urdu as and how I could but it was not yet enough for a proper conversation.

One of the peoples we heard about were the Gurkhas of Nepal. We were told that Nepal was, and always had been, a sovereign Himalayan state, nothing to do with India, with entry forbidden to all outsiders; that, ever since 1815, the Gurkhas had come down from their mountain villages to join the army because they liked service under the British. It was paradoxical that neither group could visit, let alone serve in, the country of the other's birth or domicile. Wherever else did this situation pertain? We heard that they were very loyal, very brave and tractable, and that they were apt to chop their enemies' heads off with a deadly knife called a kukri. It took a long time for an outsider to be accepted by them, after which there was nothing they would not do for that person. People said that it was a great privilege to serve with the Gurkhas who were seen as superior to most, if not all Indians, and equal to the best the British Army could produce. Some went as far as to say that they were the finest soldiers in the world.

The first time I came across a group of them at close quarters was when we went on a jungle training exercise and they acted as enemy. Short men, with skins coloured brown to wheaten, shaven-pated with smooth, round faces, high cheek bones and almond eyes, they were squatting in a group during a lull, talking. I, struggling with the compulsory Roman Urdu and not managing at all, listened in awe to the staccato grunts and atonal ululations of their normal conversation. How could anyone understand, let alone speak, such a language?

They emanated a presence and showed an inner strength which fascinated me but, so overwhelmed was I at their professionalism and high standards, I told myself I would never be good enough for service with them. Despite the initial attraction, they were not for me – or was it I was not for them?

The British subalterns in the three Gurkha regimental centres in Dehra Dun behaved arrogantly, as if they were inordinately superior to other men. I did not like them although, to be fair, I only saw them occasionally, when I went out at weekends and walked around the town or when Gurkhas acted as 'exercise enemy'. I noticed how the Gurkhas themselves clammed up when one of their young officers came upon them, how they answered in the brusquest of monosyllables. There seemed to be no rapport and yet, when a captain or a major spoke to them off parade, there would be mirth, a flashing of wonderful smiles, the intimacy of empathy, harmony and a common purpose. Was it a case of those subalterns not feeling as exalted as had they been with lesser soldiers? I later learnt that it was not so much the extra rank and a year or so in age but the confidence that the Gurkhas had in these officers and the love that their officers had for them that made such a difference. With the Gurkhas, at last, I found that those who should matter, the soldiers, did matter to their officers. I was young, immature and impressionable – and very impressed.

Six weeks or so from the end of our course, we were asked to give three regiments we would like to be commissioned into, as well as stating did we want to go to the British Army, Indian Army or be attached to an Indian regiment yet commissioned into a British regiment. I really had no idea, so I sought advice from the Company Second-in-Command, a man called Griffiths, who had been at school with my elder brother, Tim. Although I might be one of those about whom it could be said that his men would follow him if only out of curiosity, he told me to try not to go to a British unit as any experience in the Indian Army would stand me in good stead. However, I was advised not to go into the Gurkhas as 'linguistically, you're not even up to speaking Urdu', let alone my having to learn a second language, Nepali. So I decided to join an Indian not a British unit, dismissing the idea of Gurkhas entirely.

I therefore applied, along with five others and advice from Captain Griffiths, for one of three Indian regiments. A letter was sent to the depot of our first choice with our names, and recommendations. I was number five on the list. Even though there was talk about Indian independence some time in the future, it did not mean much to us. In those days, as far as I can recall, we did not read newspapers, nor did we have wirelesses. The political situation made no impression on us: we were intent on being commissioned and getting to the war, if only to prove ourselves to ourselves. However, as the future was murky (not so much as to the outcome of the war but what would happen to India and when) most of us volunteered to be commissioned into a British Army regiment and then be attached to the Indian Army. This is what I did. As I remember it, only a few of my batch were commissioned into the Indian Army.

I had nearly been relegated as I had to go into hospital with 'dhobi itch', a skin disease that makes walking a penance. I was promoted to Cadet Quarter Master Sergeant and made to look after the stores, riding to inescapably important field training in vehicles that took the hot meals out.

In early December we were told our future. I was to be commissioned into the British Army (not into the earlier 'Regiment of my Choice'!) but not posted to the Indian 'push' Griffiths had suggested. Only the first four on his list were selected. I found, to my consternation, that I had been posted to the First Gurkha Rifles – and that without passing my written Elementary Urdu examination, let alone my fears of inadequacy! Again, not the Regiment of my Choice!

None of that dulled the thrill of having 'made it'. Those little pips on my shoulders were, in themselves, only small emblems of the great journey I had made till then, however great the real change in status, purpose and knowledge they did represent. From the impersonal approach during my training in England, proud though I had been to become a lance corporal, where I never felt I belonged – 'belonging is sharing' – to being part of an extended family was another sort of change and one that stayed with me from that special day, 10 December 1944, for the rest of my service.

❦   ❧

On 27 December 1944 I reached the First Gurkha Rifles Regimental Centre at Dharmsala, later to become famous as where the Dalai Lama took residence after fleeing Tibet. The narrow-gauge track down from Simla, where I had been on leave, gave way to the broad-gauge railway in the plains. At one station I went to have a look at the engine and the driver saw 1 GR on my shoulders and asked if that stood for Indian Government Railways? This was not as bad as the British Service officer who thought that DOGRA on a shoulder title did not refer to the eponymically named regiment composed of Hindu Dogras from the Punjab but stood for Duke of Gloucester's Royal Artillery! Then I changed again on to another narrow-gauge line that wound its way through low hills to the railhead at the small town of Pathankot. From there it was a road journey of about fifty miles, along a gently rising valley until a steeper climb for the last 3,000 feet into the clear, crisp air, where pine and rhododendron forests vied for supremacy and Simla was a hundred miles away across the haze. The centre itself was situated at about 5,000 feet above sea level, sprawled over the hills that turned to mountains that were perpetually under snow. It had been built, temporarily, many years before and had been added to until it had spilled into some of the lower valleys. The men's lines had long been condemned but finance, that age-old bogey, stalked with deadening effect here as in so many other places in the Army of Hind. There was no electricity or running water and all conditions were rudimentary. A backlog of subalterns had been waiting, some for more than a year, for a posting to an active battalion. It seemed that I, too, would be stuck there for ages. Meanwhile, I was posted to a recruit training company to learn the rudiments of all that which is needed to be a commander of Gurkhas.

I had to come to terms with that quintessential aspect of the Indian Army, and indeed the Brigade of Gurkhas today, namely *kaida*, the proper way of doing things in a tightly knit, well-organised extended family that a good unit is. Each unit has its own *kaida*. In the regimental centre it was stiff and reeked of pre-war snobbery, with the introduction of 'temporary commissions' such officers were known as 'temporary gentlemen' and the toast to the King Emperor on Mess Nights was prefaced, more than once, 'Gentlemen and Temporary Officers'. Contact with soldiers was mainly during parade hours. Until a new officer is accepted, he is minutely observed, much more than he realises. Quirks and foibles are watched and, provided nothing untoward is noticed, acceptance comes sooner or later, probably with a nickname that is seldom known by the officer concerned.

In rare cases when the senior Gurkha officer, the Subedar Major, saw that a particular British officer's chemistry simply would not be in accordance with what the Gurkhas were used to or would accept, preventive action would be taken. The commanding officer would be told that, if the officer remained, the Subedar Major could not accept responsibility for any mishap. In the British Army such events happen the other way round, any misfit only being got rid of after the 'omelette hits the fan'.

That winter there was exceptionally heavy snow. We had about 14 feet in two days. Roads were blocked for miles around and, if they remained impassable, rations would be in short supply. Recruits were formed into gangs and armed with plates, there being a woeful shortage of spades and shovels, to open the road leading up from the plains. No military work could take place. The young Gurkhas had not been away from home long enough to lose their freshness so the nearest any of us got to training for war was when one gang ambushed another with a barrage of snowballs!

Those who had had boots issued wore them, sodden, uncomfortable and strange. Those with no boots wore sandals. The lads, none over eighteen years of age, had never worn boots before. One made the mistake, not only of putting the boots on the wrong feet, but lacing them together. The first step he tried to take saw him crashing down on the ground, bursting his nose open. He was taken to the hospital, admitted and issued with a shroud as well as pyjamas. The Irish doctor did not think he would die because of a sore nose but he had been found deficient of shrouds on the last inspection and was determined to leave nothing to chance. Every person admitted to the hospital had to sign for one – just in case. This practice had to be stopped soon afterwards as it was having a depressing effect on morale.

The two eldest soldiers worked in the band store. Both were reservists who had been considered too old for service in the Kaiser's War. Both wore the medal ribbon of the Tirah campaign of 1897, the elder having been enlisted in 1891, the younger in 1892.

And so the seminal year of 1944 came to its close: I had started a lifetime with the Gurkhas but, at that time, had no idea, nor could I have had. It took years to develop.

❧ 3 ❧

Bombs and More Bombs

Two days after the Atom Bombs were dropped I was ordered to go to 20 Div HQ to procure an unexpected allotment of beer, a rarity in those days. I set off accompanied by two Gurkha soldiers who asked me to tell them about this new bomb. I had as little idea as they and my Nepali was not good enough to sustain a technical conversation. On our way back we passed a mobile canteen run by the Women's Auxiliary Service (Burma), a gallant band of British ladies. The Gurkhas asked if they could stop and buy a cup of tea. They got out of the Jeep and I waited. Presently the two soldiers came back, looking slightly forlorn. They said the canteen was no good, had not got what they wanted. I sympathised. 'What was it you were looking for?' I asked. 'Did you get any tea?'

'Oh, we got our tea all right', they said, 'but we could not get any horizontal bombs.'

'Couldn't get what?' I queried. Came the same amazing reply; there were no horizontal bombs.

Despite being short of time, I was too intrigued by this enigma to leave without trying to solve it.

'Go and look again, they may have found one by now,' I told them.

Five minutes later they returned empty-handed, still dispirited. This time would I go and get 'it', whatever 'it' was. Having no idea of what to look for I asked for details. 'Describe it to me.'

'It's small and cool.'

I remembered the almost novelty capsules of compressed air and insect repellent we had recently been issued with. 'Oh, I know. It's one of those anti-mosquito squirt bombs you're after!'

Their answer was frank and emphatic. 'No, it is nothing like what you describe. Please go and find out yourself.'

So I went to find out.

I approached the truck diffidently and asked the British soldier driver what new stock there was, if any.

'Nothing much, sir, only a few so-and-sos,' and he rattled off the names of some common household toilet requisites. Obviously nothing there so, taking the bull by the horns and feeling a complete fool, I asked him; 'Have you by any chance any horizontal bombs?' He took the question as though he were always being asked for such commodities and evinced no surprise.

He answered perfectly normally. 'No sir, but if you ask one of the ladies inside, I'm sure that she'll be able to help you.'

This I did, asking for 'a horizontal bomb – one of the cool ones'.

The wretched girl was taken aback and, asking to be excused, went to consult her superior. Back they both came and asked me what it was I really wanted. As I couldn't tell them I wished that I had never stopped at the canteen, thus avoiding this embarrassing situation. I asked if one of my men could be allowed inside for he had been so sure that 'horizontal bombs' were sold.

Reluctantly permission was given. I called one of the soldiers over and said that the Memsahib had allowed him in, just this once, so be quick but she was sure there weren't any . . .

The Gurkha was not listening. He was looking around and, stiffening like a terrier scenting a rat, suddenly pounced on a small cardboard box. He put his hand in and, with the air of one who has known he was right all along, produced a small bottle.

'Lo, sahib, a horizontal bomb,' he said with quiet satisfaction. I looked at the label and there it was, clearly written – Oriental Balm.

He paid for it and we left in silence, nor did we speak until I dismissed the Jeep back in the battalion.

[1950]

❧ 4 ❧

An Unusual Secret Weapon

August–September 1945.

'All Japanese forces in French Indo-China have been ordered to fly a black flag, denoting surrender.' That edict made a great impression on me, as indeed did the rules of conduct laid down for our relations with the surrendered Japanese forces:

> . . . There will be no fraternising whatever between Japanese and Allied forces. In dealing with Japanese your behaviour will be guarded and coldly polite. You will, in the case of senior Japanese officers, use their correct titles. You will not shake hands with them . . . In no case will British and Japanese officers feed in the same room, nor will tea be offered at any meeting. Any Japanese who come to receive orders or report should be kept at arm's length, e.g. with a table between you and them, and they should not be allowed to sit at the same table . . .

All Japanese officers had to salute allied soldiers of all ranks.

To me there was something fitting and ultimate about having a black flag. For too long the Rising Sun of the Japanese flag had dominated too many places and now their sun was set. The Japanese, who had swept all before them at the start of the war, had been ordered to stop fighting. In Burma, where they had lost the war, that made sense to them. In Indo-China, where they had had no fighting, it was not easy for them to understand how they had lost the war. Luckily for the Allies the Emperor's edict was final and the Japanese conformed. The rules of conduct, the restrictions and petty embarrassments were not harsh but designed to humble by loss of face.

The Vietnamese we came into contact with, condescendingly called Annamites by the French, were small, lithe people with faces not unlike the Chinese but, in the main, darker skinned. Their language was beyond any of us; a high-pitched twittering as of many sparrows. The only way we could talk to them directly was by using French but even that had its problems as not all of them spoke it and those who did had an accent unfamiliar to our ears. If that was not enough, so little rapport was there between the locals and their colonial masters that we British had to speak French well enough to be understood but badly enough to be taken for someone who was not French. We were, initially, accepted in a friendly way.

The French, pro-Vichy colonials – and who was it who so aptly said that only French colonials like French colonials? – should have been in charge of Saigon but they were so ineffectual they soon had to hand their duties over, but to whom? We had been detailed to collect and back-load Japanese military stores from various installations so were unable to take on those French responsibilities. The only people who could were the Japanese but French national pride, or what was left of it, baulked at their soldiers handing over duties to the Japanese even if the Japanese could have been persuaded to take them over from the French. A compromise was reached: the British would take over from the French in the morning and hand over to the Japanese in the evening. In the event all went smoothly but there was one moment of tension when one Gurkha guard commander, a naik (corporal), found that his opposite number, a second lieutenant, had to draw his sword to salute with. Discipline on both sides prevailed but the Gurkha looked uncomfortable till the sword was sheathed.

Tension again surfaced that evening when the French took over from the British who were guarding the senior Frenchman's residence, General Le Clerc. A Guard of Honour from both countries was drawn up in front on either side of two flagpoles. For some reason known only to the planners, 1/1 GR (my unit) had to provide a small party of men both to haul down the Union Jack on Last Post being sounded and unfurl the Tricolor when Reveille was blown. The parade, attended by both civil and military dignitaries, was a solemn affair.

After preliminaries, arms were presented and officers saluted. Last Post was played and the Union Jack slowly hauled down. As soon as that was completed the bugler started blowing Reveille. The NCO in charge of the flags, the naik, had been briefed on the importance of the occasion but he had tied both knots on the French pole too tightly, the one at the base and the other that held the Tricolor. He could not get it open with his fingers even with frantic tugging so, horror! he bent down and undid the lower knot using his powerful teeth. The rope swung free, was tugged, but now the upper knot was seen to be too tight.

By this time Reveille had been blown and a strained look became apparent on some of the faces of both spectators and participants. The very honour of France was at stake should her flag be disgraced. Anxiety was palpable as the naik looked at the offending rope as he decided how to tackle this new and even more knotty problem. He sat down, took his boots off and then, horror of all horrors, he was observed drawing his kukri. He looked up at the tightly furled flag and, for one dreadful moment, ghastly visions of mutilated flags and ropes and flag poles must have occurred to many. But, watched by all in utter fascination – tired arms still in the saluting position – he swarmed up the pole and forced the knot open with the blade, supremely oblivious that he had saved a nation's honour.

The command 'Order Arms' was given and the ceremony continued as if nothing unusual had happened. After the parade, apart from a little stiffness in the arms, all was bonhomie. The French were full of praise, vastly impressed by this show of initiative. 'Ah, les Gorkhas, trés gallants, c'etai magnifique. Nous n'avons jamais vu . . .'

❧   ❧

Not long after we arrived it was evident that there was going to be trouble between the French civilians and the local population. The man in overall charge of the forces in the south was Major General Douglas Gracey. His orders were to control the area surrounding the two Japanese headquarters, one in Saigon itself and the other, at Dalat, a hill station not far away. Gracey found himself in an unenviable position, squeezed from many sides: by the French and the Vietminh (the shortened form of 'Vietnam League of Independence'); by Lord Louis Mountbatten, the Supreme Commander, who was not only ambitious and politically motivated but was also at 'personality odds' with him; by a Labour government in Great Britain that was not sympathetic to matters colonial and heavily in debt; by the Viceroy and Commander-in-Chief in India wanting his army back without getting involved in someone else's war; by Indian politicians to whom the presence of Indian troops helping restore French colonialism (and Dutch in Java) was anathema; and by the Japanese army which was 'undefeated'.

The situation quickly deteriorated as the Vietminh came to realise that the French were to be given back control of the country, and incidents of shooting were a nightly occurrence. Both Saigon and its Chinatown, Cholon, were dangerous places. The arrogance of the French towards their colonies has been well documented; the cruel exploitation and brutal maltreatment and contempt of the Tonkinese, Annamites and others in Indo-China shown during that phase manured seeds of bitterness and frustration already sowed and a burning desire to be rid of their masters. It was bitter irony for so many Vietnamese that, when the northern communists did eventually prevail, communism was as much a failure as it has been everywhere, with its mismanagement, corruption, privilege, repression, intransigence and cruelty on a par with the previous French colonial practice, however much Frenchmen would argue to the contrary. Their 'outrageous overestimation of their own worth' was a cardinal error.

Proof of further nastinesses was forthcoming when leaflets (I still have my copy) were smuggled into the Gia Dinh girls' school where the battalion was billeted. Headed SOLDIERS OF THE BRITISH ARMY, the message was short and to the point:

> An armed conflict may occur between French imperialists and us, the Vietnamese.
> Be prudent and never ramble about with the French.

So prudent we were, nor did we ramble about with them except occasionally when we went to swim at Le Cercle Sportif, irreverently re-christened 'The Sporting Gooly', where the women besported themselves with more faith than elastic.

One afternoon there was a film show in town that was supposed to be anti-Vichy in sentiment, and therefore unpopular with the local French inhabitants. In order to control any possible disturbances, I was ordered to take a platoon of Gurkhas to guard the cinema, inside and outside. At this unexpected display of force the audience could only give vent to their feelings with some fearsome-sounding Gallic oaths. Two hours later the crowd streamed out into the road. A car, slowly driven by a Japanese, came past and a woman cyclist, swerving to miss an obstruction, hit it. She fell off and immediately the French formed a circle around the car and started belabouring the hapless driver. Reactions pent up by frustrating inactivity in the cinema found an outlet. The Japanese sat steady, with an embarrassed smile, as blows smote him from all sides. The woman had, by this time, picked herself up and was rapidly disappearing. I was unhappy to see the luckless driver as a target of pent-up French emotions but I did not see how to redress the situation. More exploratorily than with conviction, I shouted 'Oy!' at the top of my voice and the effect was instantaneous. The Frenchmen stepped back, glaring at me as I waved the Japanese on. The engine was still ticking over and he needed no second bidding. I found myself filling the vacuum and wished I had not been so impetuous.

To stop any Gallic onslaught I put my hand out and, sub-consciously remembering being punished at school for getting a supposedly simple phrase wrong, brought it out unhesitatingly, loudly and with great authority. '"Ou sont les bagues de la reine?" which does not mean 'where are the queen's knickers', I added in English so a casual observer would not be muddled as I had been in those early days.

The effect was gratifyingly startling and, before the French crowd could realise that my message was inappropriate, albeit well timed, I had reached the safety of my platoon, now reformed nearby. 'What did you say?' the driver asked me as we drove off. For a moment I toyed with the idea of giving a Nepali rendering of my few words but regretfully decided I was not up to it. I took a side step away from the truth and said I was invoking royalty.

It may not be generally known that two Japanese battalions operated under Indian Army command during this brief campaign, both under 1/1 GR. In the Japanese army a battalion, butai, took its name from its commander, normally a major. One was the Takahashi Butai under a major; the second was the Yamagishi Butai, under a captain. Both men were experienced and shrewd operators who had spent many years fighting the Chinese. We came to know them well and found the restrictions imposed on us in our dealings with them irksome. Even so, relations were cordial. Both Japanese commanders sensed our unease and never, in any way, took advantage of our feelings. They had to come and report to us every evening. Their staff work, especially regarding reports, maps and diagrams, was faultless. As Intelligence Officer, I helped with these reports.

One day Major Takahashi and his interpreter marched in, stood to attention one side of the table behind which we were seated and saluted, bending forward from the waist as their hands came up to their hats, halfway between our army and navy salutes.

'Good evening, Gentlemen.'

'Good evening.'

'We have a report.'

'Please give us your report.'

'We have captured a Russian. Shall we kill him or bring him to you?'

'Bring him to us. How do you know he is a Russian?'

'Because of his uniform and because he is carrying a jar of coffee.'

The information was given with the quiet authority of one who talks from a position of strength because what he says is true. We did not follow the logic of the coffee but had the manners not to seem puzzled. Later on we speculated among ourselves about this curious affair. Russia was one of the 'Big Four' and an ally. We could not believe it was capable of organising clandestine operations against wartime comrades in arms, but how wrong we were.

When the Russian appeared on the morrow he was clasping a large glass jar full of roasted coffee beans. Red-haired and stocky, he was wearing khaki drill, had a yellow hammer-and-sickle emblem on a red background on each lapel, with a similar badge stuck into his khaki forage cap. He was put in the cells and kept there until Higher Authority told us to send him to Saigon. We had his clothes laundered for him but drank his coffee, which was delicious.

We sent him south to Saigon three days later, he protesting volubly that he would talk to no one except the Soviet ambassador. He would not believe us when we told him that there was no Soviet representation in Saigon. We never heard of him again.

Guerrilla activity increased in tempo. In November orders came to send a column, code-named 'Clarkol' – under Major R. W. Clark, hence its name – north to a village called Ben Cat. Its task was to locate and destroy a Vietminh force that had ambushed and caused casualties to a company of the Yamagishi Butai. The infantry element was to be our own B Company and three rifle companies of the Yamagishi. I was detailed as the column second-in-command. We moved north with a strong escort of armoured cars of the 16th Cavalry, commanded by Major Sawney, a versatile Indian officer who spoke impeccable English and quickly rose to great heights after Indian independence. The only all-British unit in the division, 114 Field Regiment, Royal Artillery, sent its contingent as did the Jat machine-gunners already with us in Thu Dau Mot, our combined base.

We reached Ben Cat that evening, after a tiring day during which many Vietminh roadblocks of felled trees had to be cleared. Major Clark went to meet the Japanese commander at his house – the largest in the village – and was kept waiting for a quarter of an hour before he came downstairs with a woman. He was dealt with curtly. Some of the Gurkhas spat their disgust as the Japanese major and his 'keep' passed them. Troops were settled for the night and orders for the next day were to be given only when a Japanese patrol returned.

At 8 o'clock that evening elements of all interested groups assembled in the house where Major Clark had set up his headquarters. It appeared that there was a group of about fifty guerrillas to our south in a triangle of country, the apex of which pointed to Saigon. The gunners were to remain on the northern 'base' road while the Jat machine-gunners and the armoured cars were to patrol the other two roads. The infantry was to sweep southwards, spread out widely at first but concentrating as the country tapered to a point. It was hoped to finish the operation in one day. Major Clark, being committed to overall command, I wondered how B Company, 1/1 GR, and the Yamagishi Butai would manage when my thoughts were rudely interrupted by hearing that 'Captain Cross is the commander of all the infantry'. We were to drive to as near where the Vietminh were suspected then patrol south of foot, searching for them.

The edict from the highest laid down that no Japanese would give orders to Allied troops. Military common sense, however, argued against me, with only ten months' commissioned service, commanding the equivalent of a battalion, three parts of which already had a commander who was battle-proven and with no common language.

I spent a restless night, going to bed with my head in a whirl. So nervous was I that I knocked over the only lamp there was in the house and we had to go to bed in the dark. I was severely cursed. In a vivid dream my elder brother, Timothy, who had been killed in Europe a year before and with whom I was very close, gave me advice on what to do on the morrow. 'Be yourself, keep calm, you'll manage,' he told me. I slept on comforted and was awoken at

3 o'clock, refreshed. I dressed and went outside to find the convoy assembling and the men falling in, an untidy jigsaw puzzle so cleverly putting itself together.

The convoy moved off at dawn. I was in the leading vehicle with three Gurkhas as bodyguards. Driving slowly along a winding road with cover on either side, shots rang out as Vietminh opened fire on us. So much on tenterhooks was I that I was out of the truck with my three men, over a bank and towards the scene of firing before I realised it was pointless my barking with so many dogs under my command. Even so, my stupidity raised my morale and luckily had a depressing effect on the opposition because they were seen, in the half-light of dawn, running away. Japanese soldiers caught me up and joined in the firefight. We did not give chase as we were on a tight movement schedule. On we drove.

We moved off on foot dead on time. With me were Yamagishi and his staff, my three Gurkha gunmen and, on my right, the company of Gurkhas. One of Yamagishi's companies was on its right and the other two away on the left. We advanced steadily through elephant grass, scrub and patches of rubber trees for about two hours with no incident.

When firing broke out I was nonplussed. It came from a rubber plantation in front of us, about 200 yards away. Between us and the guerrillas the country was reasonably open and sloped down to a small river that flowed across our front. I looked around and tried to pinpoint the fire. As I did a voice sounded in my ear and I turned to see the Japanese interpreter bending forward, hissing his respects, his solar pith helmet under his left arm, with a water bottle in his right hand and a Japanese–English dictionary in his left. He was newly appointed and quiveringly nervous. Probably we were both equally green.

'Respected sir, Captain Yamagishi sends his respects and respectfully requests you to adopt the lying position.'

Looking around I saw that we two were the only ones not lying down and, in all probability, presenting good, though small, targets. We continued our conversation in the prone position.

'Respected sir,' the interpreter hissed, looking happier now he was closer to nature than originally designed. 'Captain Yamagishi respectfully asks your respected permission to fire his mortars.'

The interpreter squirmed away to give my respected permission and the Japanese fired their mortars for about ten minutes, after which Captain Yamagishi and I, aided by the interpreter, held a short confabulation. I suggested, in my grandiose ignorance, a company attack. I was respectfully asked if I would mind if Yamagishi could have my permission to send a section. I gave it – having not much option – and was intrigued to see ten men, commanded by a second lieutenant armed only with a sword, disappear down the slope a few minutes later. After a short while they appeared some way up on the far side, near an overgrown rubber plantation. They cast about, turned and waved us forward.

The main body moved off downhill in extended line. My mind was already at the top of the hill when I reached the river so I was frightened out of my wits by seeing a Japanese head come up from between my knees and my crotch and felt myself being heaved into the air. Frightful visions of harakiri raced through my mind and I tried to kick out but my legs were firmly pinioned. I really did think I had 'had' it – miles in the middle of nowhere, yet another young and unsung embryonic hero serving King and Country – and it took a few moments to realise that I, like the Japanese officers and my three Gurkha bodyguards, were being given a piggyback across the river to save our feet from getting wet.

At the top of the hill were two casualties, both badly wounded by mortar fragments. In both cases a large lump of metal had penetrated near the top of the thigh and made a nasty hole in the neck. One was a young man, armed with a rifle; the other, a lad of about twelve, held a catapult in his hand.

About twenty yards away a section of Japanese soldiers distracted me by going through some sort of dumb pantomime. They were excitedly pointing down to something I could not see. I told the interpreter to calm them down. I was distressed on account of the wounded. We were miles from anywhere and, even to my untrained eye, there was little hope for their survival and carrying them out would badly delay us. In Yamagishi's headquarter group was a doctor with a medical satchel. He examined the casualties and spoke to the interpreter. I was approached and asked if I would authorise the doctor to despatch (I still can't use the word 'kill') the man and the boy by injecting sufficient morphia into their bloodstream for their end to be painless, as his limited medical supplies could help in no other way. I was appalled by being turned to for a decision and stalled. But apparently everything was in my hands and I made the fatal decision that I have had to live with ever since.

Feeling distraught, the antics of the Japanese soldiers, standing on the bank, grated on me.

'Stop them fooling about,' I said, angrily, to the interpreter.

'Respected sir, they are afraid.'

'Why?'

'They have seen a hand,' was the enigmatic reply.

So I went to see what it was all about. The bank, maybe three feet high, had a ditch on the other side. Rubber trees were planted on the bank and the ditch was to hold water to help their growth. But now it was full of dry leaves and a skinny brown arm was waving about, palm upwards. So the soldiers had seen a hand!

'Pull it,' I ordered callously.

'They are afraid to,' answered the interpreter.

My temper snapped and, sensing that valour was the better part of discretion, the soldiers were quickly ordered to pull the hand.

One man, braver than the rest, bent down ready to grasp it. A second man caught him round the waist and a third the second likewise. In one movement the leading soldier grasped the hand and all three pulled. I watched, fascinated, as a small, stark naked man, with the star of Tonkin tattooed on his left shoulder, was jerked upwards, carrying a brand new machine-gun of curious shape. Almost in one movement he wriggled free of his captors, looked up at the near-cloudless sky, crouched low and, just as I noticed that the gun was loaded with a tray-like magazine, he bent both ends down, so jamming the weapon. He jumped up and down, shrieking. The Japanese were on him in a flash even as I turned to my nearest Gurkha and told him to give me his kukri. I took it and made as to decapitate the naked man. He ceased his shouting and looked sullen. I asked the interpreter for an explanation.

'Respected sir, the soldiers were in micturition [some quick overtime with his dictionary there] on the leaves when the hand appeared.'

Then I understood why the man had looked at the sky on being so unexpectedly pulled out. When he felt the sudden surges of liquid wetting him he had put his hand up to see how heavily it was raining! He was part of the Vietminh stay-behind party who had left the two dying casualties as bait and presumably his mission was to shoot us up as we moved off burdened with the wounded. On seeing that there was scarcely a cloud in the sky, he was furious at having disclosed his position. The gun was of Czechoslovakian origin and, had the man not made the mistake he did, would undoubtedly have been used against us. I never knew what made him jam his weapon rather than try and kill us.

❦   ❧

Shortly afterwards I was made battalion quartermaster and had to devote my energies to the rapidly increasing amount of Japanese stores that were piling up. Their range was immense but now only a few of the more unusual items come to mind: Mauser pistols, aerial bombs, swords – at one time I had over a thousand of them in my stores – artillery pieces and unrecognisable bits of railway equipment.

By mid-December 1945 the two Japanese battalions that had supported us had to be disarmed, that is to say they had to surrender officially. By then the Takahashi Butai had returned to Saigon but Yamagishi's unit was with us. A day was fixed for the disarming ceremony.

One morning a week before the disarming parade, Yamagishi and his interpreter came to me when I was working in the stores. I had no shirt on and was hot. I was counting 60-kilogram bombs and he asked me to spare a minute. He was immaculate in clean uniform and shining leather, belt and boots. There were some Gurkha soldiers counting stores and Yamagishi signified that he wanted to see me alone. By now there was a bond between us and, although we had never gone beyond the bounds of decorum laid down by the edict, I felt that, were other situations to pre-vail, we could become firm friends. Even so, the end of the war was only four months past and a tiny and uncharitable thought struck me – was this interview going to be violent? I need not have worried.

When we were out of sight of the others and by ourselves, the interpreter told me the history of Yamagishi's sword; the 250-odd years it had been in his family, the five personal fights he had had with it against the Chinese and now, before the surrender parade, he was going to give it to me. I felt too small for the occasion as, reaching out to take it from Yamagishi's hands, the interpreter said, 'Respected sir, Captain Yamagishi says he wants to give you his sword because you are a true gentleman and a cavalier.'

I stammered my thanks, feeling that anything I said was superfluous. The sword indeed had five notches in the blade. I was also given a piece of paper on which was written:

To: Capt Cross

Q.M.A.L.F.* Thu Dau Mot

Brief History of a Sowrd

This sword was made by a famouth swardsmith called Fujiware yositoke who lived about 300 years ago in our country

We call these sword – Nippon-to, and this Nippon-to was a treasure of my house

I used this sword as my most favourite one on this great war's battlefield

Especially this sword is being kept in ancient shape, and is very sharp on its edge

Owner

Yamagishi Keisuke

18th Jan 1946 2nd Battalion Commander

[*Quarter Master Allied Land Forces]

On the eve of the parade proper, preparations were made. Towards one end of the large parade square, equidistant from both sides, a flagpole was erected. Early on the morrow the Union Jack was flown. In front of it were tables and, in the rear, a row of chairs.

For the parade, the British officers stood either side of the flagpole and the Gurkha officers sat on chairs in front, the senior Gurkha officer, the Subedar Major, in the centre. The surrender was to be Asian to Asian. At 8 o'clock the butai, let by Yamagishi, marched up the road leading into the camp and onto the square. It formed up facing the flag and the men to whom they were to surrender, the commanding officer in front, other officers six paces behind him, warrant officers six more paces behind them, then the rank and file, at open-order, with sergeants behind as supernumeraries.

Yamagishi marched up to Subedar Major Balesor Rana, saluted, unbuckled his sword – his second best – laid it on the table between him and the Gurkha officers and saluted again. His face was wet with tears. He turned about and, one by one, the officers followed suit. The Gurkha officers' faces were granite-hewn in their immobility. Their expressions were a stern mask of unrelenting unforgivingness.

At a single command the warrant officers divested themselves of their swords and laid them on the ground. The supernumeraries, rank and file, bent down and, performing the drill movement of 'ground arms', laid their rifles alongside their right feet, pointing towards the front. Erect once more, they undid their leather belts and laid them down, complete with side arms. Ranks were close-ordered, a turn to the right was made and away they marched, inscrutable no longer, as an ineffably weary slouch to their shoulders and shuffling gait poignantly expressed their inexpressible comments.

A fatigue party bundled the surrendered stuff into the store where I had to make an inventory of it. It was ironic that, within ten days of the ceremony, all the swords had to be re-issued to the same Japanese to cut the grass along the verges of the route used by the convoys to prevent Vietminh ambushes.

A quarter of a century later, when Commandant of the Jungle Warfare School, I gave South Vietnamese army students lectures and I used the 'micturition' incident as an example both of the need for constant vigilance when engaged on this type of operation and of the fact that secret weapons need not always be modern to be effective.

❦ 5 ❧

The Last Days of Empire

The North West Frontier of India has never been tamed. It is a wild, barren and hilly tract of land lying alongside Afghanistan. Its inhabitants, the Pathans, are subdivided into many families, most of whom seem to be in a state of perpetual feud with each other. They are a proud, fierce people, whose pale eyes look arrogantly on all and sundry as they lope along with easy and graceful stride. It is the visible sign of manhood to carry a rifle. The guile and patience with which it was used, whenever possible, against the military had led to a number of columns having to be sent out as punitive missions from the large garrisons that had been built at such places as Peshawar, Razmak, Damdil, Rozani, Wana and, farther south, Quetta. Apart from the garrisons there were a number of forts which housed the Scouts, groups of superbly trained Pathans who marched and fought as regular Irregulars, lovingly led by their British officers. The two most famed units were the Tochi Scouts and the South Waziristan Scouts. It must also be remembered that, whereas the King Emperor's writ was respected all over British India, it did not extend to the North West Frontier, except on the few roads that led to the garrison towns. Opportunities for skulduggery were constant and often taken.

In January 1947 the resident Gurkha battalion at Razmak was the 1st/1st Gurkha Rifles. It was an old and well-established battalion, having been raised in 1815 and allowed to incorporate 'King George V's Own' in its title. Pre-war it had done a number of tours up among these barren mountains, the peaks of which are some 12,000 feet above sea level. It had recently come up from the sweltering plains of central India and at 6,000 feet up in Razmak the difference in climate was extreme. Most of the senior ranks had 'cut their teeth' on Pathan bullets and after a war that took them to Africa, Burma and French Indo-China, here they were, back again. They knew what to expect when the road to the plains had to be opened.

But, at that time, all was rumour. Rumours of partition, rumours of leaving British India, rumours of transfers to the British Army, rumours of officers' postings – nothing but rumours.

Doubt was no new thing to live with. In the eighteen months since the end of the war we had learnt the truth of the cliché 'rumour is a lying jade'. All we could do was to carry on as though we had implicit faith in the future. Loyalty to the oath we had all sworn meant just this. None of us for a moment ever imagined we would, albeit unwittingly or unwillingly, join in the pell-mell rush to coincide with the politicians' countdown. Indianisation of Indian units meant their British officers pulling out, but not us. We had no Indian officers to hand over to in Gurkha units and we could not just leave the battalion and shove off. Abandoning men was something we never envisaged – nor had we ever been taught – but that is what was to happen. Lucky it was for our peace of mind that this dreadful occurrence could not be foreseen, was therefore never imagined.

In the isolation of the North West Frontier, with its strictly masculine population and esoteric ritual (even to calling lorries 'tretons'), much of what went on in India reached us as rumour or not at all. We knew that in the larger towns there had been rioting and it had been taken for granted that Europeans would be unmolested. However, conditions were changing rapidly and travel across India was liable to be unpleasant.

In February two of us received an invitation to go to Kathmandu. It was given by His Highness Maharaja Padma Shamsher Jang Bahadur Rana, Commander-in-Chief and Prime Minister of Nepal. This was not nearly so grand as it sounded but even so it was unusual. I believe we were about the 125th or so Britons to be so invited since contact was first made in 1793. We viewed the prospect with mixed feelings; we were thrilled at the thought of the visit but dubious about travel to and fro.

We were given a month's leave of absence. After a week's eventful journey across India – by lorry to Bannu, narrow-gauge railway to Mari Indus, broad-gauge with some changes to Lucknow, and by narrow-gauge again on the entrancingly sounding line, the Oudh and Tirhut, we eventually reached the frontier town of Raxaul. Going through India we suffered an unpleasant incident every day.

We had a night in the Legation Bungalow, then a 27-mile journey by the daily train of the Nepal Government Railway. We travelled first class, the carriage painted red with black leather. The second class coach was much gayer – a brown body, red steps, silver windows, green leather work and yellow lettering. The journey took three hours and we travelled in the company of the General Manager who 'showed us off' to the crowd at various stations on the way. At the railhead we were introduced to the provincial Governor who lent us his car for the next stage of our journey – twenty-five miles by road. Our kit went by lorry.

No sooner had we left the Governor then his car had a puncture. Protocol did not allow us to return the vehicle and travel with our kit. It was mended at last and we continued to Bhimphedi, where the road ended, passing through the tunnel at Churia. It was there that, in 1816, General Ochterlony's forces moved east into the Makwanpur valley at night, thus turning the right flank of the Gorkhalis' positions. The Nepal Government, not wishing the British in Kathmandu, thereby asked for an armistice and the Treaty of Segowli resulted. As we left having stopped to absorb this historic place one crone shrilled to an equally old gamma, 'I saw his face, I saw his face.'

In contrast to the shrill indignities of the plains, life in Kathmandu was respectfully feudal. Because they were so very seldom seen, Europeans were an object of curiosity, not scorn. On the track up to the capital of Nepal, three Tibetans, two men and a woman, came from the opposite direction. The woman stared at me, her gaze untroubled by modern notions of propriety or ancient ideas of decorum. She crossed over to me and, not speaking, took my left wrist, pulled up the sleeve of my coat and pinched me hard. On finding she had not met a bloodless ghost, she continued on her way. I stared after her thoughtfully.

Up in Kathmandu we lived in the house of the First Secretary, who arranged that we should visit the Royal Mint one afternoon. We went and were met by the officer in charge, an elderly Nepalese lieutenant colonel. My friend, being slightly senior, made the introductions. We spoke English, as to speak Nepali was considered bad manners. We were shown round and saw how coins were produced under primitive conditions. It took over an hour. We turned to thank the Colonel for all the trouble he had taken. His dismissal of my friend was perfunctory. He came over and grasped my hand.

'I am so sorry to have to say good-bye to you.' I made some non-committal remark and he continued, 'It is not often we are privileged to meet someone like you here in Kathmandu.' He pumped my arm and continued to effuse, 'Oh what a pity we cannot have Durbar so you could meet everybody and what a pity it is February so you cannot meet my wife.'

The calendary implications were lost on me. I wondered what the significance was. His next remark was easier to follow. 'Have you spare photo of yourself?'

I replied I had not and began to wonder what all this attention meant. Questions followed thick and fast. When was I returning to India?, when was I returning to Nepal?, why had I not given any prior warning of my arrival? My arm was beginning to ache.

This excessive attention and lack of respect to his two months' seniority made my friend ask why the Colonel was asking these questions.

'Because he is special man,' he replied.

'What is special about him?'

'He is first man winning Victoria Cross to visit Kathmandu,' explained the Colonel.

'No, no,' said my companion. 'He has not won Victoria Cross. His name is Lieutenant Cross.'

My arm stopped in midair. The Colonel angrily looked first at me then at the other. He muttered an expletive and threw away my hand as though he was touching some dreadful thing. He turned round and walked quickly away, anger emanating from every line of his body. My tiny moment of glory was over. We both left on our week-long return journey shortly afterwards, keeping up the average incident rate.

During the spring of 1947 large masses of Pathans moved eastwards. There was no trouble but precautions were as stringent as ever. Then, as suddenly, the mass movement ceased. Rumours proliferated and mail grew slower and slower, until it took six weeks for urgent signals to reach Razmak from Delhi. A messenger with a cleft stick would have been quicker. Mail from home also took six weeks. The local cinema showed the latest newsreel, troops crossing the Rhine during the last winter of the war.

Later on in the summer we heard news of Kashmir, which explained the influx of men through our territory. About this time it was decided to have a 'flag march', a practice column comprising most of the Brigade Group, possibly 3,000 men being involved. Razmak was left in the hands of a rear party and the column reached Damdil, two days' walk to the east. On Sunday 15 June, the battalion moved up a valley called the Mami Roga Algad. High up on the hilltops pickets had to be established. One, too weak by Frontier standards, had intermittent sniping from a position on a farther ridge. Unbeknownst to the troops, a band of Pathans, in greater strength than they, were hiding in complete silence, some twenty yards from the picket. Some time after noon the sniping Pathans noticed the waving of red flags which heralded withdrawal. Their sniping became heavier and, at a prearranged signal, they stopped firing and those in hiding ran up the hill, overcame the Gurkhas and threw them downhill, snatching two rifles and a Bren gun. One wounded man was left behind and was nobly rescued by Lieutenant Peter Davis who braved the Pathan covering fire which became more intense than ever. Davis carried the man to safety and then dashed back to get his rifle. He was nicked in the top of one finger and his almost total absence of injury was well-nigh miraculous. Those of us whose duty lay elsewhere watched agonisingly as first we saw the Pathans, mere dots of the hilltop, close and grapple with the smaller soldiers, then as we tried to make out what was happening as the soldiers rolled downhill. When, later, Davis made his lone counter-attack, with D Company giving covering fire, excitement was intense. Eyes strained through binoculars and the news was relayed to the short-sighted. Punitive action was out of the question, as politically a clamp was put on all activity and we returned prematurely to Razmak; a handful of Pathans bettering 3,000 seasoned troops. It was good to see

Davis awarded the Military Cross in 1949, one of the exceedingly rare cases of a gallantry award being allowed without its own supporting campaign medal

1/4 GR had to evacuate its camp at Wana to go to Chaklala. The few remaining Sikh workers of the Military Engineering Services had to be smuggled out of the camp in the same convoy as the soldiers. Overt riding in trucks was impossible as the Sikhs and Pathans loathed each other with a deep and bitter loathing that invited trouble. Unfortunately a Pathan naik, driver of one of the trucks, had knowledge of this. He must also have had liaison with the tribesmen. The convoy, comprising two companies, was ambushed by what was reported as over a thousand Pathans. The naik got out of his vehicle and showed the ambushers where the Sikhs were hidden. They, and the three Gurkhas with them, were overpowered and shot in cold blood. Although the naik was subsequently recognised, no action was taken. That wonderful unit, the South Waziristan Scouts, came to the rescue and gave the Gurkhas sufficient breathing space to stop fighting, collect their baggage and find sanctuary in the local Scout fort, one of the Beau Geste type buildings scattered around the Frontier. There they stayed, cramped and uncomfortable, for two days. A *laksha*, a holy war gathering of many Pathans, was waiting for their departure. The last thing that Government wanted was a full-scale war. Shortly before transport was due up to the fort to take the Gurkhas away, the Political Adviser, a dedicated and fluent Pushtu-speaking Briton, went to address the *laksha*. He was witty and cracked jokes. Men crowded around him. He so dropped his voice that those on the edge could not hear. 'Speak louder,' they cried. 'The wind is taking my voice away, come down into the shelter of this valley,' was the answer. They agreed and skilfully and slowly the Political Adviser took them out of sight and sound of the fort, with even the sentries going.

The transport arrived and slowed down to allow men to throw their bedding-rolls in before scrambling aboard themselves then driving back downhill without stopping. And as the vehicles departed a sentry noticed them and gave the alarm. The Political Adviser was completely at their mercy but so successfully had he captivated their hearts, the Pathans slapped their thighs and said, 'Wah, there goes a man.'

About this time a man of infinite patience but few resources wanted to chastise the cursed British. He was the Faqir of Ipi, who had a band of ruffians, some camels and a piece – an artillery piece. None knew the working of the sight, even if there was one. The ingenious, though mostly inaccurate, method of laying it was to take out the breech-block, look through the barrel in the required direction, elevate it and, having replaced the breech-block, fire as long as he dared or as his ammunition lasted. In Razmak there was a temptingly tall incinerator chimney which acted as an ideal aiming point. It was known by the regular inhabitants as HMS Razmak. As the British and Gurkha officers were having a group photograph taken, Ipi started shelling the camp. One shell landed not far away, between those being photographed and the brigadier's house, another in the stacked-up mule fodder. This started a fire that burnt until long after the belligerent faqir and dismantled his gun and was away. Indeed he was away before the spotter aircraft could bring down effective retaliatory fire in the suspected area of his operations.

On 9 August the long-awaited details of our future were made known. As the First Battalion of the First King George V's Own Gurkha Regiment (The Malauñ Regiment) we all thought we would be chosen for transfer to the British Army. Not only were we not chosen as a regiment, but also the men had neither the right to opt for British Service, despite previous promises, nor to go on discharge. Even leave was indefinitely postponed. Later we were told that the reason for choosing the four regiments that did join the British Army in Malaya was that three battalions, namely the 1st/6th Gurkhas, the 1st/7th Gurkhas and the 1st/10th Gurkhas, were already in Burma, so that shipping costs would be lessened. The remaining regiment, the 2nd Gurkha Rifles, had historical ties with the British Army, and were thus chosen. But at the time none of the Gurkhas understood it, nor could we for that matter. We were left without positive directions, we could therefore give none. Pressure of events obscured the heartbreak. Nor was there any properly planned hand-over to Indian officers. They never came till after the bitter end, and the end was bitter.

Within a week of hearing this sad and sombre news of our departure, on the evening of 14th August, we held a special Mess Night and at the end of the meal, quietly but with an undercurrent of deep emotion, Mr. President arose at the end of the table and, tapping his request for silence, said, 'Mr. Vice, for the last time, the King Emperor.'

Mr. Vice stood up, gripped his glass, lifted it for the loyal toast. 'Gentlemen, for the last time, the King Emperor.'

We all rose and, lifting our glasses in our right hands, intoned the solemn refrain to the litany of lament, 'For the last time, the King Emperor.'

Next day, on 15 August, Independence Day was celebrated. In Razmak a church service was held. As the minister prayed for the peace of the two new Dominions, the Pathans were sniping the camp from a neighbouring hill and the Rajputs, clad in dhotis, were pelting them with 3-inch mortar bombs. It was a bad omen. Later, during the brief sermon, it was quiet but even this was marred by a dog that had got in behind the piano, gone to sleep and was making rude noises.

A parade was held. For the first time ever the Pakistani flag was unfurled over tribal territory. The local Brigadier, the local Political

Adviser and the Parade Commander gave three cheers. The troops jubilantly responded. After the parade had marched off, they all danced around and chanted, 'We are no longer slaves, we are no longer slaves.' Wherever an 'I' appeared in the soldiers' cloth shoulder-titles, it was inked in to make a 'P'.

The weather grew colder. We were now in charge of Hindus in a religiously-motivated Muslim country, a country that had become an entity on this score. There was nothing we could do except take vigilant precautions when out of camp, on the range or opening the road. The men looked to us for further guidance, and we could give them none.

We were warned to return home. I was having my tin trunk painted one Sunday morning and was just starting a letter home, 'Dear Parents, I should be home by Christmas . . .', when the bugle blew the Officers Call, at the double. I put my pen down and ran to the Adjutant's office. There news (having taken weeks to filter through from Delhi) greeted us. We were 'frozen' and ten out of the fifteen of us were posted to 1st/7th Gurkha Rifles, to be part of the British Army, in Rangoon. Of the remaining five, three were to go to the 7th Gurkha Rifles Regimental Centre and two to remain to hand over to the Indians, who were not scheduled to arrive until after we had left. We would leave in December. I went back to my room and dismissed the painter and then I remembered my letter. I continued '. . . but not this year.'

The Rajputs left soon after that, but we 1st/1st Gurkhas stayed on until early November. As ever, prior to a move, more than one place had been announced. Calcutta was the unit's destination but by the time the new frontier between Rawalpindi and Amritsar was crossed, somewhere in the state of Jammu, south of Kashmir, was to be our home.

The comparative seclusion of the Frontier had allowed us not become involved in the horrible massacres which were sparked off by Partition. Down in the Punjab, however, grim evidence of the unbelievable turmoil, the heartlessness and the senselessness of it all hit us hard. Myriads of men, women and children, who were of the wrong faith in the wrong country, now with homes broken, impoverished and utterly without hope, made their forlorn journey from the Land of Penance to the Land of Promise. Many never saw the planned end of their journey. Thousands, each morning, would refuse to get up from the side of the road. Death, that merciful releaser, would come soon enough without having the discomfort of looking for it. It was a heart-breaking task for those involved. We passed it by on the sidelines but even so were sickened with it. On one road, 120 miles of bullock-carts were moving nose to tail, with death smelling sickly sweet the while. We saw lorries mow down whole families and the drivers drive recklessly on. When so many die, what are a few more deaths?

The battalion moved up from Gurdaspur to somewhere along the River Ravi. The only transport was one three-ton lorry abandoned by its rightful owners. It was a time of unnatural stress. Everything was of a hand-to-mouth nature, literally as regards feeding, metaphorically as regards the rest. The politicians had set 31 December as our deadline to be out of the country. I commanded C Company, which was stationed five miles over the Jammu border in a village called Kathuwa. Prime Minister Attlee had forbidden British officers of India and Pakistan to go into Jammu or Kashmir because there was a danger of their fighting each other. Even so I had to go to prepare what little I could for a new company commander when he came. I trudged the dusty five miles morning and evening. Folk had the jitters. Around the temporary camp, latrines had to be dug and this was reported within twenty-four hours by Radio Pakistan as 'Indian troops digging defensive positions at Kathuwa'.

The end was not far off. Garbled orders and incomplete messages about us leaving and Indian officers taking over never properly made sense. It seemed as though there was a conspiracy afoot to humble our departure even more than had appeared possible by not allowing us to hand over the soldiers to their new masters. However grandiose the idea behind the act of pulling out, where men meant more than cyphers and numbers, it hurt. Those who have never served in as tight-knit a community as a Gurkha battalion can have little idea of the wealth of camaraderie and the warmth of human relationship that exist. But when the soldiers asked us the whys, whens, wheres and hows, we could only give general answers that had no bearing on our limited point of view. Nothing really made sense nor could anything satisfying nor satisfactory be achieved. It was a forlorn, heartless and painful experience.

The bloodshed and the hate engendered by the cataclysmically hurried rewriting of history could never be measured. We living there, and through it, reckoned that three generations would be needed to heal the wounds of madness. And then there would have to be no further exacerbating dissension meanwhile. But within the battalion all was quiet.

Thus the end came. I spent the last two nights in Jammu territory with my company. There was no relief to hand over to and I hoped my talking with the men informally could tell them a little of what they wanted to know, without my being disloyal to my own side. Imponderables abounded. The company second-in-command understood the difficulties. Ours was a microscopic minuscule of the whole but we felt it none the less keenly for so being. On parting, tears were shed and the sorrow was genuine and hard to bear. My last view of my men (mine by proxy and mine no more) was moving out on foot and by camel on a patrol looking for Pakistani infiltrators. I walked back over the border to India, indignant at the unseemly haste of having to meet an unrealistic political deadline. I felt it a shocking and grievous way of settling affairs and my heart hung heavy. We were abandoning our men, we had broken trust and, by God, it hurt.

The next day most of the officers left for Delhi and Madras, bound for Burma. We had left Pakistan in November and now India in December. In January of the new year we were due to leave Burma for Malaya. And then, what? One unseemly rush with chaos all around; was this really the only way we could settle our affairs? As one senior Gurkha officer said, just before I left, 'Sahib, we have been serving together since 1815. Could you not have waited one month longer?'

I am still ashamed the answer had to be 'no'.

[1968]

✤ 6 ✤

An Army Schoolmaster's Challenges

From late 1949 to early 1951 I had the high-sounding title of Chief Instructor, Army School of Education (Gurkhas). We were billeted in an old lunatic asylum near Tampoi Village, not far from Johore Bahru. The wits said that that was the only time they had heard of the inmates of such an establishment administering themselves. The camp also included training facilities for jungle warfare and weapon training and was known as the FTC, short for FARELF, itself short for Far East Land Forces, Training Centre.

At about the same time embryo Gurkha sappers (more than half were from 1 GR and I had the idea of the Gurkha Engineers being King George V's Own), Signallers and Military Policemen descended on us who also came under our aegis for their English work.

The first two OCs of ASE(G), now mercifully no longer with us, were cap-badged 7 GR. Both were peace-loving people who, sensibly, preferred text books to tactics, grammars to grenades and reference books to rifles, realising that military value did not necessarily embrace military valour or virtue. When, in 1948, future Boss number 2 was recruiting in Lehra he enlisted a Darjeeling 'wide-boy' – whose local history would have prevented him being enlisted in the east. The Recruiter then came to command ASE(G) as Boss number 2, bringing with him the Darjeeling 'wide-boy', by now a Colour Sergeant. Quick promotion, if you know other channels than that of normal command. I found that besides being an ex-Indian Gorkha League man and a Communist to boot, his secret aim was to try and subvert students to be anti-British and pro-Communist.

He asked for local leave and went to Bhutan Estate (near Seremban where there is a Gurkha labour force, brought over from the Darjeeling area in 1904. There are two other estates in the area, Bute and Lothian, with a Gurkha labour force). He went with a Lt (King's Gurkha Officer – KGO), a potential instructor. The aim of his visit was to try and meet any Communist on the estate who could get him up to the Secretary General of the Malayan Communist Party, Chin Peng. He failed in that. He and the KGO had a violent quarrel and the Sergeant took his belt off and thrashed the officer who, shamed, asked to go back to his unit, 1/7 GR. He was a B Company (Royal Company as it was known from it being Ganju Lama's when he was awarded his VC) man: he asked to do an important camp recce after B Company located a large terrorist camp. This was allowed: he walked straight up to the camp and was shot dead – killer and killed on purpose.

With a certain amount of difficulty I managed to get rid of the 'wide-boy' instructor – who was clever: he could compose English sonnets – and his boss also felt it was time to go.

The third OC was a Royal Army Educational Corps (RAEC) officer who had served in 2/10 GR in Italy and, before joining up, was the reserve goal keeper for Liverpool football club. He was a friendly enough soul who passed most of his days in an alcoholic daze and whose brigadier boss, stationed in GHQ Singapore, fancied his wife as much as, if not more than, her legal owner. That ended by the OC being posted to Penang. I was blamed, rightly as it turned out, and when the brigadier was made a major-general in charge of army education in the War Office, he got his revenge by turning down my Singapore-published, later HMSO-produced,

English for Gurkha Soldiers as not being professionally produced. (I found it being used sixty years later in the hills.)

The fourth OC, also an RAEC officer, was a close relation of a legendary and ultra-left wing Welsh socialist minister who had been with the Trade Unions Movement since a lad: he told me he wanted a new sort of roll call where the men would vote for what to do the following day. I told him that the Brigade of Gurkhas had not reached its pinnacle of excellence by such methods and, grudgingly, he admitted 'perhaps they are not ready for it'.

During my early days we had an inspection by a group of earnest men from the heart of army education in Eltham Palace, London. I was asked what teacher training I had done and received tut-tuttings of disbelief when I said none but any infantry officer worth his salt was always instructing his men so I felt there was no need for any. Besides which, I added, I had started to read an educational pamphlet that on the first page asked the reader 'how long he had not thought of a steamroller for'. With such nonsense I was quite content to stay as I was. The tut-tuttings were joined by frowns and shaken heads. I did not let on that I had once got 0% for an essay at school and had also failed my School Certificate (later known, I think, as 'O' Levels) when I first sat it.

An historical note: at the end of the war, the British Military Administration (BMA) ran the country until returning or liberated colonial functionaries took over. One aspect not quickly resolved that caused difficulties was tracking those on our side reported as 'believed killed in action'. After the Japanese had taken the then-lunatic asylum over in 1942, they let most of the loonies out to fend for themselves. Some were shot, others wandered away but most loitered about till they died. Not only that, some wounded British troops being treated there were killed and their bodies buried in shallow pits without any individual markings. Low mounds were all that was visible. A hundred odd yards away from our farthest building was the jungle and in between was some open ground where we played football. The area to be looked at was where we had seen some mounds of earth just inside the edge of the jungle.

I can still vividly see one incident in early 1949: a small team from the Graves Registration Unit, comprising a few British soldiers under a time-worn if not time-expired officer, came along to see what was in those mounds of earth, to see if any skulls or skeletons could be found for identification. There was more than sentimentality in the gesture as such matters as life insurance or knowing that one was no longer a wife but a widow made a hard post-war life even harder. It was important for 'believed killed in action' to be confirmed as such. After so many years in a tropical country, it seemed a hopeless task but, if that was what was wanted, so be it.

On the morning in question I was teaching a practical map-reading lesson and so we were out of doors. We were at the top end of the football pitch, the end nearest the class rooms but, naturally, we wandered as near as we could to where the soldiers were carefully scraping at those sad-looking mounds. By that time we saw that they had dug up a number of skulls, six by one mound, and a couple each in another three. It was clear that, by then, the team had had enough and we saw that none of them was keen on his task.

We watched as the oldest of the soldiers went over to the officer and, from his pocket, produced a flask – what of? Rum? Whisky? Who knows but it was alcohol of some sort.

The officer still seemed hung over from the night before and, as he reached for the flask, we could see his hand shake. As the soldier engaged him in conversation the other men quickly lit some cigarettes and put one in the mouth of each skull. At a quick glance it looked as if the skulls had come alive and were smoking. The soldiers moved smartly away out of sight.

The officer turned, suddenly saw the appalling sight of the skulls smoking and, to everybody's amazement, did not take it as a harmless practical joke but believed the evidence of his eyes. He shrieked and fell into a dead faint. For the few seconds he was unconscious the other soldiers returned and, in a flash, removed the cigarettes from the skulls' mouths. The wretched officer obviously thought he had been hallucinating.

The last we saw of the officer was him being led away. History never related what happened to him but, according to the Gurkhas, the two things that money cannot buy are parents and self-respect. We had not thought about the former but we now knew about the latter.

We were threatened with another visitor, completely different this time, the CIGS (Chief of the Imperial General Staff). Before he arrived, during one English class, I told the students about the CIGS. 'Who knows what CIGS means?' I asked and had visions of a baton cross my eyes at the answer: 'Chief Instructor, Gurkha School'.

Although I had never been an essay writer I had to teach students how to write the wretched things. I said that their essays had to answer the questions why, where, who, how and what. Blank stares greeted that sally. Luckily we were on a veranda and a chicken was wandering around. I told one man to catch it: he did. I held it beak down on the table in front of the class, took a piece of chalk and drew a line from the end of the beak to about a foot away. The chicken squinted at it and made no movement. I gave that as an example of what to write about. Only about half a minute later did I clap my hands loud enough to wake it from its trance.

During my time at the school Britain recognised Red China. 'Any questions?' 'Yes, we did not know that Queen Victoria had promised the Chinese their inding-pinding [independence].'

However, I want to leave such dull and trivial matters and turn to what happens when confronted with madmen. The first, an ordinary student, was a rifleman from 2/10 GR, Chapalsing Rai. In those early days of the Emergency we had to carry loaded weapons with us wherever we went, the terrorists not yet having lost their zest for being pugnacious. One evening I was called from my room by the Orderly Sergeant, Sete Gurung of 2 GR, and asked to go to the canteen where Chapalsing was trying to balance beer bottles on glasses and not paying any attention to being told to desist. I was intrigued so went. 'Chapalsing,' I said, after temporarily dissuading him from not making any more mess, 'Let's go to your barrack. It is time for bed.'

He looked for his rifle, now in the Orderly Sergeant's hands, and away we went. Once out in the open Chapalsing asked me to run away with him and hide. I demurred, saying to leave it to the morrow. Reluctantly he agreed and we got to his barrack room. He sat down by his bed and tried to take his boots off without lifting his feet off the ground. Eventually we got him under his net and I left.

Next morning, early, I was sent for by my boss. 'Chapalsing has run away. Go and look for him.'

'Where are you going?'

'Back to bed as I have a cold.'

I went to below the camp buildings to the open space that we used as a football ground above the sad mounds of earth. From the far end a line of men were slowly beating up towards me. In the foreground I saw Chapalsing lying on the grass. He got up when I approached him. Six yards away he took the 'on guard' position, safety catch off, and told me that I would get shot if I came any nearer.

Over his shoulder I saw the line of men, some thirty yards away.

I spoke with him, to no effect until I used an English word. I think it was 'boot' but I can't remember. At that he lowered his rifle. I took two paces towards him and one of the advancing men, by now in earshot, used an unpleasant word that Chapalsing heard. He thought it was I who had spoken so this time I had his rifle two yards from my navel.

I used another English word when talking to him and he lowered his rifle and, from behind, was overpowered.

I looked round and saw the Major sahib looking at me from behind a bush. I waved to him and shouted out that I thought he had gone to bed with a cold. Rather shamefacedly he said it had got better before he had reached his room so he had come back.

Before we took Chapalsing to hospital the camp doctor decided to inject him with Pentathol. He went back into childhood in what he told us: fascinating! At the hospital he was found to have a tumour on his brain. He was utterly shocked when I told him about the 'incident', nor would he believe me when I told him how he had threatened to kill me, twice.

It was during my visits to him that I was asked to see a 2/7 GR man who was of unsound mind. I had to look at the name board above the beds to see which one he was in. Next week he was in a different bed and the week after yet again in a different bed. I had to look for him each time.

As I left the ward the third time a Tamil, a civilian from HM Dockyard, jumped out of his bed and came up to me and angrily accosted me. 'You are the one who is mad. You come from another ward, put on officer's clothes and look for the bed you feel you should be in. We here are the sane ones,' and I managed to run away before he clobbered me. I did not go back on any more visits.

However, one night not so long afterwards, I was woken up by a KGO in 2/7 GR. I found out later that he and a British corporal had beaten up the corporal's wife and a few others, got into a car and driven off. The car with the corporal in it was on its side in a ditch at the bottom of the hill where our Mess was and the KGO came to me for help.

'What do you want, Sahib?' I asked.

'To go and see the ship's captain and for him to take me to see Pandit Nehru and then on to see Winston Churchill.'

'Now?'

'Yes,' and hinted it would be unwise of me not to help him.

'Let me get dressed.'

Luckily my own Singer Roadster was nearby and in we got. 'Tell you what,' I said coaxingly, 'you won't be allowed on the boat if you have not been jabbed. Let's do that before we go to the docks.'

'Yes.'

I took him to the military hospital and dumped him in casualty reception, gave an adequate reason and left to catch up on my sleep.

The RAMC major in charge of him was an Irishman. 'Oh yes,' he told me later, 'I thought he'd go mad again and I wanted to see just by how much.'

As I write this I ask myself how long can I not think of a mad Gurkha for?

❧ 7 ❧

1954

My wife-to-be, Jane, arrived during the battalion's retraining period and soon after that the Commanding Officer, Lieutenant Colonel Alan Forestier-Walker, was wretchedly killed in a terrorist ambush on his way back to base after visiting us in our new locations. A large operation was mounted in deep jungle to try and find the gang responsible.

I had to take my company back to the area of our previous contacts and, on the third day out, two weeks before getting married, it was time for the midday halt and brew. I now had a golden rule that, where there was a halt, no one would be allowed to smoke for five minutes. This was in case any guerrillas were in the immediate vicinity and would otherwise be aware of our presence by cigarette smoke if not by noise. It had paid off in the past and it paid off now. An armed and uniformed Chinese youth walked straight into us and was shot. He fell to the ground. I went over to him to give succour and he died as I touched him, the death rattle, convulsing his throat, spent itself in the silence of the jungle.

I searched his belongings and found a new shirt and trousers, fifty-two new exercise books, a saw, nine maps, five letters and many diaries. Whilst a grave was being dug for him I stripped him, searching for any tell-tale tattoos or birthmarks, the better to recognise him. I also photographed him and took his fingerprints. I told headquarters what had happened.

That evening I was astonished to get a message telling me to take the body back to the nearest rubber estate, six hours' walk away, whence the man had come. In vain did I remonstrate, saying that he was obviously a courier moving the same way as we were, towards the central gang that we were looking for. To alert the rubber estate's population that their contact had been killed could easily nullify much of the information waiting to be culled from the papers I had found. The soldiers, too, were unhappy with this task, for although the body had only been buried a few hours, it would be an unpleasant and exhausting task: it had to be exhumed and carried back through the jungle, a path being hacked out.

Higher formation, in the person of Brigadier Howard, was adamant, so I detached a platoon and sent it back with the corpse. When the soldiers eventually arrived at the estate boundary it was as I had gloomily prophesied: the news spread like wildfire so everybody knew that troops were operating in the area, a secret up to then.

During the next few days I found my strength and appetite waning. By the time we were out of the jungle I felt weak. I went back to our camp at Seremban, thirty winding hill miles away, by scout car. That type of vehicle held three people, a driver and two Bren gunners. The arrangement for the gunners was simple: twin-mounted light machine guns were fixed onto a metal stalk outside on the roof and operated by remote control handle-bars from inside. The seat this gunner sat on could be elevated, so when the sliding lid-like roof was open, the whole was raised sufficiently for his head to protrude. This was cooler than being cooped up inside. The second gunner sat right down in the front of the scout car, next to the driver, at the feet of the first gunner.

Soon after we started I began to feel uncomfortable. By the time we were winding over the top of a mountain pass I felt I had to vomit. I stopped the driver, jumped out and retched emptily. I sat gloomily by the side of the road while the two Gurkhas waited patiently. Presently they suggested we move on. Once again in the scout car I felt we were moving with incredible speed. 'Slow down, slow down!' I begged the driver. Apparently we were moving slowly. I felt fish-belly cold and lowered my seat to get warm. A dizziness assailed me and I must have started behaving queerly. The driver turned to the other man and said something I could not fully catch, '. . . has affected him.' An uncontrollable impulse made me bend forward and embrace the gunner for warmth. I dimly heard the answer, 'But he is a Christian. His church will protect him.'

Any effect my religion might have had was thought to have worn off so I was told to sit up and, shakily, I did. Because I had to be smart in Seremban I wore polished shoes but they had got muddy when I left the vehicle earlier. The driver, Kalibahadur Limbu, a shaman in his own right, turned and snicked some earth from my shoes onto his finger, then scratched some polish off both toe-caps.

Kalibahadur spat on the mixture, making a paste of it. He began to mutter but I was too uninterested and remote to care how he was driving or to listen to what he was saying. He dabbed my forearms, my forehead and the tip of my tongue with the paste. 'That should do it,' he told his companion.

Almost immediately I felt a ball inside the pit of my stomach pushing up and up. I gasped as it struggled against my throat, choking me. As it burst through I started sobbing out loud. I pulled myself together and, feeling warmer, told the drive to drive normally. This he did, saying nothing.

Within ten minutes I was much better, although I felt utterly worn out. I was to learn that the dead man's soul had entered into mine when I was touching him as he died. I have since learnt that Christian exorcism has the same effect as Kalibahadur's had on me.

As we drove into the camp the two Gurkhas saw my fiancée and waved to her through the port holes in the side of the vehicle. I, sitting with my head above the scout car, was so slow in reacting that I did not wave and I saw a shadow cross her face. She scolded me when we met later on that evening. I apologised. During the next few days we completed the arrangements for our accommodation and, finally, bought the ring and a wedding veil. However, with only a few days to go, Brigadier Howard himself ordered me back into the jungle. Information from the captured diaries and my personal knowledge of the area meant I had to be there to take advantage of the situation.

It was too much for Jane. She wrote me a letter, unsigned, to be air-dropped to me, telling me she would have left Malaya by the time I got it. I was unexpectedly flown out of the jungle; we had a torrid meeting and she left the next day. A woman, speaking in English, later telephoned me from Singapore but I was not there to answer. 'When love is over, what of love does even the lover understand?'

After the brigadier had intervened in my marriage plans bad luck had it that he came to see me one afternoon. 'John, I'm browned off,' was his opening remark. Without a second thought I forgot my military manners and unthinkingly said, 'That's because you're a brigadier and a brigadier is the most useless rank in the army.'

'Why?' he asked, glacially.

Inspiration! 'Because, sir, you are not near enough ground level to influence the fighting nor are you near enough the top to influence planning.'

I felt properly vindicated to learn that after he had retired the brigadier said that if only he could have his time again he would have been more than happy to have listened to company commanders' advice from the very beginning.

❦ ❧

I was walking down the aisle in full ceremonial uniform, not wanting to go through the bother of it but faced with the inevitability of the foredoomed. The best man, whom I could not recognise, whispered to me that my laces were undone. I bent down to tie them up and found I was bare-footed. I turned back to look for my shoes and, to my dismay, found they were jungle boots. Then I found I had no coat. 'Here, take mine,' someone said and gave his to me with a slight shove. I woke up sweating, aware of the night noises of the Malayan jungle, the sighs, chirrupings and rustles, and the smell of my clothes after some time on operations. A hand gently shook me again. I turned over on the leaf 'mattress' and sat up. 'Are you all right, Sahib?'

'What is it, Balbahadur?' It was my batman, a cheerful, strong lad, hard-working and a friend. 'What are you doing here? What do you want? It's not morning yet, surely? What is the time?'

It was around 1 o'clock. The jungle had had its nightly wash of rain. Moonbeams danced on the floor, mixing with the phosphorus of decaying undergrowth.

'No, I'm not the sentry. I came to see how you are. You were in trouble and I had to save you from it.' He spoke softly, out of habit when in the jungle, and partly so that the tired, sleeping men would not be disturbed.

'Yes, I again had the bad dream that has been haunting me.' Bits of similar recurring themes cluttered my mind: the walking up the aisle, wrong or missing clothing; the preparations that never properly materialised; the subterfuges others resorted to in order that I should not escape again. 'Sit down and have a chat,' I said.

He did. It was several weeks since that telephone call had been made to me, three days after Jane had gone, and my company, which had returned to base on the eve of my planned wedding day, was preparing to go into the jungle again. From the time Jane left me I started going on double the number of patrols that I sent my junior commanders, believing that physical exhaustion and a good night's sleep were therapeutic and banished other worries. It also allowed the whole company to reach as high a standard, so I believed, as any in countering Communist Revolutionary Warfare at company level: patrolling, ambushing, watermanship, surrounding enemy camps or whatever the requirement was. It was not easy, as a company commander, always to find the type of target or terrain to deploy a company of between sixty to eighty men but I generally managed to as, even had I not wanted to work Jane out of my system, I quailed at the idea of commanding some of the world's finest soldiers from my office chair.

I now learnt that every night between midnight and three Balbahadur would visit my room, or stay by where I slept, to stop me doing myself a damage during that part of the night when one is at one's lowest. I was immensely touched and told him that I was burning my anger out by hard physical work in the day and as good a sleep as possible at night; he should not worry about me anymore and should try and get enough sleep himself from now onwards.

Five years later he came to me and said: 'I'm going on home leave and I won't be coming back. Please look after my sons.'

I repaid my debt by educating both of them to university level as Balbahadur did indeed die within ten days of getting home. Over the next twelve years I 'launched' both of them.

❧ 8 ❧

One Winter: A Simple Story

I. Thought

They came to the inn at dusk, three tired and foot-sore men. It was cold and the strong wind was like ice. They had been on the road for a month, so were used to long and hard walks. They had, that day, walked since dawn. Now they searched for a place to spend the night. Of the three, two knew the road well, but the third man did not as he was new to the place, on trek for the first time. They were firm friends and could speak the same tongue. This was a great help. The third man had, at times, feigned that he could not speak with men he met on the road. This, too, had been of use.

The inn was small and not much more than a large hut, but it had mud walls and a thatch roof and looked, to the tired men, snug. It stood by the side of the track and was there for those whose need was food, drink and rest: at a price. At the door they stopped and asked the man of the house if they could buy drink and a meal as well as have a place to spend the night. He bade them come in and in they went. It was dark in the one room and full of smoke so, for a while, it was hard to see. At least it was warm and a change from the ice-cold wind. The men took off their hats, coats and shoes and groped their way to the wall where they sat and eased their legs. The man's wife came from the one small room at the back and sought their needs. They asked for rice-wine and tea, each to his

71

own taste, and a meal for all three. Drink was brought and with slow sips they soon felt warm once more. The man of the house then joined them. His talk was coarse, his voice was harsh and he coughed and coughed. He was a loud-mouthed man and looked none too clean. His wife, though plump, was ill-kempt and kept her two small boys at bay with sweeps of her arm while she cooked, brewed and stirred at the fire-place, which was made of three large stones set in the floor. Both small boys were in rags and looked ill. They wept as if they were cold and had scant love shown them. The son and heir, a youth of a score or so years, had been lame since he was a few months old. He had learnt to walk, with the aid of a stick, when he was nine so was not much use at all, but he could do some odd jobs in the house and in the fields as well, or so he said. He had cut his right hand with a sharp knife that same day when he had gone out to get some food for the goats. He had tried to reach some grass high on a bank by the side of the road. The cut was deep and he had lost some blood, so he would be of no use for a few days as the wound throbbed and hurt when he tried to use his hand.

It was the grown-up girl who seemed to do the most work. She went to the well, she cut the wood for the fire, she fetched plates, pots and pans. She then cleaned, wiped and stacked them. And all with such poise, grace and ease, and so calm! With no word said, with no haste yet with due speed she did more work than all the rest of her folk. It was her face that was so sweet, so full of charm, bright yet coy, that drew men's eyes to her eyes which knew her to be pure. The man who did not know the road glanced at her, more than once, and at last she met his gaze. Both smiled and her eyes dropped. He tried to talk with her but she took no heed and went on with her chores. Strange, he mused. In this place where all seem to be ill-starred what quirk of fate has sired so fair and sweet a girl from what looks like dross? Give her a chance to get clean, dress her with good taste and she would have no par here nor far nor wide. In that she does not talk to me just shows that she is shy and that she knows her place.

The meal had, by this time, been set in front of them, on the floor where they sat. They rinsed their hands then ate the rice, pulse and bean that had been cooked for them. Mats and rugs were then brought out and they lay down for the night on the hard floor, full, warm and in need of a good night's rest. They talked a while, then, wrapped in their own thoughts, shut their eyes and slept.

At dawn the three men rose, drank tea, packed up for a new day on the road, paid their dues and left. There was thick hoar-frost on the ground but the wind had dropped and the sky was a rich, deep blue. As they left those of the house came to see them off. The girl was not there. They saw her at work in the back room and she glanced up and met their gaze. Once more she smiled but said no word, though she joined her hands in front of her and bowed her head. She then went on with her work.

On the road no one spoke for a while then the third man asked his two friends why it was that the girl did not talk, worked so hard and yet seemed so calm? 'Oh, we thought you knew,' they said, 'she has been deaf and dumb from birth.

II. Word

It was the Stranger's first visit to the Hills. He had served for over twenty years in one or other of the regiments whose ranks are filled with men from these same hills and he could speak their language well, besides knowing about their customs in some detail, yet he wondered if his knowledge was enough to do justice to his visit. On the way up to a village where he was going to meet one already on pension, he was elated by the crisp, clear and almost heady air as opposed to the muggy, clammy, stuffy atmosphere of places nearer the Equator. The long views up to the snows thrilled him as did the sudden, sharp-edged sky-lines met with as a corner was turned or an incline mounted, all so excitingly different. Certain scenes etched themselves on his mind as he journeyed north: the staggering loads carried alike by man, woman and child, who in bare feet and unharmed by sharp stones, walked with shuffling gait as they picked their way with unhurried speed over the rougher patches. Then there was the small boy, no more than six years old, holding a sapling branch that would have merely tickled any tough-skinned dog. The boy was trying to urge on a large and cumbersome buffalo by swipes of the stick, shrieking shrilly, and probably vilely, as he did. The buffalo, unperturbed, turned its head slowly, almost gently and gazed momentarily at its minute oppressor then plodded on, entirely of its own volition, but with the small boy triumphant. The houses, also, coloured red and white, looking spick-and-span on the hill-sides were, from afar, a picture. Nearer by the poverty, the improvisation and, above all, the industry of the people struck him forcibly. He was fascinated by the row after row of terraced fields, draping the hills now shorn of foliage and the product of who knows how much sweat, toil and back-ache? And other things caught his eye and fascinated him: the long scar of a recent landslide; the kites, soaring so lazily in the currents of air with never so much as a flap of a wing, dropping with so sudden a rush onto some unsuspecting fluff of a chick below. There were sadnesses too. A dog dying by the side of the track with grubby-nosed children playing heedlessly around; the coarse-voiced lunatic, chained to the post of a cow shed, stark naked except for his hat; and in another place a cow suffering from a broken leg with a jagged wound unhealed. But, of course, there were also happinesses. Three small girls so sweetly singing as they gathered kindling in the still evening high up on the hillside; the small, highly-coloured birds playing hide-and-seek in a clump of bamboo and, above all, the infectious smile and laughing responses both men and women gave as the Stranger passed them.

He reached the village on the evening of the third day. The last half mile was steep and he followed some of the villagers who were carrying large loads of straw from an outlying field. Only strong, firm legs were visible under each load, so it was impossible to tell who was who from behind. At a stone resting place just short of the village the bales started putting themselves on the ledge set at knee height and, in so doing, turned into dusty and tired men who, relieved of their burdens, stood erect, wiping the sweat and dust from their faces. They stared at the Stranger and asked him whom he sought and where he was going.

'I am on my way to meet one Bhimraj who lives in the village called Cloves, which I believe lies yonder,' was the answer and a gleam of understanding flicked in their eyes.

'Follow us, you are expected,' said one of them and, rested, burdens were once more picked up. The Stranger followed them up into the village now growing obscure in the gathering dusk. The village was a thick cluster of houses, separated by narrow, winding lanes and each with its own forecourt. By the time they reached Bhimraj's house, it was dark.

It was a happy reunion for they had served together for some time and the Stranger counted himself Friend. Mat and rug were set down and there the Stranger (for it was all rather strange) sat and waited until the excitement had subsided. Then, one by one, mother, father, wife, sons, daughters and many others were introduced.

Outside it became cold and brilliant stars pierced a jet black night but inside the house it was warm and cheerful. As news of a visitor spread a number of people came to see if they knew who he was or if, by any chance, news of an old friend could be given. Soon the room was full and there was a lot of laughter as conversation flowed to and fro. Shadows from two flickering lamps lit up strong, animated faces, smiling and bright of eye. In the background, apart from normal household knick-knacks, stood a row of large ewers. It was explained that they were used only at marriages when many guests were fed and much water was needed to cook for so many. The Stranger found that everybody was delighted to impart such knowledge to him and he looked forward to the next day when it would be light enough to see much more. After a lot more talk he was shown to a small room above a cattle shed where a bed and blankets had been made ready. After his long walk he was tired and soon fell fast asleep.

The next day, early, the Stranger and Bhimraj went to the village spring for their morning wash. One flow of water was for the men and one for the women. They, with shy glances at first, but with full face later, bravely spoke and even japed with the two friends. It augured well for a happy stay. Later on, after a meal, the two men wandered around the village, followed by a crowd of curious but friendly children. They met all of note; dignitaries, old soldiers, their families and many who were of lesser importance. But kindliness was ever present because at every house they visited the unbreakable laws of hospitality had to be observed; a little food, a little drink, politenesses and then more normal conversation. It was late in the day when they returned to Bhimraj's house, with full heart and fuller belly. A short rest and then the evening meal. If I don't start walking soon, thought the Stranger, I'll burst.

That night many of the villagers assembled in the house and an impromptu sing-song was started:

> I was due back from leave on the twenty-first
> It is now the twenty-fourth

And because of you my darling
The Colonel will be wrath.

The woman's answer was:

Take me if you're going to
When you go tomorrow
If you don't I'll kill myself
To everybody's sorrow.

And the soldier sang:

My darling says she'll go with me
Whatever else I urge.
But I have not brought a family pass
They're bound to start a purge.

The chorus, sung between every verse, was:

Oh stay you here and make no fuss
On service I'll not marry.
In one year's time I'll be right back
To fetch you I'll not tarry.

An old soldier leaned across to the Stranger and told him that he had been almost stone-deaf for sixteen years and what were they singing? So the song was explained and the Stranger added, 'You may be deaf, but your hands and feet are still strong,' for he had seen the old man at work earlier in the day.

This was taken as an invitation to get up and join in, so, the old soldier stood up and, in rumbustious style but creaking joints and panting voice, sang:

Oh go my darling fry the fish
And make a wholesome curry.
Or otherwise I'll miss my train
You'll really have to hurry.

There were shrills of delighted laughter as the old man had been known as a 'regular card' in his younger days and all were delighted to see him performing once more. He continued:

A jet black goat with good crisp meat
And we'll all eat a part.
Yet a woman with looks however sweet
Must have a golden heart.

and after a pause:

Pure gold needs no touchstone
And a good man's heart is pure.
And if only I could raise a loan
I'd marry that girl for sure.

'Sit down, old man,' said the Stranger. 'You're short of breath. Save what's left for later on.' And even as he finished talking he realised that it was his turn next, that the others were telling him that he and the deaf man must take it in turns. So the Stranger got stiffly to his feet and, clearing his throat a little nervously, sang:

To the village of Cloves high on the hill
An English stranger came.
One night a deaf old man and he
Danced and sang with great acclaim.
On his arrival in the place

Of fluttering hand and smiling face
With flowered garlands, as of lace,
The maidens comely, one by one,
Gave him a welcome – then were gone.

Of course a second verse was requested and, after due deliberation, it came:

It was in the jungle that we heard them
Then we saw the bandit camp.
I fired a round but my rifle jammed
And away they all did scamp
And I realised to my sorrow
That my gun had played me tricks
Just like the type of woman
Who leaves one in a fix.

It was straining it to add a third verse, but it was inevitable. So the Stranger let the chorus be sung several times while he forced himself to think. And this was the result:

Some have to stay and farm the land
While others' fate it is to roam.
The life you lead is in your hand
If in the Regiment or at home.
Despite the way of life you choose
One thing only can you trust.
There's one command you can't refuse
And when you're called, then go you must.

The Stranger was bidding farewell to the people of the Village of Cloves a few days later. As an expression of friendship he was escorted by about fifty people to the village limits, old and young, hale and lame, man, woman and child. Eight garlands had been hung around his neck and many nice things had been said. But none struck nicer than the woman who gave him a hat to wear, saying, 'You talk like us and you sing like us, we see you as one of us. Never let it be said that a friend of all of us in the Village of Cloves left like a man suffering a bereavement – hatless. We have enjoyed your staying with us. You are ever welcome to return.'

III. Deed

On his way south the Stranger went to spend a few short days with a soldier who was finishing his leave. This had been easy to arrange as the two men were serving in the same regiment and they had previously decided to return together.

In the soldier's home lived widowed mother, unwed sister, young wife and small son. There was also a younger brother and a small black dog. The house, made of stone, had a thatch roof, an upper story and boasted a separate kitchen. It was daubed dull red on the outside. Being set on the edge of a main track, there was a constant stream of folk passing both ways, often stopping and asking for floor space to spend the night as it was known over a wide area as being a hospitable house. The soldier's mother was of uncertain years and even more uncertain temper but she nursed her year-old grandson with obvious devotion. He, poor mite, was puny and querulous. His mother did all the work in the house. The night the Stranger arrived, the village maidens came to sing their welcome. They sat outside under a bright moon and sang, a drum beat helping to keep the rhythm. Their strong, young voices, the slow, haunting melody with its repetitive chant and warmth of message, unexpectedly spell-binding, made a great impression on the Stranger who sat, a little apart, head bowed, untroubled by a cold wind. Later the tempo quickened and he joined in, singing and dancing, till well into the night.

All too soon came the day when both soldier and Stranger had to leave; the former son, father, husband and brother; the latter, by now, a friend.

'Look after my son,' the mother was saying to the Stranger as final preparations for leaving were being made. 'I have never spared myself for him since his father died many years ago. I have worked myself thin to provide for him and he has never gone hungry nor have I ever been in debt. Look after him as though he were yours,' and a tear rolled down her cheek. The Stranger remembered an old village saying:

A mother's love for her son never dies,
Nor can a son ever repay his mother's milk.

A little later two brass jars were filled with water and had a marigold bud popped into each. They were then set on either side of the door, on the lintel. There was tension in the air and a little impatience was shown as in all imminent separations anywhere in the world with 'time, so precious, unwanted'. The two men were called forward and, as he came, the soldier picked up his baby boy (who still regarded his father as a complete stranger) and, with a wonderful smile, said his own farewell in his own sweet way, the infant resisting furiously. Then, the mother to her son and the sister to the Stranger, first a garland round the neck, then a dab of rice, milk and saffron on the forehead and finally a brass bowl, filled with curds, guided to each man's lips without letting go, the age-old ritual of farewell was once more enacted. Four pairs of hands moved, fluttered, joined in salutation, then dropped in poise and counter-poise as the simple ceremony came to a close. The women stepped aside and in two short paces forward son, brother, husband and father bent to the brass ewers by the door. He flicked water round about as well as on his head and over his shoulders, muttering prayers softly as he did. The Stranger stole a glance at the three women. The mother and sister were standing and the mother suckling her baby as she sat on the floor. Three pairs of eyes were fixed on their man and they wept, silently, effortlessly and forlornly. Then it was the Stranger's turn to cross the threshold and, feeling bogus, he merely bent his head and momentarily clasped his upturned hands together as he stepped outside, slightly at a loss, but relieved when the tension broke as last minute instructions were given about, of all things, a transistor radio licence

[1967]

❦ 9 ❧

The Border Scouts

Consequent upon the loyal support shown by certain of the races in Sarawak during the Brunei rebellion, it was thought that if more people with a similar purpose in life could be raised along the entire border between Kalimantan and the Borneo Territories, the difficulties in dealing with any possible future incursions from the South would be much the easier to counteract. This far-sighted idea initially had only a few supporters amongst the permanent senior members of the European community and it was only after considerable deliberation that the go-ahead was given.

In Sarawak, the people involved Land Dyaks, Ibans, Kayans, Kenyahs, Kelabits and Muruts. In Sabah, the majority of people in the affected areas are Muruts, but of a different type from their neighbours. With much diversity of races considerable differences of capabilities and potential emerge, apart from differing language, customs and temperament.

Despite the prevalence of rivers and jungle, Borneo is a land of contrasts, if not contradictions. For the former, uplands, mountains, grand scenery and longhouses are more alluring than the less exciting plains and more humble dwellings which, being nearer civilisation, tend to have less appeal. The contradictions lie in the varying opinions held by those whose opinion in sought. These are diverse and stem from whether the indigenous population has been looked on as fodder for missionaries, anthropological survey material, taxpaying natives or merely as adjuncts of the tourist trade. Working hand in glove with them all as Border Scouts, much of what has been said or read about appears dull and inaccurate.

By June, 1963, training for men in the First and Second Divisions of Sarawak had started. Under officer supervision, men of the Gurkha Independent Parachute Company and 22 Special Air Service Regiment trained the Scouts in basic section tactics and weapon training. Language difficulties were not as acute as could be imagined. English, Nepali and Malay, with a retranslation by a Malay- or English-speaking member of the Scouts into one of the five Land Dyak languages or Iban, was indeed a slow, cumbersome and often inaccurate method of instruction, but it worked.

The British soldiers moved on and the Gurkha soldiers remained as Section Commanders to the newly-formed and trained Scouts. Spread along the frontier, often as satellite to a remote longhouse, using a language that did not come easily to him, the Gurkha found it lonely, uncomfortable, primitive and strange. His charges were frightened by the possibility of an armed enemy incursion resulting in a fire fight and were unused to Gurkha-type discipline. Results achieved and steadfastness shown by the great majority, for the most part unsung, was most gratifying. At places in the western part of the First Division, the Border Scout Sections lived with the Marine Commandos. Here the jargon was confusing at first. This is best illustrated by when a Marine Sergeant said to a Gurkha Corporal, 'I want four hands on watch at eight o'clock,' and received the reply, 'My watch has two hands at eight o'clock.'

Supervision of the sections proved difficult. In some areas there were roads. There Land Rovers were invaluable, but otherwise helicopters, fixed-wing aeroplanes and longboats, combined with much hard walking, were the normal methods of travel.

Border Scouts are now all along the border except in certain places. Teething troubles there have been, obviously, but in the main the Scouts are just like anyone else in the world: the more that there is put into them, the more than can be got out of them. They are of extreme importance to the future of the country and the measure of their present success is to the credit and enhancement of those Gurkha soldiers who, in the early formative days, had greatness thrust upon them and accepted it with never the flicker of an eyelid.

[1964]

❧ 10 ❧

Four Fragments

I. A One-Track Mind

The area of operations lay in the northern part of Johore State. The Forest Reserve held plentiful game, ranging from wild buffalo, tiger and bear to monkey and otter. Mountain and valley were jungle-clad in profusion while stream and river were plentiful and limpid. Nature was majestic and Official Man had kept away to the extent that the region had yet to be surveyed and the map sheet was white. Unofficial Man, however, in the shape of terrorists, had found uses for it.

We entered the jungle from a neighbouring oil-palm estate and started on an extensive patrolling programme which took us towards the higher ground. Evening reports became monotonous in their negative repetition. We took an airdrop of a further five days, ready to move even deeper than hitherto and well into the white map sheet. Giving out details of my plan for this stage one of the corporals, Jasbahadur Rai, flashed me a wicked little smile at me and said, 'We'll meet animals, nothing else!'

Jasbahadur was a slight man, perennially cheerful, indefatigable, brave and a friend of some years standing. I was stung by the implied rebuke of there being no real point in searching that part of the jungle so I said I would take my own patrol on the morrow and check for myself.

I set off next morning with two men and an hour or so later happened on a log across a patch of swamp. There, both on the wood and the soft ground, were footprints, heel and toe, starkly visible. We followed the tracks heading in the general direction of the high hills before losing them. We then returned.

All the other patrols had nothing to report, even Jasbahadur's. When I told the other patrol leaders what I had found, polite scepticism greeted me, except in Jasbahadur's case. 'Bears,' he said scornfully. 'You never noticed the marks of the claws on the heels – nor, probably, did you examine the toes and see that they were of equal length.'

However shaken I may have been inwardly at this forceful display of jungle lore, I resolutely stuck to my story.

The following day I moved the base to a point whence, were my diagnosis correct, we would have a fair chance of picking the tracks up again. Once more I took two men, once more I found similar tracks which seemed to us more man-shaped than bear-shaped, and once more none of the rest found anything.

That evening Jasbahadur was more restrained than normal but not by much, correspondingly I may have shown a trace of satisfaction although I tried to hide it.

By then we were well within the confines of the near-useless map sheet and intuition played an even greater part than normal in our subsequent moves. I felt convinced we were going to meet the tracks again and, sure enough, next morning, when we were moving as a company, we did. The lead scout suddenly stopped, stared at the ground, made his mind up and signalled his discovery down the line of men to me. I went forward and there, for all to see, were firm prints for two men, this time wearing shoes. The tracks were not old and we had to press on but before we did that I sent down the column for Jasbahadur. He came, grinning broadly and infectiously. 'So you want to point out to me, sahib,' he said, 'that your bears are now wearing canvas shoes?' I gave him an apt answer and we continued on our way.

The following morning the patrol I went out with saw four pairs of trousers hanging out to dry. As ill luck would have it, an Auster aircraft on a separate mission circled the spot once which meant, for the terrorists, stand-to and be ready to leave at immediate notice. I cursed my ill fortune: speed was obviously essential when stealth would be far more likely to bring results.

Two hours later we started to encircle the terrorist camp. Jasbahadur's group went round to the rear as cut-off troops and a third group moved to a flank. The group that stayed with me was the assault group. I had set the deadline for the assault as late as I possibly dared and, to make matters worse, no rain had fallen for some time and silent movement was only possible extemely slowly. I waited for the third group to get into position but after the appointed time there was still no sign of them so, reluctantly and stupidly, I tried to hurry matters up. This involved getting to the other side of the small stream that lay between us and the terrorist camp and, hopefully in dead ground from any chance sentry, to try and make visual contact with my third and overdue group. Telling Ramansing, the nearest Bren gunner, to cover me but not to open fire until I signalled him, I crawled forward down the slope to the stream. At the foot of the far bank I started to inch my way up the slope until I adjudged I had reached a spot whence I could attract the attention of the missing group, who should by then have been in sight. They were not, so thinking my only chance of making any contact at all was to worm my way even nearer to the lip of the bank, I continued upwards. My resolve was steeled by their non-appearance making success most unlikely and because we had already seen Chinese movement and had realised that they were on the point of departure.

Six yards from the top of the bank I craned my neck to try and spot the others. I was unaware that I had been heard by one of the departing terrorists who had turned back and was kneeling behind a tree, ready for me to show myself again. My escort a little lower down did not see him either but Ramansing did. He saw the sentry draw a bead of where I was about to emerge and, on tenterhooks, got ready to fire. He saw the danger of my ignorance and realised that, for him to be first to open fire, he had to be split-second quick.

Still in ignorance of what lay before me I crawled on up another two yards, craned my neck again; neither the terrorist nor Ramansing could curb his impatience any longer. At four yards' range the terrorist opened fire on me, fractionally first, and how he missed I'll never know but miss he did. So did Ramansing. I thought the terrorist was hit as he disappeared up the hill but I could not be sure as I lay sweating under my own men's fire, head benumbed by the nearness of the shooting and seeing the bullets pepper the trees around me.

I had to get up and get on so I yelled 'Cease fire!' at the top of my voice, several times, over the noise. In the shattering silence I rose, staggered forward, my knees jelly. I was unable to continue the chase. Both the terrorist and I had our lucky day.

That evening, in the bitter aftermath, I gave orders for the chase to continue on the morrow. Jasbahadur still clung to his bear theory, much to Ramansing's annoyance.

II. A Split Second

Another time there were five of us on patrol. Already deep into the jungle we had been given further orders to extend our company boundary north to the Sungei Serting, a small but well-defined stream in the flat jungle to the north of Bahau, in Negri Sembilan, Malaya. I had queried the order, not in any spirit of indiscipline, but because we were under command of another battalion and I wanted to make absolutely sure there were no snags; that, for instance, the rifle company to our north had been similarly warned and so had adjusted their own limit of permitted movement.

'All OK,' had been the laconic confirmation to my query. 'Move north to the Serting. Troops to your north have been briefed accordingly.'

We were expectant: my patrol found a camp for fifty and more, heavily bunkered and difficult of approach. It had an armourer's store, cleverly hidden near a stream. Cultivations abounded in the general area and contact had been made with the terrorists several times already. It seemed to us that we were not far from their main body so we were tense as we moved out on patrol that overcast afternoon in May 1954.

It was a hot, muggy and oppressive day, with not a breath of wind. Not having rained for some time it was too dry and noisy underfoot even for the normal slow and deliberate rate of advance for patrolling. We therefore moved unusually slowly and deliberately northwards to the line of the River Serting.

About an hour away from our overnight base camp and not far from the Serting I suddenly froze, standing stock still, signalling silence. I had heard a noise off to our right that could have been man-made, like something striking a hard object. After a short wait Jasbahadur smiled and muttered that it was a bird – who would make a noise like that in the jungle? On we moved, I not convinced by Jasbahadur's reasoning. A few minutes later I heard it again – nearer and louder, a cracking noise, almost a report, over to our right.

Again we listened – again we waited and again Jasbahadur broke the tension by smiling and muttering, 'This time it was the branch of a tree,' but none of us was convinced. I wanted to investigate further so ordered a change of direction, over to the east.

Alongside the slight rise in the ground on which we were when the suspicious noises had been heard was a swamp, filled with American aloes, those giant, serrated, thick fronds that crackle when rubbed against and which catch on skin, clothing and equipment alike. They are hateful and extremely nasty things through which to have to move, needing to be treated with the greatest respect.

As carefully, slowly and quietly as possible, we started to cross the swamp. Our feet oozed filth, our clothing was blackened with sweat in the oppressive dampness and our senses cursed the fevered orchestra of a myriad insects, plangent and strident in their whining, croaking and aimlessly repetitive cacophony.

Some twenty yards of swamp had been delicately traversed when we heard the unmistakable clink of metal against metal, followed by a low buzz of indistinguishable but Chinese-sounding conversation. Men, not birds or branches! I caught Jasbahadur's eye and looked at him haughtily. A rapid appraisal was required . . . were they coming our way? . . . could we reach them undetected? . . . how many were they? They started moving towards us.

We had been in single file and thus we stayed, frozen in our tracks, weapons at the ready; then we slowly turned towards the noise of men who were approaching us at an oblique angle across our front. Then suddenly, there they were, passing us within yards, unaware of us – one, two, three . . . seven of them.

'Fire only when I order,' I whispered – tense and expectant. It was Jasbahadur on my right who hissed at me, 'Don't fire!' It was not the reaction that I expected although, curiously enough, they were wearing clothes of a pattern darker than the uniform the terrorists usually wore but then it was well known they had recently got through Security Force positions using captured uniforms and thus clad had successfully ambushed unsuspecting soldiers . . . Then, as one man, those seven turned towards us and saw five men, in standing fire positions, covering them. As they turned I saw they had red Communist-type stars in their hats. Instantaneously and instinctively they levelled their weapons at us, utterly taken by surprise by our presence.

I was in an agony of suspense – were they Chinese or Gurkha? It had become too dark to see clearly. Doubt, anger, fear all chased through my mind with a speed that made split seconds long, slow and leaden. I must do something positive and fast. NOW. Forcing myself to act I took off my hat, the better to identify myself, lowered my weapon and, still as one movement, made towards them.

'Don't shoot! Don't shoot!' I cried in Nepali . . . and they didn't.

I later realised my reasoning to be 'if I speak in Chinese and they are Gurkhas, shoot they will and miss they won't: if I speak in Nepali and they are Chinese, shoot they will and miss they might . . . the latter is the safer', but at the time it was animal survival at work. Gurkhas they were and lower their weapons they did.

We were all badly shaken and, atypically, mutual recrimination set in. We both accused the others of poaching. It transpired that our clearance had not been notified to them. Their red star was an anti-Chinese ruse, worn only in the jungle, never in the lines. The Chinese-sounding speech happened to be that of a Gurkha Sergeant, nicknamed, I later learnt, 'China'. The noises I had heard were made by the patrol finding and piercing tins of rice that the terrorists had hidden, thus allowing water to seep into them, spoil the contents and so deny them to the enemy.

We decided to part, moving back to our original areas. Our relief at not shooting each other was only tempered by disappointment at being robbed of a contact. Unhappy thoughts chased each other through my mind as we went back to our base camp. That evening, after an acrimonious session on 'the blower', I called Jasbahadur over to me.

'Why did you tell me not to open fire?' I queried. He looked up at me and answered simply. 'Because I recognised my brother.'

III. *The Third and Last Time of Asking*

The jungles around South Johore had seen a fair share of terrorist activity as well as the more mundane manoeuvrings of soldiers from all five continents during their training at the Jungle Warfare School. For my part, much of the time in 1971 was spent on problems concerning the setting up of what the school was to become; the Commonwealth Jungle Warfare Centre. However, I did manage some time on training as when a delegation from the Army of the Republic of Vietnam, known as ARVN, came to see the final phase of the very last course run for their soldiers, and I took them into the jungle, supposedly for a 24-hour period. The delegation head was a Colonel of Rangers, in charge, so he said, of more than thirty battalions. He had three officers with him so, counting the five Guiding Officers for the ARVN students, we were a larger than normal party. A complicated fly-in by helicopter took them to the focal point of the exercise. They made a desultory walk round the positions and even spoke to some of the students. We then brewed up tea for them. After pleasantries and a few throw-away remarks about the superiority of ARVN to British Army tactics, the Colonel suddenly announced that they all had an important dinner date in Singapore and had to leave for it there and then. They would not be back in time for the final attack in the morning. After frantic re-scheduling of helicopters the group was flown away. In truth, I was not at all surprised when they did not stay, nor were the students. As an earnest of a ten-year training programme coming to its close, however, it left something to be desired.

The 'enemy' on these exercises were Gurkha soldiers from the school demonstration company. Theirs was a thankless task, involving long periods of patient practice for demonstrations as well as even longer periods of setting up and coping with tactical incidents when the students almost always won. In the former role they dressed in normal issue green; in the latter they wore black pyjamas, simulating the Viet Cong.

The final attack always took place in the early morning. This was the culminating event after a week's exercise when the 'enemy' hide-out had to be destroyed having been finally discovered the previous day: the 'enemy' either ran away or lay 'dead' after the victorious students had assaulted. All went according to plan on this last day until one of the students came across Bhakté lying 'dead' by a trench. Maybe the sight of the black 'uniform' mesmerised him into forgetting himself or maybe it was just the excitement of the moment; he rolled Bhakté over with his foot and kicked him sharply in the teeth. The hand-to-hand struggle that ensued was in deadly earnest. As they were being separated the exercise was abruptly terminated and the other students sent some distance away. Bhakté then went berserk. A small man, he was unbelievably strong. It took four of us to get him under control.

Gradually he quietened. I got the others helpers to stand aside and I sat beside him, holding his sleeve, talking to him. Accumulated tensions from being exercise-enemy welled up and out. Bhakté had been hit by a wad of blank ammunition at five yards' range by an ARVN student only three weeks prior. His resentment was bitter and determined but fervently unrealistic.

'Either you let me kick him in the teeth or you let me cut him.' Even if an eye was not for an eye, a tooth was definitely needed for a tooth. As a skilled tactician who knows when he is on favourable ground, he declined to budge at all.

In vain did I explain as best I could the ramifications and

subtleties of the complex international situation: I had no jurisdiction over any ARVN man, nor could I accommodate Bhakté in his lust for revenge. He repeated his ultimatum. I countered; 'Either you accept his apology or you'll let me report the whole matter to ARVN HQ in Saigon.'

'No.'

He got up and went over to where his hoochy was and packed up his kit. He then sat down again, took out his kukri and started honing the blade. I realised I must defuse the situation, and quickly at that.

I called over Corporal Minbahadur, as tall and strong a man as I knew. I explained my plan to him. 'You will take your squad down to the river, along the path where the ARVN students are waiting for further orders. You will stay behind Bhakté all the time and not let him draw his kukri – whatever happens. Once we have reached the Vietnamese, I'll get the man who kicked him to shake hands.' I showed more confidence that I felt. Minbahadur, a man I had long known, showed no emotion.

So we moved off down the path towards the river and the Vietnamese students, just ten Gurkhas and myself. The ARVN Guiding Officer, who had stayed back to help the exercise, declined to go with us. Some distance down the track, in a glade, we came across the thirty ARVN students. The leading Gurkha hesitated but I ordered him on. At the end of the group Bhakté stayed where he was, eyeing every student balefully, looking for his target. I felt that, were there to be another set-to, we would be unwise to remain split. I urged Bhakté forward. We passed through the Vietnamese who stayed silent. On the farther side of the students the Gurkhas stopped and turned towards me, faces impassive. I turned towards the Vietnamese who, politely and in chorus, wished me good morning. They refused to say anything until their Guiding Officer arrived, anxiously breathless, obviously an unwilling participant.

He immediately launched into an effusion of collective sympathy, shock and shame, and ended up by offering a corporate apology. I translated. Bhakté declined. 'The one who kicked me must come forward,' he said.

No one stirred when I turned to Captain Minh and declined his offer. At that he left me to manage the situation by myself. Tension mounted. Suddenly Bhakté pointed at one of the students. 'He's the one!' he growled. The man so singled out went green and slowly got to his feet. Bhakté equally slowly took his pack off, laid it on the ground and felt for his kukri. I glanced at Minbahadur who put his hand very firmly on the handle.

'Come here,' I said to the Vietnamese. Hesitantly, unwillingly, he came forward. I caught hold of his right wrist with my left hand. 'Come here,' I said to Bhakté. With equal difficulty I caught hold of his right wrist with my right hand.

Rather like the referee in a tug-of-war competition trying to align the centre of the rope over the centre of the pulling area, I tried to bring two hands together. I failed. The two men jerked away from me. Two paces to me left for the Vietnamese, two paces to my right for Bhakté. 'Shake hands!' I rasped out twice as I tugged them towards each other. I failed again.

By now all the students had a hard look in their eyes, while the man who had kicked Bhakté looked hunted and near to breaking point. Bhakté looked ferociously red-eyed. The other Gurkhas were tense. I felt desperate.

'Come here!' I snapped at the Vietnamese, lunged at him and pulled him towards me. 'Give me your hand and shake his, or else . . .' I snarled at Bhakté and, my fear at failure transmuting into strength, I did get them to shake hands.

I turned and dismissed the Gurkhas, sending them on down the track. I turned back, thanked the students for the apology and said that tempers would now cool.

Inwardly blessing all those weary hours learning Vietnamese, I left the students to rejoin the Gurkhas, sweatingly thankful that I had managed at the third and last time of asking.

IV. *The Fourth Fragment*

So much of our work in the jungle, especially in the middle 1950s, was repetitive, monotonous and unproductive. One statistic gleaned from some arcane source revealed that the average rifle company needed a million man hours to achieve one kill or capture of a terrorist during the years 1953 to 1956. Certainly, contacts were usually so fleeting that time actually spent in combat could be measured in seconds rather than minutes.

During this period it was hard to acquire up-to-date evidence, collateral or otherwise, of the 'baddies' and their intentions so any documentary evidence available was, by definition and of necessity, grist to the mill.

One morning, having received five days' rations the previous day, we set off on yet another leg of our prophylactic and so-far-unrewarded patrolling. That evening we camped near a large stream. There was no evidence of enemy movement and the area seemed dead.

The next morning two of us awoke with a gut ache, myself and a young soldier called Dharmajit so, instead of making the planned early start, I decided to wait until after the morning meal before making any decision to move. In the meantime I ordered perimeter guards to be doubled and placed irregularly. No sooner had this been done when firing broke out as two terrorists walked to the far bank of the stream. Vision was obscured by cordite smoke mixing with the mist over the water and only one of the pair was killed. Both packs were picked up. They were stuffed full of documents.

In the ensuing excitement my gut ache must have transferred itself to Dharmajit, for I recovered and he got worse. I contacted HQ, photographed, finger-printed and buried the dead man and then inspected the contents of the two packs. Around me I heard the last round of congratulations and recriminations finally peter out. I found most of the documents were standard Communist propaganda tracts with, in English and Chinese, such titles as 'Freedom News' and 'Red Star'. These seemed uninteresting but there were some exciting-looking letters, wrapped up into cone-shaped spills. The former were bulky and, I felt, not really worth taking back, despite stringent orders that everything was required. We moved off slowly as we still had four days' rations with us and Dharmajit was ill.

That evening we were still two days' march from another dropping zone and I was ordered to be there by noon on the second day, take my resupply there and be ready to receive a helicopter which was coming to take the documents away. By getting there by noon, I could secure the area for the helicopter to land safely. I said it could also take Dharmajit away. I made my plans to arrive there at 11 o'clock which would give me ample time to make the landing site safe. Imagine my horror when I heard the helicopter coming while I was still half an hour or so from the landing site. I threw caution to the winds; we put our heads down and went like the clappers. Helicopters were scarce then and to have missed it would have entailed greater inconveniences.

It was uncomfortable while it lasted. Navigation was no problem as we made for the direction that the helicopter was circling. Other than that the undergrowth and thorns tore us and our clothing as we pushed through, while the carriage of weapons, packs, something taken as normal, became burdensome, especially for the men carrying those wretched tracts.

We just got to the site in time as the pilot, apparently, only had five minutes' fuel spare before he would have to return. He had landed as soon as the fastest movers had come into view. He was now out of his machine and was disconsolately looking around as I came up, breathless, thorn-torn and sweating heavily. He commiserated and said he understood. Dharmajit arrived half an hour later, looking ghastly. Soon after both he and the documents were loaded and the aircraft flew away.

As we were tired and because a river flowed temptingly nearby, I declared a holiday and we bathed and laundered our clothes. Next day we took our airdrop and were ordered to walk out to the road, twenty miles away, during the next five days, patrolling as we went.

Meanwhile the documents had been sent to Special Branch in Segamat, North Johore, where the exciting-looking spills turned out to the less than exciting, a bitter blow, and, as expected, the propaganda tracts were valueless.

We continued patrolling to the jungle edge without incident and returned to our company base. I reported to the CO the next day who, surprisingly, thanked me from Special Branch for bringing out those bulky tracts. It transpired that Special Branch, Johore, the next senior to that in Segamat, had, at the last moment, asked for them. Their best man had cursorily glanced through them. At first he too had wondered why I had bothered to report their discovery but then a worm of suspicion had entered his mind and he had examined them with greater care and growing excitement.

Two days later he had managed to break the code the tracts concealed and found they revealed the latest Politburo directive for infiltrating schools, trade unions and local government. By prompt action, taken in forestalling these planned developments, much trouble was avoided in Malaya where it was reckoned that Authority had learnt about the new directive maybe a year before otherwise might have been the case. Singapore, also a target, disregarded the evidence and suffered from student anarchy.

The code was that only every fourth word was used to spell out the orders of the Politburo, while the whole text seamlessly managed to obfuscate the real message by making sense in its own right.

I realised neither I, nor anyone else for that matter, would ever have known about any of this had I thrown the tracts away but, even so, I shuddered at the thought of what might have been the results of my initial impetuosity – and had I not had gut ache!

[1977]

❧ *11* ❧

The Breakthrough

A small boat with a noisy out-board engine came into sight around the river bend. In the fading light the two men on the bank saw the passenger glance at his watch, look up and wave. There was a feeling of relief – another ten minutes and the boat would have been benighted downstream. The boat crunched to a halt on the little sandy spit, the forward boatman jumped out and made fast. The driver stopped the engine and the evening cicadas were heard once more. The passenger stood up awkwardly and stiffly, obviously cramped after his long journey from the riverine town of Grik, some six hours away. Those on the bank saw a Malay, dressed in jungle green, carrying a carbine. He was of medium height, of stocky build and still quite young. He smiled cheerfully, revealing wide-set teeth, and walked up to the small group, now swelled to six, who had come down to the river's edge. He held his hand out.

'*Selamat datang!*' It was the Englishman who gave the greeting and stepped forward with out-stretched hand. He, too, was wearing jungle green and carried a weapon. The salutation was answered, and the Malay asked softly in English, 'Is this him?' The Englishman nodded and turned round to the Temiar headman standing silently behind him and said, smiling kindly, '*Na Gob-doh, na chepchiib, je ha tuug, Tata.*' ['That is the Malay due in. Do not fear, Old Man.'] The man gave the ghost of a grin and padded forward soundlessly

101

to meet the Malay. They greeted each other Malay style, touching their chest with their right hand after the handshake. A few words of Malay were mumbled to each other.

By now it was dark, the boat had been secured for the night and three fires had been lit some fifty yards in from the river, in a small jungle clearing. Three fires for three groups. The Englishman, a British officer, with two Gurkha soldiers, comprised one group. The second consisted of the Malay, a Special Branch officer, and his two boatmen. The third also had three people in it, the Temiar headman, his younger wife and a small son. There was enough light to complete the chores. Shadows flickered, men moved purposefully about, there was an occasional clink of mess tins and finishing touches were put to rude shelters.

It was February 1962, during the month of the Fast, the Puasa. The Malays hungrily ate their fill, not having touched food all day. The officer and soldiers were less hungry, but were also ready for their meal. It was the Temiar cooking which was the most drawn-out. The headman's wife had carried with her a rattan back-basket containing bamboo cylinders for water, and tapioca. Earlier on she had carried the bamboos into the water and, legs apart and sarong above her knees, washed them out as she stood, then filled them. Later she built a small fire to bake the tapioca. First she had to clean the tubers. She peeled them, squatting down, holding a bamboo container between her knees lest it spill. As each piece of tapioca was ready for washing, she tilted the container up to her mouth, took a swig, replaced the bamboo between her knees, and picked up the piece of tapioca, holding it a little away from her. She then squirted the water out, jet-like, on to the tapioca, deftly cleaning it before her supply ran dry. It was then put into the ashes to roast, with a slight dowsing of the flame until it dried off.

It was an unusual gathering. The officer and the headman had been living together for some time and had gained each other's confidence and respect. Imperceptibly and unobtrusively the Englishman had led the Temiar on to commit himself into helping to combat those few elusive Chinese terrorists, still active, still with considerable influence, still a problem to Government, still a target for the Security forces. Kerinching, for that was his name, had unwittingly crossed the point of no return and had not wanted anyone else to know of the help he was prepared to give, but was persuaded that a Malay known as Ismail also had to know. Kerinching had reluctantly agreed to a meeting, but only in secret, hence the six-hour boat ride for Ismail and a walk of an hour and a half for the others. This meeting would arrange details of how the officer could combine military and police aspects as well as making full use of the trusted men Kerinching would provide to work with the officer. This chance would not easily occur again.

And so, after the meal, a long confabulation took place. Ismail, the Special Branch officer, sat with Kerinching on his right and the British officer on his left. He said, in English, 'Let me do the talking, you just listen.' There was a nodded assent.

Then, in painstakingly simple Malay, with simple question and simpler answer, were ideas, hopes, fears and finally plans drawn out of the headman.

'Before, in the past, is a man. Man sick, strongly. I fear he die, his woman also. This one,' he pointed to the Englishman, 'make well with medicine. Already well but weak. After strong will walk with this one.' Again he gesticulated to the Englishman. 'My son, my brother, also go. They will be this one's men. I am Kerinching, all Inland Men know me, known my men, will talk. But difficult. Walk far. Eat tapioca. No andrup ['airdrop']. Difficult. My three men, few Gurkhas, this one Tuan only. If another, my men not go. I do not know, I do not trust, I do not like; only this one.' He paused. 'Will go look for fish, with two legs,' He chuckled. 'I hope strongly, good luck, meet and kill. If not . . .' and by the light of the

fire the shadows emphasised his expressive shrug. 'If not . . . what
more can I do?'

The Special Branch officer excitedly nudged the Englishman.
'We're through!' he said, 'Now at last we have the key, or rather,'
he corrected himself, 'you have the key which opens all doors.
Maybe you don't realise that the one you made well has worked
for the Chinese before, and was on a mission for them when he
fell ill. Those three with you will act as your screen. This has never
happened before – ever.' He went on to embrace Kerinching and,
after a few pleasantries, the meeting broke up.

They went to settle down for the night. The officer moved over
to where his two Gurkhas sat, weapons over their knees. 'Perhaps
it will work out. We talked much and the "bare one" is satisfied.
Maybe all this time living with mangy dogs and jumping fleas has
not been wasted. Now I am tired.'

The Gurkha turned and one said, 'You spoke too quietly for us to
hear. We, too, hope for success. Now let us sleep.'

But sleep does not come at a man's bidding. The officer lay quiet,
turning over in his mind the events of the past months leading
up to today's meeting. Why is there still trouble? Who are these
Temiar? He lay on his back, musing . . .

❧ ❧

Banditry in Malaya is endemic. Even during the 1948–1960 Emergency there were many instances when fewer acts of violence were
perpetrated in any one month than in the corresponding month
twenty years previously. It would therefore have been naïve to
expect a complete cessation of nefarious activities when post-
Emergency conditions prevailed. A new 'peacetime' phenomenon
appeared – a Chinese Communist presence on the Malay-Thai
border. This was a continuation of activities started during the

Japanese occupation and was never stamped out during the Emergency. The mid-twentieth century aspirations of the Overseas Chinese are worthy of a far more detailed scrutiny than dismissal by a mere bald statement of fact. It is certainly true to say that the aftermath of the Emergency resulted in conditions favourable to Chinese influence and pressures on the Malay-Thai border, and whether or not Communism is the cause or effect of Chinese expansion does not greatly matter here.

Overseas Chinese are known to be proud of their ancestors' country, the Middle Kingdom. It may be long-term Chinese strategy wholly to dominate South East Asia, starting with the fringe lands around China, either in a Communist guise or by stirring up indigenous nationalist feelings. It was certainly long-standing Communist pressure and influence from the southern Thai states which resulted in the apparent ease with which Chinese terrorists maintained their sway over the aboriginal population living in the remoter areas of north Malaya. So friendly had the Chinese become with the local inhabitants and so ineffectual did Government representation seem, that Chinese movement was completely screened while any information about them was scanty, nebulous and stale.

To many in Malaya the problem, even if it was regarded as such, was so quiescent that it did not merit attention. To the thinking few there was a potential danger, but methods used to counteract it were not wholly successful. Mao Tse-tung had spent thirty years in the wilderness before making a comeback. His representative in the Kra Isthmus, Chin Peng, had only spent twenty by 1962. Was there a parallel? And if so, did only Chin Peng remember it?

The Communists had, in effect, established a bridgehead in the centre of north Malaya. It was one of influence rather than of physical occupation, but none the less useful for all that. In the event of any future incursion from Thailand into Malaya, the aboriginal population, already completely won over by the Chinese, would be able to provide intelligence, porterage and food to a degree which would be imperative for Communist plans and without which they could well result in failure. To reverse this situation realistic and long-term Government planning backed up by steady, persuasive and sympathetic action was essential. There was no mechanical panacea for success, the hearts and minds of the aborigines had to be weaned from the Chinese and, not the same thing, won over by Government.

The term used to describe the many and varied groups of aboriginal and prototype people in South East Asia is Nesiot. Characteristically they are found in the deep jungles of 'rain forest' countries. Jetsam of old civilisations and flotsam of primitive nomads, the world has passed them by. Some remained undiscovered until after World War II (as in Burma), others were the subject of considerable research, sincere and accurate in some cases, sensational in others, but efforts were, in the main, uncoordinated, individualistic and limited. A belated interest is now being taken in those in Malaya, possibly not entirely governed by purely altruistic motives.

Nesiot peoples in Malaya have been classified, by some, into as many as ten separate groups, all of which were known, until recently, as Sakai. This name is now resented by the aborigines as it implies a person of inferior status, possibly even 'slave', although in Borneo it can mean, 'friend', 'stranger' or 'traveller'.

The main group dominated by Chinese in north Malaya were the Temiar who, with the more southern Semai, form the Senoi. ('*Senoi*' is the Temiar for 'man' generally; they refer to themselves as '*serok*', meaning 'inlander'.) They, and other tribes even less civilised, stretch north into Thailand. In appearance they are small, dark and frail, and are timorous by nature. They live in communities varying from under a score to over a hundred. A headman ('*penghulu*') and a priest ('*shaman*') have the most influence over a group, but many matters are decided by common assent. Intimate family affairs are normally not the concern of anybody other than the siblings (which for this purpose can be taken as the basic hearth group, parents and children), but in matters of love and dreams there are wider repercussions. For the former, the Temiar equivalent to the Table of Kindred and Affinity has it that a man must seek his bride from another community, otherwise even the marrying of a non-relation is regarded as tantamount to incest. There is no actual marriage ceremony (or so it is thought), and the advent of the first child is normally accepted as the binding factor between two partners. Unlike any Western counterpart, a wife's sisters and cousins are fair game for any husband yet sanity is shown by a complete avoidance taboo regarding one's parents-in-law. To look on them is to court disaster, accidentally to speak to them is to wed it. It is believed that this will result in thunder and lightning, headaches and upset stomachs, each only being relieved by the offending person, normally the younger generation, cutting and drawing blood from their shin bone. Many Western civilisations may well applaud the sentiment behind the deed.

As for dreams, the shaman, who would be better described as medicine man, community name-giver and song-maker, as well as official interpreter of dreams, has the task of relating an individual's dreams to any particular situation, more than likely affecting the whole community. As medicine man alone, the shaman has great status. Western medicines are now known about but obtained with difficulty, and then little understood. Ancient remedies may be less efficacious but are simpler to come by. Certain complaints, for instance ringworm, yaws, elephantiasis, have to be lived with. Fevers, headaches and stomach upsets may be caused by the individual or collective offending of the spirits by breaking a taboo. Here the shaman diagnoses the remedy which includes the evil spirit causing the upset to be starved, smoked out by being blown on (tobacco or fire), frightened out by noises, charmed out by songs or painted out by various red and white emblems daubed on the patient's head and body. It has been the practice for many years for a community to move when someone dies of illness. This entails burning down the houses and, it is hoped, the disease. Placating the homeless spirit, which wanders through the jungle, sometimes hooting like an owl, deciding whether to build temporary huts or more permanent houses, when to start felling the jungle and many other details are the shaman's responsibility.

Children are given names by the shaman, who is told, in a dream by an animal spirit, what they are. This animal also becomes the child's guardian spirit, and this relationship lasts a lifetime. There is a pact between the person and the animal, the one not killing the other. How seriously this relationship is taken is not known but a few years ago a tiger entered a temporary hut in which some people were sleeping on the ground and, ignoring the first two people, pounced on and dragged out the third. The two people ignored by the tiger claimed to be 'were-tigers' and, as such, were safe from such accidents.

As for names, being part of a person's soul, these should never be mentioned. Among themselves the relationship between people is the most often used for calling and for reference, much less frequently is use made of a second name or a nickname. Quite often a hint or reference in conversation is considered sufficient. Many Temiar are, for instance, called Busu, Aloi or Pedik (the second or 'un-soul' name) and so confusing to a newcomer because the name can refer to so many different people, but even so this is much easier than the intricacies of half-brothers, son's fathers, second wife's offspring or a maze of cousins.

Being animists superstition prevails. New troops and aspiring anthropologists are taught not to laugh in front of butterflies, not to flash mirrors in the open, nor to touch the head of anyone. Each person has his own god in his own head and butterflies (at least the larger varieties) are said to be a soul in transit, while a mirror flashed in the sun is a magnet for lightening. It is open to question how much of this prevails now.

Temiar live in family groups and their houses are fashioned accordingly. The description 'longhouse' gives a false comparison with the much longer longhouses in certain parts of Borneo, lived in by Iban, Kayan, Kenyah and Kelabit, but equate with those of some recently-settled Punans. Temiar, like Malays, build their houses on stilts and, except for the main uprights and the thatch, bamboo is used. Rattan takes the place of nails. The whole structure is rickety and, even though there are flimsy partitions between families, there can be no privacy, even at night. Normally there is a cleared space in the middle of the house, often used for meetings. Dancing sessions last all night with the step, left left right right, man following woman following man, in a tight circle. Leaves are stuck in the back of loin cloths and crowns of rice straw are worn on heads, essential to the Temiar community spirit. Men and women sing in chorus, and the accompaniment is the two-toned 'plonking' noise made by the women holding upright long and short bamboo cylinders and bringing them sharply into contact with a piece of log at their feet. With dim and flickering illumination, the male dancers work themselves into a trance, falling to the floor with a frightening crash, immediately to be jumped on and held down by the women and ignored by the other men. This condition may not last long; if however it persists, then a friend of the distressed one may pull his head three times, the headman once and finally the shaman once. If none of this is efficacious the man, so it is said, dies. Alcohol plays no part in Temiar life whatsoever. Trances are all self-inspired.

All are materially poor by any standards. Men wear a loincloth and sometimes a shirt. Women wear the Malay-type 'kain sarong' rolled waist-high for comfort or with breast covered in front of most foreigners. For decoration rice straw is used, so is the red juice of a berry which, with a white juice, is daubed on the face in a polka dot pattern. All ages smoke and betel nut in very popular.

There is no beast of burden, no ploughing, no milk, no manure. For many the first wheel ever seen is that of a helicopter and for most their mother's milk is the only milk ever tasted. Food can be hard to come by. Apart from jungle produce, knowledge of which the Temiar have untold, their staple diet is tapioca and hill rice. To plant these the jungle is felled. It is an inspiring sight to see them do this. Trees are only half cut through on the upper side, starting from downhill. When the clearing to be is adjudged big enough, the top trees are fully cut. The jungle collapses like a house of cards, with a horrific din. Caladium, gourd, taro, sweet potato, sugar cane, plantains and, surprisingly, spinach are grown. Cooking is confined to baking (in ashes) and boiling. Where possible the Temiar hunt and fish to augment and vary their diet. They have a gift for walking through the jungle in silence armed, for the most part, with blow pipes, the darts of which are tipped with the black poisonous juice of the Ipoh tree. They are skilful in hunting small game. They catch fish with trap, spear and rod, also by stunning them by poisoning the rivers with the juice of certain plants. When using a rod they do not stay in one place. They walk quite fast along the river's edge or in the shallows and use, as bait, (if they have no grasshoppers or prawns) the berries of the trees above them. They claim that the fish know where each sort of berry comes plopping down and an unusual berry is never taken as bait. The efficacy and speed of this method, contrasted with the slowness of any more orthodox way, bear this out.

Nowadays the Department of Aborigines has started schools using Malay as the teaching medium. There is also a medical service comprising resident dressers and a visiting doctor who makes monthly rounds by helicopter. It is likely that a generation will grow up who may resent the communal existence now enjoyed and a real effort will surely be made to spread Islam. At present most influence has been spread by troops visiting the clearing, or ladang, where aborigines live. Many present the picture of a rural slum, with starvation, disease and death never far away. As would be expected, many aborigines are reticent about things that concern them deeply, and that which is known about them (indeed most of the details given here), is due to efforts made by the brothers Pat and Dick Noone and Dr. Iskandar Carey, the present Protector.

The Temiar speak a language thought to be an off-shoot of the Mon-Khmer group, centred in Indo-China. Except for loan words it is completely separate from present-day Malay, although some words are similar to those found in Proto Malay as well as the Jagoi dialect of Land Dayak found southwest of Kuching in Sarawak. This language, like those who speak it, is primitive. The archaic dual person is retained, Malay words are needed to count above three, while everything talked about has to be related to the stream (either actual or non-existent) which lies in relation to the object, speaker and listener. Time and distance mean nothing.

Any time more than two days in the past is undesignated, likewise any future happening more than four days ahead is too remote to need specification. In distances, as in depths and heights, a blanket word *jeruq* (the 'q' being a heavily accented glottal stop) signifies, to the speaker, almost anything and, to the listener, almost nothing. Even the concept of an animal is too much to understand. Certainly individual animals have names, but they have no generic word. Birds are better treated, as are trees, but this

111

is an illusion, as the classification needed for accuracy demands a far larger vocabulary than the English counterpart. Such is the social pattern of behaviour that there are two words for child, *papööd* for any child (unspecified), but *kuëësh* for when the father, with a touch of justifiable pride, can identify the offspring as his own. Nowadays many Temiar understand Malay, but it is only the words of a song which lead us to believe that 'you don't have to know the language'.

Efforts have been made from the end of the Emergency to win over the hearts and minds of the remaining recalcitrant Temiar from the Chinese, whose commander, Ah Soo Chye, was reputed to have eleven wives scattered around various ladangs. Contact between Security Forces and the Chinese almost never happened, so Chinese influence remained superior. Unfortunately in earlier years the Malays, if they thought at all, regarded the 'Sakai' as a minority with problems that were no concern of theirs; the Sakai were too jungly to bother about. This was reciprocated by the aborigines regarding Malays as 'city slickers'. There was also a deep-rooted suspicion of Government which resulted from the ill-starred attempt to resettle the aborigines in villages along the pattern adopted in the early years of the Emergency when an effort was made to overcome the Chinese squatter problem. The Temiar hated leaving their beloved jungle and were not accustomed to living in strong sunlight. Many became ill and far too many died. Those remaining alive were allowed to leave and a whole number of them were out of contact with Government for five or more years. Naturally the Chinese played on their fears, so when Government eventually made contact again they had to start anew. Antipathy even extended toward the Thais as typified by the following incident. At the turn of the century, the King commissioned a Scottish doctor to design a bullet, and produce some medicine, to help him in his sport of shooting the natives who were, of course, the inferior Sakai. Being, at heart, a kind man, the King did not want unnecessarily to hurt people and the bullet was to have been such that it hardly penetrated the target's skin, while the medicine was to be an embrocation to soothe what little discomfort there was. On the doctor refusing to cooperate, the King was annoyed, feeling that the doctor was an unnecessary spoilsport. Also, rumour has it that the last Sakai hunt for sport by Malay royalty, using, it is said, elephants, was as late as 1920. So despite their inability to have any proper idea of time, the Temiar, cognisant of six generations of ancestry, may well have recollections that rankle. Their creed could be described as 'anything for a quiet life'. Coolness, because they want to be left alone, inherent fear and latent antipathy also extend to a certain degree towards the Security Forces as these are Government men. This reserve has broken down considerably over the years but was evident as late as 1961, as was the obvious trait of being adept at taking anything offered, but unwilling to show any positive initiative if it entailed effort of giving.

The only real military problem was the actual deployment against the Chinese. Anything else was an extension of the Department's policy of winning over the hearts and minds of the aborigines, and troops were as good as any to implement much of it. Titbits from rations, medical supplies and cast-off clothing, to say nothing of the natural friendliness of soldiery, were an attraction if not a magnet for the aborigines. For the troops, periods spent in the jungle had value for training purposes but palled heavily after a time. Monotony, discomfort and squalor, often seemingly to no purpose, were hard to combat. And up to the end of 1961 there had been no positive results; it was virtually a position of stalemate.

❦ ❧

'. . . stalemate?' I asked myself, just before I dropped off to sleep, 'this surely is the breakthrough . . .'

[1965]

✦ 12 ✦

Brave Prince

During the uneasy lull between the Brunei rebellion and the founding of Malaysia in 1963, the Border Scouts were raised. As their name implies they were scouts on the border and the border was the frontier of British and Indonesian Borneo. They were to be the 'eyes and ears' of the Security Forces. Being local men, based on their own longhouse, knowing their own fields and backwoods, recognising friend and foreigner, it was hoped that they would provide adequate early warning of Indonesian incursions for positive action speedily to be taken.

However, it was not easy. There were two colonies involved, Sarawak and North Borneo, both of which dealt directly with London, but never with Kuala Lumpur or Singapore. Neither had much longer as colonies and understandably did not want to become involved in something that a new state might not want. Despite misgivings at high level, there was a real need for such an organisation, so plans had been made to raise them.

I was recalled from leave in England to be the Commandant, enormously challenging in concept but woefully vague in detail. It was rumoured that the Scouts were policemen. Would I therefore also be a policeman? If they were and I was not, could I be put under arrest by one of my own men? I was told that the 22nd Special Air Service Regiment and the Gurkha Independent Parachute

Company were raising and training the Scouts. As a policeman, how would I fit in?

I flew to Singapore, thence to Brunei where the controlling headquarters was. I was briefed about the country, the political situation and about the task. It appeared that Indonesian Confrontation would succeed if so much pressure was brought to bear on the Border peoples that either they were absorbed by the opposition or forced to evacuate their border homelands. If the border peoples could be made to feel that they were taking an active part in their own defence and the Government was behind them, then Confrontation would probably fail. If not, Confrontation would probably succeed. The Border Scouts, besides being what their name implied, would so associate the border peoples with their own defence that a successful Border Scouts could spell the doom of Confrontation as far as the border peoples were concerned. The converse was also true. I was told that it was up to me to make the organisation work. I realised all too plainly the enormous responsibility given to me: it was an enormous challenge.

But I was unique. No terms of service existed for a British Army officer to be seconded to the Sarawak Constabulary. I was posted out of my battalion and, by way of a non-existent appointment, was temporarily attached back to my battalion. In the meantime I had been sworn in as a Superintendent of Sarawak Constabulary. The Treasury of Great Britain was only happy to pay me as long as Sarawak was a Crown Colony and I a soldier, but Sarawak wanted me as a policeman. I was made a local Lieutenant Colonel in the British Army and the Constabulary offered me a Captain's salary. This I refused. Sarawak then said as they would soon no longer exist they could offer me nothing. I went across to Kuala Lumpur and asked what Malaysia would offer. I was told that as Malaysia did not then exist they could tell me nothing. So I asked what Malaya thought and was equally politely told that, as far as Malaya

Frontline Books
FREEPOST SF5
47 Church Street
BARNSLEY
South Yorkshire
S70 2BR

DISCOVER MORE ABOUT MILITARY HISTORY

Frontline Books is an imprint of Pen & Sword Books, which has more than 1500 titles in print covering all aspects of military history on land, sea and air. If you would like to receive more information and special offers on your preferred interests from time to time, along with our standard catalogue, please indicate your areas of interest below and return this card (no stamp required in the UK). Alternatively, register online at www.frontline-books.com. Thank you.

PLEASE NOTE: We do not sell data information to any third party companies

Mr/Mrs/Ms/Other................ Name..

Address...

.... Postcode.................

Email address..

If you wish to receive our email newsletter, please tick here ❏

PLEASE SELECT YOUR AREAS OF INTEREST

Ancient History ❏	Medieval History ❏	English Civil War ❏
Napoleonic ❏	Pre World War One ❏	World War One ❏
World War Two ❏	Post World War Two ❏	Falklands ❏
Aviation ❏	Maritime ❏	Battlefield Guides ❏
Regimental History ❏	Military Reference ❏	Military Biography ❏

Website: www.frontline-books.com • Email: info@frontline-books.com
Telephone: 01226 734555 • Fax: 01226 734438

was concerned, Sarawak's affairs interested them not one whit. I returned to Kuching gloomily.

On Malaysia becoming a country I was attached to the Federation Army as an acting Lieutenant Colonel, posted to the Ministry of Defence, who posted me to the Ministry of Internal Security, who posted me to the Royal Malaysia Police who could not post me to the Sarawak Constabulary because I was there already. By that time I had been sworn in as a Superintendent of the Sabah Police Force. Belonging then to two different armies and three different Police Contingents, the next step was obvious – no one wanted to pay me. I had broken the rules. I had beaten the system. I was a headache. I wasted far more time than I was ever worth. The month before I was due to leave it was decided who was going to pay me.

Sarawak is divided into five Divisions, numbered one to five. In the Fifth Division lie the two enclaves of Brunei. North Borneo, later to be renamed Sabah, is split into four Residencies, named the Interior, Tawau, East Coast and West Coast. This last contained the capital, named Jessleton, and the island of Labuan. My parish at first only covered Sarawak, but later included, for a few months, the border areas of the Interior and Tawau Residences, with thirty different tongues spoken. My main language was Malay, modified to meet local peculiarities. I also used Iban extensively and, when I had to, English.

My life was one continuous move. In one year and two days, I spent no longer that three days in any one place at any one time, except in August when I was five days in one place, the last two waiting for a helicopter to pick me up. I should have walked out. Every longhouse I went to the head man there had to be the one man who mattered. My diet ranged from bully to rotting monkey via dollops of pig fat and rice cakes. I remonstrated with Residents, argued with army officers, pleaded with policemen and genially gesticulated with generals. Slowly, ever so slowly, the Border Scouts took shape. In my questings and journeyings I learnt much, saw much, had much to be thankful for – and once a month on average only the dhobi and myself knew how frightened I was.

Mostly I wore uniform. On one occasion I wandered around part of Sabah in civilian clothes, unarmed, as a member of the North Borneo Trading Company. I carried an umbrella, more as a paraplui than a parasol. There I was asked why it was that the Japanese had not yet surrendered.

When in uniform I wore a hornbill emblem on my left arm. I called into my office in Kuching sometimes. My official code name was 'Brave Prince'. I played ducks and drakes with the opposition. I travelled by road a little, river and air much – and walked well over a thousand miles. I am not a vain man but the only time I would ever describe myself as 'soft and attractive' was when I referred to myself as a military target in the border areas.

I remember some incidents more clearly than others.

❧   ❧

In his youth Jimbuan had dreamed brave dreams about proving his Iban manhood. He saw himself lopping off his enemies' heads and thereby being allowed to tattoo the joints of all five fingers of his left hand. And sure enough, while he was still strong even after the first flush of youth was over, his chance came. During the Pacific War he killed a number of Japanese soldiers, including at least one officer. He strung the skulls up in his longhouse, a total of nineteen, kept the officer's sword as a souvenir and, after the war, collected a British Empire Medal for gallantry from the Governor of Sarawak. He later became Penghulu and later still, leader of a number of Penghulus, known as a Pengara. He drew a Government wage. Nothing more militant than cock-fighting and pig-hunting occupied his time for rising twenty years, but Jimbuan basked in his old glory and revelled in the respect all paid him.

By the time of Confrontation, Jimbuan was an old man, a 'character', pensioned off by the Government and fretting at lost authority. This means much to the mercurial Iban, surely one of the more extrovert of people. Jimbuan felt it keenly, especially so when it was decreed by far-off Kuching that certain border areas would have to be evacuated, hence longhouses moved. Reaction against this was strong. The border between the British and Dutch in Borneo had divided the Iban population with the minority only in British territory. Except for normal family feuds, quarrels about hunting rights or tempers lost over misplaced favours given by voluptuously nubile maidens, Iban had no quarrel with Iban. The larger political issues were normally too remote for the longhouse population to be affected, but when they were, parochial opinions militated against them so strongly that most Government edicts, orders, plans and ideas were greeted with vociferous antipathy or mute disdain, normally the former. Certainly, the order about moving back from familiar houses and beloved hunting grounds gave Jimbuan an excuse to exert his personal influence to a degree which threatened to override the authority of the Pengara who had been appointed in Jimbuan's place. Feelings were running high and tempers explosive.

I was invited down by Jimbuan himself to his longhouse. I had been witness at a painful meeting between the old Iban and a high official of Government and I feared that Jimbuan thought I wielded sufficient weight to be able to reverse this unpopular decision. The journey to the longhouse was made by long boat, skilfully navigated down river, over many rapids, by two Iban youths who looked magnificently piratical with their distinctive hairstyle, fringe in front and long, to the shoulders at the back; bare-buff and rippling muscles, legs, pectoral and shoulder. It took forty minutes from the military outpost to reach the house, which had about twenty doors, that is to say twenty family groups lived there. In front of the house ran a long veranda, approachable only up a pole with notches cut in it, where all communal intercourse took place. Outside each door was a fine fighting cockerel, tied by a piece of string. Sometimes the proud owner would take his bird with him when he went to wash in the river. Even without the motley crowd of all ages, talking, singing, laughing and arguing, ever arguing, it was ever noisy and smelly.

I was shown some floor space opposite Jimbuan's door. I put down my pack then went to wash in the river, but it was muddy due to recent rain, so I returned, feeling stale. I was invited into Jimbuan's room and was taken to the small part that was to serve for our eating place. It was between the main room and the kitchen. I had already taken my shoes off. We sat down on the bamboo-slatted floor. Drink was offered in two glasses, one small and one large. It was rice-beer. The smaller glass was lifted first and, having been brought to the mouth as though to be drunk, was then poured through the slats onto the ground under the house. This, apparently, was to appease some of Jimbuan's gods. The larger glass was for us and I was ordered to drink. Despite being teetotal, I drank it, because I did not wish to cause offence. It was bitter. I refused any more but ate the meal that was brought in. Jimbuan was old enough not to worry about drinking more than his guest. I had no means of knowing how much he could stomach but I guessed an all-night session would be normal.

It was either pique that I had told him that I could in no way influence the unpleasant and unpopular decision about moving the longhouse, chagrin at my refusal of more drink, or that, having been drinking all day, his recent consumption had induced a state of combativeness but, whatever the reason, Jimbuan started to pick a quarrel with me. He took me outside onto the veranda. It was now dark and raining. The longhouse was built about ten feet off the ground. We went and sat with our backs to the outer wall. Gradually the men of the longhouse came and sat in serried ranks, facing us. They were a strong-looking bunch, and in the dim light the flickering shadows made their unsmiling faces look relentlessly stern. Young and old, there were about fifty of them. They sat, silent and staring.

Jimbuan then started a litany of frustration. Rights and wrongs, imagined or real, he spoke at me. In twenty minutes he worked himself into a towering rage. In brief, his message ran thus:

'The enemy are not those who live over the border. Those are Ibans and our friends. The enemy live in Kuching, their name is Government. You are from Kuching, you are the enemy. You should therefore be killed. You should be killed like Jimbuan killed the enemy of yesteryear . . . with this sword.' So saying, the old man, with surprising agility, got to his feet and, from where I did not see, produced a Japanese sword. He unsheathed it and brandished it over my head. He continued, his voice shaking with anger, 'I will do to you what I did to my enemies . . . look up above you!' and so insistent was he I looked up. And there, unnoticed before, were Jimbuan's bunch of nineteen sightless, grinning skulls, blackened with age, dumb witness to former acts of violence, hanging above my head, ready to act as witness again. I turned my gaze from them, to Jimbuan, to the faces of his men, every one of them staring unwaveringly at me. Their expression was without regard, without remorse, without regret. They were at one with Jimbuan. I was horror struck. The old man still had his sword above me. 'What have you to say? Why should not I treat you the same as those?' he queried with a nod of his head at the skulls. The atmosphere was tense, my throat was dry and I was sweating. Escape was completely impossible.

'No reason at all, old man. I am your guest, but tonight I am tired. Put your sword away and use it tomorrow when it is light. Your aim will be better then.'

And my soft answer turned away his wrath.

❧   ❧

In the upper reaches of the River Baram, in Sarawak, lies a cluster of four Kayan longhouses. Two of the houses are Christian, two remain proudly pagan. Outside one of the pagan houses stands a totem pole, said to be a representation of the God of War. As the annual celebration in aid of the god was in progress, a small patrol of British soldiers arrived. They were asked to join in. No sooner had they joined the procession when a deer broke out of the jungle on the far bank of the river alongside which the houses were built and swam across to the near bank. As it climbed up the bank it was shot. The whole incident was regarded as a good omen and the four British soldiers were regarded most favourably. They were invited in, given the corner of a room and there they stayed for a week.

On the last but one day of their stay I arrived by boat from upstream with my Gurkha bodyguard, Tanké Rai. I met certain of the dignitaries of the houses as well as these four British soldiers. A sergeant was in command and the patrol's medical orderly had done good work in ministering to the sick. A large crowd sat around the four men who spoke to each other in Malay so that the longhouse folk could understand what they were saying.

That night these four men gave a small feast for the elders of the community. They had bought some chickens and had made an acceptable mess of pottage with their own tinned rations. Guests brought their own rice. A rum punch had been brewed, using rum, boiled sweets and sugar. It did not last long but long enough to get things started.

After the meal was over, hosts and guests moved out to the veranda. Liberal supplies of native hooch started flowing and, to the accompaniment of flutes and drums, the girls started dancing, most gracefully. They pirouetted elegantly in flowing, easy movements in honour of the hornbill, for they wore feathers of that bird draped over their shoulders. This was in sharp contrast to the jabbing, lunging, jerking tempo of Iban bird-dances. The music was as enchanting as the dancing. I sat with Tanké on one side, for it was the sergeant's farewell party, not mine. One of the maidens came up to me and gently brushed my face with her wing tips. Delighted laughter greeted this sally. I met her twinkling eyes unblinkingly. She danced off and I was left alone.

Later I noticed a slight commotion on the other side of the veranda. The Kayan headman was talking to the sergeant, who seemed reluctant. The headman then made a sudden movement with his hands and put a monkey skin hat on the sergeant's head, the tail hanging rakishly behind one ear. The sergeant pointed to himself, then at the hat, then all around, amazement and disbelief chasing each other across his features. The headman appeared to be telling the sergeant something. The sergeant then espied me and came over. He leaned over and said, in an Irish brogue that sounded strangely out of place, 'Sir, sir, do you see this monkey skin hat on my head? Do you know what it means?' He saw I did not and carried on, in a rush, 'This monkey skin hat means that every virgin and every married woman in this house can be a mother to my children. There are over two hundred here but I cannot touch one of them.'

'Why not?' I asked.

'Sorr, sorr,' he lapsed into purer Irish, 'under other circumstances possibly yes but I'm away tomorrow morning and I daren't discriminate . . . and anyway, sorr, I'm still a soldier of the Queen.'

I translated that to Tanké, who smiled neutrally.

◆   ◆

There was a longhouse near the border of Sabah and Sarawak. It was in a remote place, set in the uplands near a large, ice-cold river and seldom ever visited by any of the Administration. Missionaries had been to it before Confrontation but when the troubles broke out there was no help even from an alien God. More trade had been done with Indonesian Borneo than with the coastal areas around Jessleton to the north but even so the house lay halfway between two spheres of influence. It was natural, therefore, that efforts from both sides should be made and that the hapless inmates should react to whichever side maintained the greater pressure. In due course some British troops were sent to the area and, intent on winning both the hearts and minds of the locals, treated them well. Biscuits and cast-off clothing ensured a steady contact being maintained. It was bad luck that one of the visitors who was shown round the camp by a proud platoon commander was an enemy sergeant on a reconnaissance. When this was realised, feelings were hurt and tension engendered. Human nature being liable to certain reactions it was not long before equally certain avoidable, and regrettable, restrictions were imposed on the longhouse dwellers. Thus were the seeds of reprisal sown, as it was done ham-handedly.

Shortly afterwards I arrived. By this time the enemy had arrived from Indonesia, had a battle, lost some men, but pressed on north. A few of the enemy were believed to be skulking in the rain forest an hour's walk from the longhouse. I was asked to walk down to where the headman and one of his henchmen were harvesting their rice crop. Both men were restricted in their movements and had to get permission from the local military commander before they could move away.

I was travelling with a Gurkha soldier, Tanké, who spoke Malay. There was a local Border Scout section living in the house but, due to some mix-up, they not only spoke a different language but also did not understand the local patois. We took two of these men on the twenty-minute walk to the harvest area. A small, stilt-raised platform was where the two men lived and we climbed up and sat on the rickety bamboo floor. Questions were asked and answers given. It was general conversation until I began to be questioned closely as to my future movements. I told them and the two locals immediately put their heads together and, for the first time, started talking in their own patois. If I felt uneasy, so did the Gurkha. The headman then said he would like to talk with me further, on the morrow, and he would come to the longhouse that evening to fix the time. It was then ten in the morning.

We left. On the way back Tanké said, 'Sahib, why did you have to tell them everything? You know this trip we are on is a two-month one and that we are at a disadvantage as we walk along the border. You and I cannot afford to get involved in a fight. I don't like it one bit.'

Privately I agreed with him. I told him to ask the Border Scouts how they read the situation, then I would determine what course of action we should take. By the time the headman had arrived that evening I had had it from three sources that we would be ambushed the following day with the headman or the day after that if I stuck to my proclaimed programme of walking the twenty miles to the next house over the border in Sarawak. At five that evening the headman came and fixed an appointment for eleven the next morning. He would not have time to come himself but if I were to go down that jungle track, he pointed in a direction that lay away from the camp and the harvesting, I would meet him near a stream. Please would I go alone?

Had I been brave, had I not taken counsel of my fears, had I not listened to the advice of others, I would have gone the following morning. But I did not go. Instead I waited till 5 o'clock in the morning and, rousing two Border Scouts as guides, told them we were moving at six, across into Sarawak. As I was packing up, a figure came out of a room opposite and joined me on the veranda. He was a Murut, a middle-aged man who claimed he had been given a gold medal for helping some American airmen during the Pacific War. 'This is the correct decision,' he said. 'I will guide you. He with whom you spoke yesterday is not to be trusted. He is up to no good.' It was to this man that I had put my quandary, as a hypothetical question, the previous day.

There were five of us in the party. Myself, Tanké Rai, the guide and two Border Scouts. These had already been detailed as guides before the Murut's kind offer.

Eleven hours and twenty miles later we were well out of the known danger area and across in a friendly house in Sarawak. The march had been tiring but uneventful. We rested our legs on a raised platform that ran the length of the nine-doored house. The head man, a young convert, lived, as befitting his status, in the middle room. When we arrived he was away in the fields, harvesting his rice. Here was irrigation and rice could be sown in the same fields each year. This was much easier than cutting down the jungle and planting hill rice.

We went away for a wash in the local stream in the almost ice-cold local stream, which acted as a tonic.

Back in the house, dressed once more, we were ready for a meal, our first that day. Being guests, albeit uninvited, it was against the laws of hospitality to do anything except wait to be invited. An old crone came from the end room and shyly invited us in for a meal. I was surprised that the headman had not reappeared but was glad of a chance to assuage my hunger. She said grace and we uncovered our eyes. The meal consisted of rice, wrapped in a banana leaf, and a spinach-like vegetable. It tasted plain but filled us both. We rose, thanked the woman and left. As we passed the second door it opened and a young smiling Murut said, 'Come and eat in my place.' I said that we had just eaten but he seemed to think that no reason for not eating again. So grace was said once more and more rice was offered, as well as a sliver of meat in a watery soup, and vegetables. It was hard work but we both made a brave showing and flatulently patted our distended guts as we left.

My one aim was to sit quietly and digest my meals but it was not to be. No sooner were we out of the second door and opposite the third when that, too, opened and yet another invitation was given. For the third time that evening we shut our eyes and bowed our heads as grace was said. Food was then offered. Quite how we managed to do any justice to it, I do not remember, but eventually, belching merrily and feeling gross, we eased ourselves off the mats and, with profuse thanks, left the room.

The Gurkha said, as we passed the fourth door, 'You know, they are very hospitable here, but I am glad we have finished for this evening.' He had hardly stopped speaking when, to our horror, we were confronted with an open doorway and a polite invitation to come and eat. In vain did I protest. I was told, firmly and politely, that it was many years since he had had the honour of entertaining a European and how could I refuse his wish? How could I, I mused, and dejectedly followed him in. What under normal circumstances would have been a pleasant meal, tasty, served by a pretty young Murut girl, now took on the qualities of a nightmare. Grace was said for a fourth time. 'Please eat,' said our host. Tanké giggled feebly and we made great efforts to eat something. I was seized by a recklessness unusual in me and, with one eye on the nearest door leading into the darkness, bet myself I could eat ten mouthfuls. I just managed to and looked around in a torpor. The Gurkha was emulating me and manfully showing appreciation of this unwanted hospitality. Once more we hoisted ourselves off the floor. Once more we took leave and once more, as we passed the fifth, the middle, the headman's door, it opened and we were invited in for a meal.

It lay on the floor, lovingly put out by his wife. Lord knows they were poor, but it was obvious that they had gone to great pains to produce little delicacies they could ill afford. It was a difficult situation. I knew that great store was set on proper appreciation of hospitality. I also knew that they were a proud people and it would do no good to offend. So I said, 'Tanké, we must! Let us go through the motions. Let him say his thank-you prayers. Let us join in. After all, eating ourselves to death is less frightening than being ambushed by the opposition.' We shared a plate of rice. It was unusual, but so were the circumstances. The headman joined us as we forlornly pecked at what he had given us. I hope he understood. The taut skin of my belly rebelled at being further punished. I stood up. 'Headman,' I said. 'Please eat slowly and in peace. I go and wait outside.'

The male inhabitants of the longhouse gathered round me a few minutes later when I reappeared out of the darkness. For four hours they questioned me on various aspects of Confrontation and Malaysia as well as such matters that normally concern the District Officers about which I knew nothing. It was hard work and at midnight I had to ask their forgivingness as sleep overtook me. I do not believe that I even finished the sentence. Someone must have covered me with a blanket, it was 3,000 feet above sea level and cold, for I had one round me when I awoke soon after dawn.

As the people left the house to continue with the harvest, we gave them our heartfelt thanks. The three from Sabah then returned and Tanké and I continued on our long journey, regaled, refreshed, replete – and safe.

❧   ❧

It was a small village set a mile back from the frontier, one of those places that lie dormant for a thousand years and then, through the perverse fortunes of fate, famine, earthquake or war, suddenly spring into world headlines. It would have been termed a nodal point by military thinkers. It lay on the direct route from Kuching and in 1857 when Chinese rioters fled, then again in 1945 when the Japanese did likewise, they passed through it. During Confrontation the Security Forces garrisoned the place. When I visited it there was a Marine presence as well as a mixed Gurkha and Border Scout one. None of 'romantic Borneo' was to be found here. No invigorating upland climate, no absurd straw hats or complicated tattoos pricked out over manly, warlike bodies. Here dwelt the gentler Land Dyak who had been driven there by, from the east, the more ebullient Iban, and who had been harassed from the west by marauding pirates. But they were good people and, once shown how, became capable leaders and scouts. Like so much of Borneo life, real knowledge was at a premium, individual personalities could hold tremendous sway and hearsay was endemic.

The houses of the village were built on stilts. The one I stayed in was a separate entity, and primitive. Everybody slept in one room on the floor – father, mother, elder daughter and 'cubs, one and one'. The house, like the others, had a central room, an off-shoot kitchen and a partitioned room with a door, possibly a bridal suite. On the walls were the inevitable information posters and, as always, the Queen and Prince Philip. England was never known as England, always 'the queen's country'. Some of the posters were useful. In the local lingo as well as Malay, folk were shown how to grow rice and rubber. However, of less use was a highly-coloured one of Industrial Motor Vehicles of Great Britain. As the nearest road head was five hours' walk away, it was decidedly futuristic. There was an out-of-date calendar of the Vicariate

Apostolic of Kuching and a handless clock. Toilet arrangements were primitive in the extreme. Many of the houses were joined together by rickety wooden 'paths' which allowed easy access. Privacy was negligible. The raised wooden spaces in front of each house were used for gossiping as well as drying grain, making leaves into thatch and providing play grounds for children. Fowls scavenged and dogs basked. It was peaceful, friendly and slightly smelly. Then an enemy agent gave notice that an attack would be made.

Brutality suddenly erupted. One old man was seized, as he worked in his fields, by a gang from the other side. His clothes were set alight, then dowsed with boiling water. He was forced to eat a hot coal and was finally beheaded, many hours later. Refugees started to pour in, also from the other side. The villagers became angry and decided to go across themselves and show their mettle to the opposition. They asked me to escort them to the border. It took two hours to gather twenty militant men. We moved out from the village confines. Within two hundred yards they stopped with one accord. An ex-policeman, called Jihed, who had had considerable experience, showed his intense disgust by firing his shotgun into the bushes. This made everybody more jittery still. Suddenly a voice was heard crying from the village, 'Return! Return!' Gongs, the warning of an enemy attack, were beaten, clangingly metallic. The effect was instant. All turned and rushed back to their houses. Jihed and myself, along with a Gurkha of Border Scouts, stared at one another. Once more in the village, we found it deserted. Shamefacedly they emerged from hiding when it was realised that the 'attack' was Jihed firing his shotgun. I assembled the group again and harangued them – 'Are you chickens, fish, women or men?' I glowered ferociously. 'Hands up those who will go with me'? There was a furtive showing, a majority vote. We tiptoed away towards the border.

Nothing constructive was achieved and we returned to camp that evening where I spent the night, instead of in the village itself.

At times it was not an easy war.

❧   ❧

And so my time came to an end and I was posted back to my battalion. Tired, thin and still slightly surprised to be alive, I was given a farewell present by the Constabulary. It was an ash-tray and, as a non-smoker, I felt the gesture subtle. In my little answer of thanks I said;

> He wanders here, he wanders there
> That Hornbill wanders everywhere
> So seldom in, so often out
> That demned elusive Border Scout.

Achievements? Yes, those who had never known service and leadership were taught both, and responded. Also much positive information was collected and successfully passed on. Confrontation never properly got a foothold in the Border areas.

Mistakes? Of course, but not so many as to be detrimental, nor too bad not to be put down to experience.

As for myself, the brief days of my martial snobbery were at an end and I reverted to that level where my friends still recognised me, my enemies disdained me even more and many of my elders, and some of my betters, felt I should remain.

[1969]

13

Ooty Interlude

I was one of the first Brigade of Gurkhas officers to reach Malaya on 12 January 1948. I was the last to leave it on 3 December 1971, from the Jungle Warfare School. The day was damp and cloudy; the camp, a mere shell by then, would be handed over a few days later. As a last chore paper was being burnt as files, no longer wanted, were being destroyed. What was once a thriving, cheerful camp now looked deserted with wisps of smoke, competing against the drizzle, adding to the melancholy we remaining folk felt.

For me it was the end of an era: the reduction within the Brigade, the disbandment of the Gurkha Independent Parachute Company, the metamorphosis of the Jungle Warfare School, the final evacuation of Peninsular Malaysia all made 31 December 1971 a date so final that 1 January 1972 seemed an impossibility. There also seemed no further chance of ever serving with Gurkhas. Thus I planned the first half of my overdue long leave to take place in the Hills, with visits to a friend in Assam and to the old First Gurkha cantonment in Dharmsala. My hopes were that I could unwind (having had seven weeks' home leave in seven years) by saying farewell to the men in my own way and retire, unhurt.

The gathering war clouds over the subcontinent made my visits within and my transit through India questionable. When I left Singapore on 4 December 1971 for India via Bangkok, India was 'in'. On arrival in Bangkok, India was 'out'. I managed, however, to get to Bombay whence, two days later, I travelled, via Madras, to Ootacamund. Excitement was intense and in most of the train compartments transistor radios gave Pakistani air losses as though they were scores in a subcontinental Test Match.

At Ootacamund I tried to find accommodation. At the first port of call two Indian ladies from South Africa were holding forth at the reception desk about the colour bar. I, as the only European in a bunch of Dravidians, was eyed suspiciously. 'Tell me, mister,' importuned one of the ladies in her sing-song accent, 'why is colour bar?' I looked at her, wondering how best not to become involved. 'I know where is this Malabar,' I countered, 'but I am not knowing where is this colour bar.' I abruptly left with my baggage, seeking other accommodation, before my audience could further react.

This I found at the Savoy Hotel, a European-owned and run institution twenty-five years out of date but still surviving. The manageress still spoke of Home, read her English newspapers disdainfully, took tea exactly at half past four every afternoon in her office (knees rug-draped to ward off the cold as fuel was so expensive) and fed her fat and pampered Pekinese pet dog on paper-thin jam sandwiches.

Cashing money in a bank is normally a laborious process in India. The first two banks I tried were not authorised to change sterling travellers' cheques. Only the State Bank of India was, so there I went. I was shown to a desk where an important-looking man sat. He eyed me coldly. I foresaw a difficult time ahead. 'Whose fault is this war?' he asked directly. 'Mountbatten and Muhammad Ali Jinnah's,' I answered unhesitatingly. Not only did I get prompt service but I even got a letter authorising any surplus rupees to be transferred to sterling, an accolade if ever there was one.

I called in at the Nilgiri Library. It was a fascinating place. Except for a few recent daily papers, it was a monument to 1947; nothing had changed, so it seemed. I was allowed into a smaller room, where the *Encyclopædia Britannica* (1929 edition) was kept. Here, sternly staring from a frame on the opposite wall, was a painting of the Queen Empress, presented to the library on the occasion of her Golden Jubilee in 1887. All else was much older. Dust was the only post-independence addition to the old magazines and periodicals: *Nineteenth Century* from 1878, *Fraser's Magazine* from 1864, with *Bailey's* and *Badminton* equally old. Tantalisingly, *Blackwood's* started with volume 2, dated 1817, and continued intact until 1915. What farthest ripple of the Great War lapped into that bleak room, putting an end to a 98-year collection?

I saw what I thought was a man's name, Neil Gherey, but I learnt it was the old Anglo-Indian spelling of Nilgiri, the 'Blue Hills'. I was also told that Ootacamund was the bastardised version of the local aboriginal Toda otha-ka-mand, the Village of the One Big Stone. Victoriana spoke of the place as 'Snooty Ooty'.

My musings were interrupted by the secretary introducing himself, an ex-Major Son Dutt. Urbane, impeccable English and friendly, here indeed was a living link with the past. More links were made manifest when, next evening, I was called to the telephone by a staccato and dictatorial voice (which failed to identify itself) asking me my business and inviting me to breakfast on the morrow with the Maharaja of Porbandar. The latter then came to the telephone when the invitation was repeated and, mystery settled, General Cariappa would also be there. It was the General who had heard from Major Son Dutt that a British Army officer was in Ooty. The General, the first Commander-in-Chief after the British left India, had retired some years before. He was in Ooty giving a lecture to the Indian Union Club Cultural Centre on 'Mother India'.

Breakfast the next morning was good. The General and I had fruit, porridge and cream, scrambled eggs, followed by toast, butter and the Maharani's home-made marmalade. However, it was fasting day for the Maharaja, who nibbled a raw carrot, and for the Maharani, who toyed with a banana. The General monopolised the conversation. He suggested to the Maharani, who was the secretary of the Indian Union Club Cultural Centre, that I give them a talk. I demurred, pleading a clash of dates. The proposed lecture was then brought forward to a Thursday ('the first time in our Club's history') and I was obliged to name my subject. I chose 'South-East Asia – Historic and Prophetic'. Thus it was that many little notices appeared all over Ooty during the next few days, advertising this supposed attraction.

Soon after this the party dispersed. The General drove down into the Plains, escorted for the first few miles by the Maharaja and Maharani, who showed him a short cut. There farewells were said. I accompanied the General some distance in his car before returning to Ooty. 'What wonderful English the Maharani speaks,' I ventured. 'Should do,' he said, 'she's a Welsh woman.' I learnt that the Maharaja had captained the first Indian Test XI to England in 1932 as well as being an international squash player, an author, an artist and a composer. Talented and positive, the ex-ruler was one of the Old School.

I was invited to the Porbandar residence, Fir Grove, two days later to meet a Guru Nataraj at a lunch ('Strictly vegetarian, of course,' cooed the Maharani). The guru, a portly, heavily moustached 76-year-old, was dressed in orange pyjamas and a brown dressing gown, the belt of which was upside down, inside out and had 'Made in England' imprinted thereon. His European flock wore holy robes. The men had long hair up over their heads, bun-fashion, some with a head band. Two women, Dutch, shivered in home-spun. A pitiful creature next to the chair I was shown to sat on the floor, feet and knees tight together, hands dutifully upright in his lap – a hard drug case.

Conversation was desultory. The guru had travelled extensively. I gently pulled his leg, to the evident amusement of the Maharaja. 'What,' asked the guru, 'is freedom? Constitution says India is free but also says 199 things I cannot do. What is freedom?' The Maharaja answered that, to him, freedom was being able to do the things one was allowed to do.

At lunch (tomato juice, vegetable soup, pumpkin, gourd, cabbage, brinjal, egg-plant, rice and cheese, apple and cake, laced with the Maharani's home-made marmalade) news of the cease-fire in East Pakistan was relayed by the BBC. Later the guru asked me why certain people in Canada had objected to a statue being in the nude? Having no better answer than 'Guruji, that is freedom,' I took leave of my host and hostess and left.

My next port of call was tea at the vicar's, meeting those old Koi Hais who could be dug out. The vicar's lady was scathing about Mrs Porbandar and I detected a feud. I made a merry jape about her militant Christianity and continued with my sticky bun. A dear old quavering colonel was there, the doyen of the small, introspective, dwindling, back-biting English community. 'Know your face,' he piped. 'know it anywhere. Arakan, Poonah, Delhi?' he continued asking as I shook my head. 'Where then?' he asked. 'At Mohan's General Stores this morning, when you were asking for Tutty-Frutty,' I answered, glad, at that juncture, that the Porbandar car came to take me to the cultural centre, it being time to give my lecture.

I was introduced to a nondescript audience of some thirty people and monopolised forty minutes of their time. A pretty but long-winded summing up by the Maharani was followed by a cup of Nescafé (bought, I gathered, especially at Mohan's that morning).

The good people of Ooty were certainly living in a whirl. I left the following day for the Hills by way of Madras, Calcutta and Dharan and when 1 January 1972 did come I was ready for it, meeting old friends in Taplejung.

[1975]

❧ 14 ❧

Free as a Bird

It hardly seems like twenty years ago that Malaya became independent. I was on the staff then (for the first and last time in my service) and not enjoying it so, when I was ordered to do a special job over the independence celebrations, I was pleased. I was sent on a mission.

It had been thought that Chin Peng might well start some skulduggery during this period, knowing that by then there were fewer troops in the country and most of them had to be taking part in the celebrations thereby giving him (Chin Peng) a head start. British Army HQ in Kuala Lumpur had been sent down to Seremban and the Malayan Army, more correctly the Federation Military Forces, now reigned (almost) supreme where before they had been but junior and embryo partners.

The theorists had thought thus: if Chin Peng came down into Malaya on the west side of the country, which was unlikely, there were good roads for reinforcements as well as airfields. If he chose the centre of the country, below the Betong Salient, as the jutting-down part of Thailand is known, there was little or nothing that could be done about it, even if it were heard about.

That left the east, with a road that had then to cross ten ferries, so was too slow for any rapidly required deployment but which did have a good airfield at a place called Kota Bahru. This area was unlikely to be used but there had been a misappreciation of the threat (the uncharitable called it something else), so precautions were taken. In order for there to be transport at the airfield in the event of an emergency, I was ordered to move up the road with a convoy of seventeen Land Rovers and their trailers.

It was a hotchpotch assortment of drivers, British and Gurkha, that assembled at Seremban. We were escorted by armoured cars for the first part of the journey, which was slow, hot and, in places, pervasively dusty.

On the second day we had to cross the majority of the ferries. In places the road jinked inland so the river to be crossed was narrow, thus operations were comparatively speedy even though only two Land Rovers and their trailers were able to be handled at one time. More often than not the ferries were placed at the mouths of the rivers, where the crossings were affected by the tides to an extent that one particular river took seven hours to cross. The convoy became uncontrollably spread out.

Towards the end of that day, 30 August 1957, I had gone forward to choose a site for that night and eventually settled on an area by the beach at the edge of the Kuala Trengganu club. Having fixed up details as well as I could, I drove back down the road, hoping to gather everyone in by dusk.

Heavy rain and breakdowns resulted in the last vehicle arriving at midnight with, for me, that morning's meal. The ground around the clubhouse was inches deep in water. Thunder and lightning were almost continuous. The only dry place for the Gurkha driver and myself was a table we found. Up we clambered, having ushered in Independence Day in the most dismal of circumstances.

Next morning we dried ourselves out as best we could and drove off northwards. I gathered later that our progress out of the town caused quite a stir. A parade was being held to mark the end of British colonial rule with Police, Home Guard, Boy Scouts, Girl Guides, Boys' Brigade and the First Aid fraternities, were all in three ranks, with school children less well marshalled and a watching crowd of spectators dressed in their finery – Malay and European. A Malay speech had been made and now an English one was being given. A clipped, staccato voice was saying, '... and now we are looking after ourselves having shaken the British off ...' when a low rumble of transport was heard. All heads craned as the first, then second Land Rover and trailer hove into sight along the road abutting the parade ground. No interest in the parade was paid until the seventeenth had been counted and was out of sight. Just having moved off the spacing between the vehicles was equidistant and most impressive. Damp and bored soldiers scowled as they drove past, giving an unwarranted impression of power and control. The noise died away and the reedy voice resumed its paean of self-praise to the multitude: '... from now on we are on our own.'

Up in Kota Bahru the celebration parade had been, if anything, less successful. A cage of pigeons, mounted on a stand, was in front of and to one side of the main dais. Men in traditional warrior dress, carrying staves, were its escort. An artillery piece was to boom out independence joy as the pigeons were liberated when the roof of the cage was lifted back. The Chief Minister of Kelantan had, unfortunately, muddled his notes up and reached the climax of his speech before he should have done. A recording of the new national anthem, which had only arrived the day before, was started at the previously notified juncture, but alas! the record was cracked and no one had realised it. In the embarrassingly unrehearsed hiatus before it had dawned on anyone to turn the thing off or to jolt it on a revolution, the Chief Minister realised that he had skipped a page or two and turned back. His fluttering hands were mistaken for the signal for the artillery piece to boom, which it did, several times. There was no stopping it. Back was flung the lid of the pigeons' cage but so frightened were the birds by the noise that they remained just where they were. The last boom died away, the shrill scratch of the record was becoming even more scratchy, when an old retainer, one of the warriors guarding the pigeons' cage, took the initiative. Lifting up his staff he ignominiously poked it through the bars, thinking presumably that that would cause the recalcitrant birds to become airborne. The birds, however, had different ideas on the subject. They bounced and shuffled to the far end of the cage only to be poked back again, ignominiously, by their staff-wielding keeper. Only after considerable effort did he manage to get the birds away but at least he had the crowd's sympathy as the ill-omened birds rose into the air, only to flutter down nearby and start waddling petulantly, looking for food.

We stayed in Kota Bahru for a few days and carried out some reconnaissances. After watching the celebrations, which included kite-flying and boat-racing, we drove back to Seremban. We were not best pleased to learn that the expedition would never have been sent if the person who had originally assessed the situation had not been on leave at the time and his 'stand-in' had read the small print. But thus is history written – and anyway it got me away from my desk for a few days.

[1977]

The End of an Era

The high hills of Laos are breath-taking in their beauty and their immensity, far more so than, say, in Borneo. Rising to a height of 9,000 feet vast cliffs of lime stone vie with majestic jungle-covered peaks. On the upper slopes of many hills are Meo and other tribesmen who, by choice, live a remote life, cultivating their poppies and just living, minding their own business. Evidence of decades of 'slash and burn' cultivation are all too apparent. One saying of the Meo, who have migrated from Yunnan during the last few decades, is that 'there is always another hill'. Uglier scars remain; patches burnt out by napalm give silent witness to the bombing that has taken place over the years. In the valleys from which there has been no exodus of refugees there are rice fields, farms, small villages and rural activity that has remained unchanged for many centuries. Communications are scarce but paradoxically the areas where there has been fighting have been opened up by considerable road construction. The newer roads have been built by the Chinese, Americans and Vietnamese – notably the Ho Chi Minh trail road system. The older roads were built by the French and, for the most part, are still laterite, dusty during the dry season and treacherously muddy in the rainy season.

One of these roads, Route 7, snakes its way from the North Vietnamese border, north of the Plain of Jars, towards a strategically important road junction called Sala Phou Khoun. There it joins the important Route 13 that runs all the way from Saigon, first through Cambodia, then right up Laos, parallel with the River Mekong, reaching the administrative capital, Vientiane, then turns north away from the river and on up to the royal capital, Luang Prabang, one of the most beautiful towns in the world. It so happened that at the time of the cease-fire of 1962, the road junction was in the hands of the 'pro-Communist Pathet Lao' forces, but during the ensuing ten years it had changed hands a number of times until, by the time of the 1973 cease-fire, it was virtually on the zonal boundary of the two sides but occupied by the pro-Government forces, the Royal Lao Army. It also had the distinction of being the only piece of real estate in Government hands that had belonged to the Pathet Lao in 1962. It was an especially sensitive area, both politically and militarily.

Scattered around the road junction was a unit of the Royal Lao Army, mainly an infantry battalion but also a sprinkling of armoured cars, a few pieces of light artillery and the local queen of the battlefield, a piece of medium artillery. It pointed towards the enemy, was the pride and joy of its crew and the main reason why the commander thought it unlikely that the enemy would be so stupid and attack the place. It was superbly camouflaged, so well so that, to the casual observer, its presence was a secret. It was also hoped that the enemy spies and agents were similarly in the dark. Unfortunately it was unserviceable and had been so for an embarrassingly long time. The American who was in charge of the funds that were paying for the Royal Lao Army went to Sala Phou Khoun one day in April 1975 and asked the proud commander whether the previously given advice about having the gun either changed or repaired *in situ* was going to be followed or not. The astonishing (to some) reply was that the commander, a colonel, was loth to disturb the camouflage around the gun 'as the enemy might then know that we had it, be angry with us and punish us by attacking the position which we would then lose, and the Headquarters would also be angry with me. It is much better and easier to leave things as they are.' This extraordinary answer typified so much that was horribly wrong. His visitor asked him about his strength and was told that, although some men were away, there was a platoon's worth of soldiers defending the road junction. The visitor then brought their minds back to more interesting things by pulling out of his briefcase a quart bottle of whisky and several issues of *Playboy*, complete with pull-out pin-ups. Having made his contribution to help stabilise the situation and leaving a huddled, excited group of officers sitting round a ration box that served as their Mess table, he jumped into his helicopter and, for the last time ever, flew away.

On 30 March 1975 Danang fell and things were never the same again. Saigon fell a month later, on 30 April, thereby spreading panic and gloom in the ranks of the Royal Lao Army, from the topmost to the lowest. On the morrow, taking advantage of Labour Day manifestations to drive home their message, the local 'rent-a-crowd' students in Vientiane paraded with placards and banners on which were listed the most hated sixteen men of the 'right wing', civilians in the Coalition Government and soldiers alike. Rumour and fear were already manifest in a large segment of the public and the May Day warnings did not go unheeded for long. The Pathet Lao attacked the Sala Phou Khoun feature on 5 May and, not surprisingly, took it without much difficulty. The Royal Lao Army units in the area melted away. A company of Pathet Lao soldiers moved some way south down Route 13, coming to a halt about 120 miles to the north of Vientiane. Simultaneously there were rumours of assassins having infiltrated into the capital and so, when one prominent man was assassinated, the inhabitants of Vientiane had their worst fears realised: death was everywhere. There was an exodus across the

Mekong to the comparative safety of Thailand. The population visibly dwindled.

On 9 May other Pathet Lao forces moved out of the hills about fifty miles north of Vientiane and cut Route 13, thereby preventing any reinforcement from the north by the one group of Royal Lao Army troops that might have been capable of a show of force. By that time the majority of the sixteen 'traitors' had fled the country and the northern force also crumbled. These were the remnants of the Central Intelligence Agency secret army that had had so much publicity.

May 11th was Constitution Day and the normal military activity that was a feature of the occasion was noticeably absent. It was during his speech to His Majesty the King that the Prime Minister, Prince Souvanna Phouma, gave strong hints that there would soon be more political changes to reconcile with the new situation. The very next day the Pathet Lao Secretary of State for War was appointed Acting Minister of Defence in place of the man who had been high on the list of sixteen and who had also fled the country. The first order that the new man gave was to the Royal Lao Army to stay where it was and not to fight. At the same time orders were given for the Pathet Lao forces (correctly named as the Lao People's Liberation Army) for a general advance into the zone occupied by the pro-Government forces, which militarily they had never taken, up to the western frontier of Laos' border with Thailand. Only the two capitals were spared at that juncture as they were officially already neutral and there were plans to deal with them separately. Between 16 and 23 May all the other towns had been occupied or, as we quickly learnt to say, 'liberated', for the first time ever. There was no opposition – the Royal Lao Army was utterly useless, utterly broken and only too thankful to have an excuse not to fight any more.

The evening before the Constitution Day ceremony, a new development occurred when the cadets from the Military

Academy, which was a few miles east of Vientiane and in the same complex as the 'reactionaries' heartland, staged a demonstration against their Commandant and the Deputy Commander-in-Chief, saying that they did not want to be used as coup troops by the 'reactionary traitors' and pledging their loyalty to the Prime Minister, under whose direct orders they placed themselves. Carefully prepared and well organised, they set a pattern that was to be closely followed in every department and unit of the armed services, the civil administration and various commercial organisations.

The case of the cadets attracted the attention of the world press who had gathered in Vientiane a week or so earlier when news of the capture of Sala Phou Khoun broke. The venue the cadets chose (or had chosen for them) was the Lao-German Technical School, which lay halfway between their camp, itself the prime target during the abortive coup of 20 August 1973, and the town centre, close to the Prime Minister's residence. This was deliberate because the Prime Minister was a 'neutralist' and still a revered figure. The whole show lasted three days and nights. Groups of students took turns to stop passers-by and give them leaflets. Their banners and placards set the tone for all later 'manifestations', as they were called; 'ultra rightists', a phrase unknown before, and 'imperialist America', as well as 'traitorous lackeys' and many others. A loud hailer was used the more blatantly, if not the more clearly, to put over the protesters' point of view. A later refinement, introduced by the Signal Regiment, was the use of a tape recorder, but this was when such antics were commonplace and had lost what little interest there ever had been. That is not to say that all the manifestations had no point, when a man's destiny is in the balance, joining the crowd can be the most expedient. Even so it was a curious sensation to visit the Ministry of Defence and come across placards outside every office (even the guard commander's cubby hole) condemning the man who used to be within and demanding that he be replaced. Other aspects of a cultural revolution that were aimed at reshaping the lives of all, change the government at every level as well as including such details as the banning of male long hair, forcibly cutting it off if necessary, and the abandonment of flared trousers – both obnoxious and typical of 'imperial and reactionary' habits.

Another feature of the revolution was the way in which various commanding officers were replaced by those considered more revolutionary, less corrupt and fitted to be leaders in the New Order. In the case of an Engineer unit, the CO, a colonel, was a good and popular man. At a mass meeting of the unit, during the three-day manifestation so necessary for the people's wishes to be known, a show of hands was requested for one of two candidates to be the new CO; the old commander or a captain, the latter being the Pathet Lao favourite. There was a representative of the Pathet Lao at the election, at which the colonel was re-elected by 80% of the vote. The ballot was immediately declared null and void. An hour's break was ordered by the representative at the end of which (surprise! surprise!) the results were exactly opposite and the colonel found himself out of a job. In the case of the Military Police, the Provost Marshal was replaced by a sergeant. I spoke to a lieutenant who had been responsible for getting rid of the entire local hierarchy, the Sub-Divisional Commander, a colonel, the local Police Chief and the local Administrator whose HQ was fifty-five minutes' drive north from Vientiane. When I asked him what he now proposed to do, he replied that he would escape to France if conditions became too difficult. In answer to my observing that it seemed strange to plan on that course having been so successful, so why had he bothered in the first place, he engagingly admitted that he had only been looking after himself and that seemed the most prudent way of doing it.

There were many jobless officers, not drawing any pay, too poor to run away and start a new life in another country and too tarred with reactionary stigma to be absorbed into the new regime. That, however, was to be only one of their worries – in the early days the implication of the euphemistic word 'seminar' had yet to conjure up visions of forced labour, hunger and pre-dawn knocks on the door or hungry, terrified and deserted wives and children not knowing where father was nor when he would return; seminar still meant a short two-week period of re-education. Even those who cleared the first hurdle were by no means home or dry. That which had happened to date was merely a clever way for the Old Order, with a bit of self-engendered help, to define itself into various categories of self-acceptability. It in no way altered the inevitable second stage, helpful though events so far had been, which had its roots in history.

The war in Indo-China had been going on, in varying degrees of intensity, for thirty years. A lull in the middle 1950s neatly divided the period for some historians to call the period until Dien Bien Phu in 1954 'The First Indo-China War' and thereafter 'The Second Indo-China War'. Be that as it may. During that time many changes had occurred but not the political aims of the various major contestants and their clients, except that the French had wanted to restore a lost empire and the Americans to fight Communism on the mainland of Asia. From 1954 onwards, at least as far as Laos was concerned, its problems were, in the main, exacerbated by it being an independent state with no method of being a viable entity in its own right and politically hopelessly divided. After the debacle of Dien Bien Phu, the Royal Lao Army found itself in no way prepared for fighting any kind of war, as there was no one with any training or knowledge of what should be done, especially at any level above platoon. There were a number of coups as rival factions sought to gain some advantage or other, such as political benefits or a hand in the opium trade that was such a lucrative and flourishing concern. Likewise, the war in Laos was always regarded as an adjunct to the main struggle farther to the east in Vietnam. Neither was the threat properly analysed: the West would call it Communist Revolutionary Warfare, they called it People's Revolutionary War, but at times it was so heavily disguised by actions on a major scale that it fooled the analysts. Thus was the threat wrongly seen, thus was there a faulty conclusion as to the correct counter. These are brave words and have the advantages of hindsight but even before much of the fighting the works of General Giap and Ho Chi Minh were available for study. A People's Revolutionary War, controlled by an authoritarian state, puts its main emphasis on a firm political base from which to operate and not in any mere military solution. Thus while such devices as, for instance, people sniffers and infra-red aids helped bombing and main force attacks to inflict horrendous casualties, the very nature of the military effort was largely counter-productive. (Witness the bombing of London by the Germans in the '39-'45 war.) Whatever role the Pathet Lao played during the two Indo-China wars, they had one policy and one aim, unlike the other side, the Royal Lao Government, which seemingly had none but was beset by family quarrels, feudal barons exploiting the situation to their personal advantage and military incompetence to a debilitating degree from top to bottom. It is small wonder that there was no united support of any value to the legitimate government. A fear of the opposition was in no way a proper alternative to a firm policy, despite (or because of) being told the dangers of this countless times by their sponsors. A death wish of incompetence and inertia by those who should have had a completely opposite slant on life had they foreseen how quickly they were losing the war resulted in nothing positive being done, but a series of bumbling 'ad hocery' always too little and too late. Thus one unkind wit remarked that it was 'a case of the Pathet Lao versus the Pathetic Lao'.

During 1973, 1974 and the first four months of 1975 I visited sixty-eight different places in Laos and, of these, two were in the 'liberated' zone, at the invitation of the Central Committee. The other sixty-six were under the control of the Royal Lao Government, and many were visited often, thus affording me the opportunity to monitor their morale. Despite much kindness and hospitality, coupled with what I felt to be genuine friendship and appreciation of my visits, it was depressing in the extreme to see the state of affairs: underfed soldiers, some aged twelve or thirteen years; whole platoons who were suffering from malaria (despite there being ample preventive drugs at source); rusty weapons; decrepit hovels as semi-permanent accommodation; six months in arrears of pay; death by starvation on patrol because the helicopter pilots would not fly in to bring the patrol out without being paid 'danger money' that the local commander either could not or would not pay . . . but why continue the dreary catalogue? As month succeeded month, morale dropped lower and lower. Many and high-ranking were the people who asked advice on what should be done to avert a situation that was looming more and more ominously. The rules of the game were strict and had to be followed. The diplomatic and other constraints placed even on so lowly a creature as a Defence Attaché completely forbade putting Britain's impartial posture in jeopardy, even were the truth of the advice to be believed.

I was nothing but the accredited military representative for the collection of military information by overt means, not a disguised adviser, however much private feeling rebelled against such constraints and one's own military judgement cried out in protest at what was there and military hackles rose on countless occasions. It simply was not my business, nor was it worth upsetting the system

1. Lt Col J. P. Cross, Chief Instructor, Jungle Warfare School, 1968.

2. The Yamagishi Butai surrendering to 1st Bn 1st KGV's Own Gurkha Rifles, Thu Dau Mot, Cochin-China, November 1945. (*Courtesy of G. W. J. Wheatley*).

3. 'This is my nose'. J. P. Cross as Chief Instructor, Army School of Education (Gurkhas), some time between mid-1949 and late 1951.

4. Field Marshal Sir John Harding with Pipe Major Shamsher Gurung 7GR (one of the Coronation Contingent), at Pirbright in England in 1953. (*Copyright © The Gurkha Museum*)

5. Visit of QMG General Sir Ouvry Roberts (with GOC General Stockwell) to Sungei Besi, Kuala Lumpur, Malaya, 2/7 Gurkha Rifles on 8 October 1953. (*Copyright © The Gurkha Museum*)

11. Members of the aboriginal Temiar tribe give a demo to Lt Col John Heelis and the Colonel of the Pacific Island Regiment (affiliated to 7GR) at Fort Kemar, north Malaya, while the battalion was on Op Bamboo, operating from Grik in 1962. They were extremely accurate! (*Lt Col R. Holworthy*)

12. Army Air Corps Sioux helicopter drops in to B coy base at the school in Paduan, 5th Division, Sarawak. 1963. (*Lt Col R. Holworthy*)

13. A Border Scout at the village of Long Jawi in Malaysia. Later, the post here was attacked by the Indonesians and the twenty-odd Border Scouts there were either captured or killed. (*Copyright © The Gurkha Museum*)

14. Men of J. P. Cross's Para Company practising river crossing, Brunei, 1966. (*Copyright © The Gurkha Museum*)

15. Parachute training, Changi, Singapore, early 1962. Members of 1/7 GR contingent prepare to jump from an RAF Hastings at Kuantan airfield. These men, together with some from 10 GR, later formed the nucleus of the Gurkha Independent Parachute Company. (*Lt Col R. Holworthy*)

16. Major J. P. Cross, the OC, attending Maj Gen A. G. Patterson in handing out 'red berets' instead of the normal rifle green ones to men of the Gurkha Para Company at Kluang, on 7 July 1966.(*Copyright © The Gurkha Museum*)

17. Member of Gurkha Independent Parachute Company based in Brunei practising abseiling on 200 feet of line, February 1966. (*Copyright © The Gurkha Museum*)

18. Qualifying descent: OC Gurkha Independent Parachute Company, Major J. P. Cross, gives out red beret to successful soldier Rfm Sombahadur Thapa. (*Copyright © The Gurkha Museum*)

19. Now as Commandant, a press briefing at the Jungle Warfare School, Johore Bahru, Peninsular Malaysia, 1970.

20. Demonstration at the Jungle Warfare School, 1970. (*Copyright © The Gurkha Museum*)

21. Swimming contest at the British Gurkha Centre, Paklihawa, Nepal, in 1978.

22. J. P. Cross with the 6GR pipes and drums, Gillingham, 24 July 1987. (*Colin Hoare*)

23. Father and son in Pokhara Camp. (*Alison Locke*)

24. J. P. Cross and family, 1996.

25. J. P. Cross with his one-time Gurkha Major, Birkaraj Gurung, MBE 6GR.

26. J. P. Cross working on comparing modern Nepali with that of seventy years ago in the university in Kathmandu, a younger version of today by 27½ years, alas! (*Nirmalman Tuladhar*)

by interfering, although pressures were applied and opportunities offered. Thus there were awkward moments, even long after the cease-fire, when it would have been so easy to have disregarded the little bell that started ringing in the back of my head when such situations arose. In a civil war, agents on the other side are bound to exist – and I was representing Britain for the whole of Laos, not just for one side. One awkward moment is vivid still . . .

There was an innocent-looking and unobtrusive group of humble buildings set to one side of a feeder road, fifty-five minutes' drive north from Vientiane. A Resettlement Centre for the local troops, or so the notice board proclaimed. Being interested in Gurkha resettlement, I wanted to visit it. It so happened that I managed to pay a visit when I was with the local Sub-Divisional Commander, a colonel. As we were driving past it on the way somewhere else, I asked about it and suggested we drop in on our way back. The Colonel seemed to forget as we drove past it but, on my reminding him of our earlier conversation, we reversed and entered the place. All was 'shoe-string' simplicity. The Captain in command gave me a briefing, which was as lacklustre as himself, but which was hardly surprising considering that he had been in command for ten years. What was far more surprising was when the Colonel interrupted the Captain and told me that the resettlement aspect was but a cover for certain clandestine activities, and so secret was it that even the Ministry of Defence was officially unaware of its existence. It was, in fact, what might be termed a school for agents operating 'behind the lines' and he then proceeded to describe activities in interesting detail. On the way back to the Sub-District camp I asked the Colonel if I could pay the school an in-depth visit some time. 'If Military Region HQ have no objections, please come back.'

Some weeks later another visit was arranged, only mysteriously to be cancelled at short notice. This was so typical that I was not unduly worried. Another date was fixed but the Colonel was ill and I was not wanted. I could have been escorted by his deputy, but no. Back in Vientiane, I went to the Military Region HQ again and met the Chief of Staff, whom I knew well. 'Colonen,' I said (there is a tendency to change a final 'l' to an 'n' in Lao, whether speaking Lao or a foreign language), 'if I am an embarrassment, please tell me and I will desist in trying to revisit the school.' 'Colonen,' he replied, 'you are a great help to us, we would like you to go.' 'Help', I mused later, had I misunderstood him?

A third visit was fixed. I arrived at the Sub-District HQ dead on the stroke of 9 o'clock, where I was greeted by the Colonel and surprisingly, (but hadn't I learnt never to be surprised in Laos?) by the local Police Chief and the local Administrator. I was invited into the office and offered a seat. The Colonel went to his desk and searched for a piece of paper. 'The programme,' he proudly proclaimed. This time I was amazed, though I tried not to show it. In all the visits I had ever paid the Royal Lao Army, it was always the case that I was asked what I wanted to do and for how long. How refreshing to have met a man who had arranged a programme for me. Go to the school, meet the staff, talk with the students, take questions, walk around the area and return to the HQ. The Colonel suggested we go in my staff car. I was amazed yet again when the Police Chief and the Administrator also got it. Perhaps they were stranded, otherwise surely they would not be allowed to go to such a sensitive place? Away we drove – past the turning to the school. By that time I realised that anything might happen and I was in the hands of the Colonel. We were making for the open countryside and I had been in the game long enough to know that it was best to roll with the punch; so I said nothing. It could be that we were ahead of schedule, and that we were passing time by going on a joy ride. We drove on till we reached the end of the road where there was a village. We reached a group of new buildings on the far side and turned into the compound. I glanced up at the largest and read Fa Ngum Comprehensive School, written in English. It had 'aid' stamped everywhere. Still the penny did not drop. We drove past the main buildings and stopped near a roofed but wall-less edifice outside which were some twenty local dignitaries to whom I was introduced, whilst inside I saw serried rows of teenage school children, about 400 of them. I was escorted to a raised platform and, as I was being shown the obvious chair of honour, the penny finally did drop. The 'school' had been changed and here was I as guest of honour, if not guest speaker. I had been hijacked!

I numbly noticed a tape recorder at the rostrum and dimly realised all eyes were on me as I racked my brains for a subject suitable for my young audience. The Colonel was the first of four to go to the rostrum to welcome me. A glowing and, to my mind, unnecessarily detailed description of my linguistic ability was given as I was introduced as the English Military Attaché, along with a brief resume of what the Colonel thought I had so far done in Laos. After the other three had had their say, and I obviously was the guest speaker, there was nothing else to do but to accept the nightmarish situation with as good grace as possible. When it was my inevitable and unenviable turn to stand up and address the crowd all I felt was missing was a roll of drums; the nearest to that noise was my heart beating. One problem in speaking Lao is the marked regional differences that abound. I had had my initial sixty hours' introduction to the Lao language at the hands of the king's niece, Princess Golden Fairy, when still in London and she taught me her dialect, the royal dialect, which is more musical than any other and has an unusual vowel sound that brings smiles to others. Of its six tones, only one is similar to the Vientiane dialect which my audience spoke, as well as other complexities. Would what I tried to say be understood?

In the opening remarks I deliberately made them laugh, thus breaking the ice and I then talked generalities for about fifteen minutes, when I made to regain my seat. I was neatly intercepted by the Colonel who politely ushered me back to the rostrum, took the microphone and told the audience that the English 'Colonen' would tell them what Prince Souvanouvong (the 'Red Prince') had discussed with the English ambassador when, eighteen months previously, we were in the caves of the remote Pathet Lao capital, the first non-Communists to be invited for about ten years. If nothing else that gave me a clue of what to talk about as none of my audience had ever been there and so wanted to know about the place. I was therefore able to spend about twenty minutes in describing the place, the bomb damage, the caves, the razed town, the terrain and all.

Smugly I felt I had acquitted myself gallantly and turned to leave once more. Alas, the Lao Colonel was more tenacious than his English counterpart and once more my passage was blocked. Smiling benignly, he took the microphone and told the long-suffering audience that Laos was a monarchy as was England. Furthermore, Laos had a Communist problem as had England. He therefore wanted to know what the English 'Colonen' advised as to the remedies for the two countries.

What, indeed? Even had I had time to prepare an answer to that question in my own language, I felt I was not really qualified to give a reasoned and considered opinion – in a language as imperfectly known as Lao and with an audience so ill-prepared for such a dreary topic, anything I said would probably be wrong. But above all, I had to forget my audience and remember that my voice was being recorded, so no silly throw-away remarks could be indulged in. But an answer I had to give, and cursing the Colonel under my breath, I again reminded my audience that I was an impartial and apolitical Defence Attaché, so it would be wrong of me to give too

154

many details. I re-quoted to them that the price of freedom was eternal vigilance (or words possibly to that effect) and continued in an uninteresting and neutral strain until I adjudged that a few more minutes had passed.

I then made a resolute move back to my seat. 'But not so fast, Colonen, I have another question for you.' He must have seen the face I pulled but behaved as though he hadn't. Certainly the children did and they howled with mirth. However the Colonel was not to be deflected and this time he told the students, who to their credit were well behaved and long-suffering, that the English 'Colonen' would discuss the future of the monarchy in both countries and the part it could play in preventing the spread of Communism.

But I'd had enough. I'd gone to the limits of my charter already and heaven help me if there were agents in the audience; how could I have foretold that the three of those who had travelled with me in my car to the school would be some of the very first casualties of the cultural revolution and kicked out by the lieutenant who had organised the tape-recorder? In the event I limited myself to thanking the students for being so patient and how honoured I was to have been invited to talk to them.

I then sat down with the utmost relief having been on my feet for forty-five minutes. Three people made thank-you speeches and I was asked a supplementary question. I was a little slow in winding myself up to answer it and I was surprised when the audience started a slow hand clap. The last person to get up and speak was the student leader, who wanted to know what was the population of England, how old was I and could I be extended in post for another year? The students then sang the school song and I was taken on a conducted tour of the area before going back to the camp where, to my intense embarrassment, the whole proceedings were played back to me over a meal of sticky rice and chickens' legs from the knee down. I made as quick a get-away as I decently could . . . and had an early night that night, feeling whacked. I was later told that 80% of what I'd said had been understood. The Lao are by nature polite!

When eventually I did get to the military school, I could only again marvel that anybody could achieve anything in the way of training for an arduous, dangerous and skilful task when there were no training aids, no artificial lighting of any sort, no administrative back-up such as cooking facilities in the camp itself, nothing that I had been brought up to believe was an inescapable minimum for any training concern. My visit there was as painful as so many others were, seeing the pitiable efforts of the inmates trying to make the best of an appallingly difficult and hopeless situation. As ever, I had constantly to remind myself that it was not my business and that I was there at the invitation of the Lao authorities, that it was not Britain's quarrel, and importantly, with so much to occupy a harassed Government at home, all unnecessary embarrassment (such as becoming 'involved') had to be avoided. But even so . . .

My final series of visits around that part of the country where I was still welcome took place in the latter half of April 1975. Those who had previously been reticent were garrulous, those who had been pessimistic were 'windy' to a degree that it was unkind to keep them in charge of soldiers, those who had been full of brave talk were grave-stone silent among the chatter and rumour-spreading of their fellows. Leadership from the topmost downwards was, as ever, non-existent and in the lower echelons rapidly dwindling to meaningless proportions as realisation of their actual plight sank in. Even had the army been prepared to fight how many of the 50,000 men on the strength were available? Depressed commanders had told me how, in order that their families could survive, at least as many as a third of the force was always away at another job, if the unit was near a town or just foraging at any one time. In the remoter areas where the local commander was little more than a petty despot, units were estimated to be at a tenth of their strength as no one either bothered or was allowed to check on the rolls of phantom soldiers; thus the effective, if that is the right word to use, strength was, maybe, 10,000. Anything that might have been done to rectify the situation was ten to twelve years too late, so when the end did come it came with lightning speed: foundations made of sand have never been known to last.

Those who had been in the army and in the administration had suffered under a regime that had taught them such bad thoughts that everybody had to be retaught the correct approach. Everybody, did I say? Well, almost everybody; certainly servicemen, Government employees, schoolmasters, manual labourers, skilled workers, farmers, even taxi drivers, prostitutes and my house-boy's mother-in-law, seemingly there was no category left out, except the rent-a-crowd students that so oppressed the American community. Their activities were rigidly controlled and had a mingling of Pathet Lao in plain clothes to help. They represented 'the people', so were an essential part of the revolutionary process, and had to be present at negotiations between the two sides when, for instance, American aid had to be wound up. All the processions, the manifestations, the demonstrations were skilfully stage-managed by hard-liners, who had done their homework thoroughly. Despite no casualties, it was a deeply humiliating process. The Lao people were punishing the Americans so they said. As soon as the students had served their purpose, their organisation was disbanded and the activists dispersed, with, so it seemed, some feeling that their fun and games had not gone on long enough . . . so maybe there were seminars for everybody after all!

It was interesting to be in a position to observe it going on before one's eyes. I spoke at length to my Chinese colleague about how 'controlled' it was but he professed himself well pleased to see how copy-book were developments. The lesson to be learnt and the lesson to be applied and the lesson never to be forgotten was, first and foremost, that everything had to come from the people, as the people's will. It was in no way to appear as a small group of activists manipulating events alone as such a happening could not, by definition, be the will of the people, so it was plainly absurd (on my part, I was told) to express such sentiments. Any such activists represented the people because the people had to understand the true revolutionary line, the true political base from which, on which, by which and with which, in endless, mindless repetition, all depended, and without which revolution could never be won. In the old days no Inquisitor worthy of his Holy Office could have been so zealous, no recent convert so quickly learn his catechism as were the eighteen political points read, marked, learnt and inwardly digested. There is a stark and puritanical revulsion away from all signs of the old order: traditional dress, short back and sides, no 'Western' style dancing are some examples of the new imperative. Cars are not the method for ordinary folk to go to work; bicycles or walking is the new requirement.

Aversion therapy is applied to those unreceptive to warnings and whose attitudes are manifestly incorrect, such as those whose human frailty allows them to like playing cards – non-stop for seventy-two hours under the watchful eyes of vigilant guards (and this for elderly women) who allow them six hours sleep every twenty-four. Too many awkward questions at seminars result in the asker having to listen to the correct answer, in solitary confinement, for seventy-two hours, played to him by a tape-recorder that is only silent for six hours of the twenty-four. This so far has done the trick. One hapless man who had this treatment later said it nearly sent him mad and he would never ask another question in his life. At the airport one morning I was talking to a young Pathet Lao soldier (for all the world a Gurkha hill man in a different uniform as far as looks were concerned) when two young Thai girls, dependants of an official in the Thai embassy, teetered across the apron to their aeroplane in shoes with monstrously high heels but otherwise demure. The soldier, an airport guard, looked down his nose at them and said, 'They're an insult to their country.' It is hard to imagine many other young men anywhere else in the world (except possibly China?) with revolutionary ardour so ingrained that such a reaction is forthcoming and, to them, natural.

I make a practice of speaking to these men as much as possible, which the majority of them seem to appreciate, with only the real hard-core political commissar-type eyeing me suspiciously, at least initially, and apart from this latter category they are simple men, polite, with a developed sense of dedication and purpose and who obviously regard themselves as the true representatives of their country. What little they know about Britain they seem to like. A socialist country, sloughed from a colonial past with, so I have often been told, a record second-to-none and keeping the old mores and traditions, as exemplified by the Monarchy. Ah well, who am I to teach them about our export rejects?

The question has to be asked, how long will it all last? I believe it will be a feature of life in this part of the world for an indefinite period. Politically it is important in the battle for influence in the region so that any means at the disposal of the hard men be utilised to their advantage. The Public Enemy No 1 is the American and is likely so to be for a long, long time and school text books are prepared around the myth that the Pathet Lao beat the 'Imperialist Americans' single-handed. Such impressions will never be eradicated although possibly modified, so, fairly or unfairly, they will always influence at least one generation. The French are also a good, albeit a more restrained, target, so are the Japanese who are branded as 'fascists', though I never did find anyone who could tell me what he meant by 'fascist'. Similarly, a reactionary is not one who reacts against a change in the situation but one who reacts against a reaction. Such a heresy as that would make me worth of having to attend a seminar for several weeks as, if the Big God is Politics, then the Godling is Semantics. If anyone doubts that, let him or her read any major pronouncement of any Communist – endless and soul-destroying repetition but every word used with its own invariable and exact meaning.

In conclusion it is my considered opinion that the outward spread of the sea change that has occurred in Laos and the rest of south Indo-China during 1975 has a long way to go until it can he halted, but that it can never be mopped up. And the saddest part of it all, as I see it, is that what has taken over from the old regime had, initially, to be better than that which it had replaced. That which could not sensibly evolve by its own peaceful methods was ripe for change to be brought upon it by violent means – in other words, the political base of the old regime was not firm enough. Decent men and women had ceased to have faith in their own institutions yet were powerless to root out the enemy in their own midst, let alone prevent the external pressures that were applied, to say nothing of the defeat of the 'Free World' that has left all of us in the West the poorer, just because the leaders gave them no sign that they had understood either the problems of any of the dangers that were besetting them, nor that there was enough willpower to change what a few good men and true had already realised needed changing. Is Laos the only country in that unenviable position?

Vientiane, Laos
October, 1975
[1976]

❦ *16* ❧

Thirty Years of Change and Challenge

In February 1947 my friend and I crossed the Indo-Nepalese border at Raxaul, boarded the quaint little train there and went to Amlekhganj where the local Governor, whom we happened to meet, lent us his car for the next stage of our journey to Kathmandu. The unmetalled road ended at Bhimphedi and the rest of the way, until the brim of the Valley was reached, was on foot.

On our way back to India we saw a car being carried over the rough track by a horde of porters, ant-like in their scurrying. Once in India we were jogged back into modern-day reality by the ugliness of the pre-partition crowds we met everywhere. Back in the battalion (where it was only one year after the men stopped having shaven pates) we recounted our adventures and felt a tinge of (probably unmerited) heroism.

Not until thirty years later did I once more drive along part of the Raxaul-Kathmandu road, this time on my way from Paklihawa to Dharan. I had not seen those bare, serrated hills for many more years than a dog's lifetime and as I drove along the east-west highway I mused as to whether those hills were the only constant features in Nepal, in an age when change has never been so rapid nor challenge more demanding.

In 1947 we were still part of the Indian Army. Even six months before partition such an event was neither decided upon nor even believed possible. In Britain the uglinesses and sadnesses of losing the peace having won the war were not yet apparent. The last great Chief of the Imperial General Staff was still Mr Slim, number two in the infant British Railways. The scars of the Red Fort Indian National Army trials and the mutiny of the Royal Indian Navy, to say nothing of our own Royal Air Force and Parachute Regiment euphemistically 'going on strike' were still so fresh we were benumbed by them; let alone by some atypically grave acts of Gurkha indiscipline in Santa Cruz and Dehra Dun. Thankfully the vastness of a disintegrating India and the total personal enmeshment made these and much else pass by unrealised by many, as indeed were the appalling massacres in the Punjab later in the year: 'the greatest act of British statesmanship in the twentieth century,' pontificated the Premier; 'apartheid in the name of God,' thought others. Even so, how many of us then realised the cataclysmic changes that were about to swamp us and whose disciples still gloatingly want more?

In early 1947 many in England (we had yet to learn to call our country by that less restrictive name Britain) felt that the world owed us a living: in 1977 no such thoughts exist except in the minds of the Lunatic Left, and then for different reasons. Empire, Patriotism, Enterprise and Religion (and many more) are dirty words – yet we still have that strange anachronism, the Brigade of Gurkhas, integrally in the British Army. The narrow-minded, regimentally dogmatic outlook of some of the British officers is a subject for bored smiles and tired grins in the offices of sophisticated but, if it were not for the laser-like intensity of the dedication and regimental pride of such people, along with the backbone of solidness of the Gurkha himself, such an institution as ours would never have lasted so long. In the same context it could be postulated that only by even more singleness of purpose have the Jewish people retained their identity for over forty centuries.

It would, however, be unrealistic in the extreme to pretend that change has not touched us to a significant degree. I often wonder if those amongst us who live in their Ivory Towers of Isolation (another name for them could be the Maintainers of the Myth) fully realise just how much change there has been in Nepal hence amongst her citizens: 'what do they know of Nepal who only Gurkhas know?' is not an unkind paraphrase.

In Nepal alone there have been such landmarks as the Palace Revolution that overthrew the Ranas, civil unrest, to say nothing of such measures as the land-reform programme, the emancipation of the under-privileged, the introduction of the Panchayat system and the Back to the Village campaign; nor should such aspects as the increase in the diplomatic community from the sole foreigners of 1947, the British, to the seventy-five accredited nations of (April) 1977 (of whom nineteen have resident missions in Kathmandu), the addition to the country's infrastructure of such organisations as UNESCO, the Peace Corps and Voluntary Service Overseas workers, to name but three of many who, in turn, are dwarfed by the flock of Do-Gooders to the Third World that scratch away with missionary zeal and who, in turn, are overshadowed by the crores of rupees poured in by interested Big Brothers, God-Fathers and other members of the Guilty-Conscience Syndrome – and the ungracious influx of tourists. From good to loathsome they descend on the country. The better ones are too polite (maybe) fully to remonstrate when necessary (or too ignorant), whilst the latter category cannot be worse than the pair of European hippies copulating in the village street at noon. The Jomoson air was their excuse but we are all the poorer because of it.

Nowadays the Ranas are never mentioned except with vituperation, yet were they wholly bad? Education is regarded as the paramount criterion for success by many but how few of them even know the sad half-truth that the spread of education is the spread of unhappiness? In land-hungry, land-locked Nepal, where

deforestation and soil-erosion are driving many to the dusty heat of
the Tarai the better to provide for their families, the tribal pattern
of resilience, parental authority, influence and prestige can be said
to have become weakened to the extent that the progeny of such
sibling off-shoots are not considered suitable for enlistment. But
the question I ask is what proportion of ex-servicemen die before
their due time through back-breaking, soul-searing overwork?
Those migrants or those left up in the Hills? I think the answer is
the former.

And does the magic of the Hills still exert its influence as it
did? Take the ethical standard of any village anywhere along the
tourist trail or the purlieus of any of the larger towns such as
Pokhara and Bhojpur, and you would be struck by the heightened
awareness for the 'quick buck': you are no longer a Traveller, you
are a Tourist. And although these lads have cut their teeth early
in an environment of easier gain than hitherto and all that stands
for, is the mere fact that the snows can be seen from their villages
going to be an overriding factor in allowing them to join the army,
instead of the lowlander pioneer?

'Know your men!' some say: 'know yourself!' others echo. The
Panchayat system and the drive in education have led to a fusion
of Aryan and Mongoloid Nepalis (we irrationally still call all the
latter Gurkhas) where characteristics of the one rub off against
the other – with what results? Ask any sapper what happens if you
remove one snag from a river and he will tell you that another is
formed elsewhere. And therein lies the problem for today, namely
recognising the problems of tomorrow.

The more rigid the pattern the less free the movement, while
no movement is tantamount to death: and as we are living in an
age when change has never been so fast, the art must be to keep
fluid movement within the rigid pattern and, where necessary, to
change that pattern so it becomes a skin and not a straitjacket.

I myself believe that for British and Gurkha alike our areas for enhancement lie not in the rigid boundaries of hitherto but need an empirical flexibility that is a happy mixture of necessity, experience and opportunity. We may not be far off true balance (otherwise how could we have survived so long?) but everything we have taken for granted in the past now needs looking at more circumspectly, needs appreciating its nuances more finely, needs a freer ranging mind to look beyond the present formalised concepts. And the final mixture must still have the correct proportions of discipline, skills and loyalty, seasoned with an act of faith and blessed by luck.

If that is what is happening now, we will make good: if not, we still have a little time left to adjust. If never – Amen.

[1978]

17

Five Fateful Flaws

The time has come, the Teacher said,
To see, when natural things
Are parodied or spoilt by man,
What consequence it brings,
Of leaves and limes and jungle camps
And where what bird call rings
And untold deeds by unsung men
Of whom some once wore wings.

'It's amazing what a lot of people take for granted,' said the Teacher. 'There's nothing more natural than nature and yet, when an aberration does occur, even if you do notice it, it probably never crosses your mind that you should ask yourself about it, why a pattern has been broken up, when, how and by whom? Such inquisitiveness is part of soldier's heritage.'

The young soldiers listened with great attention and respect for here was one laden with honours, rich in experience, renowned for his wisdom and famous for his teaching. 'If there is a flaw, it can be fateful, if not fatal. If you want to construe what probably happened before you came on the scene, notice nature. If nature didn't do something itself then someone did so for it or even against it. Life – yours, your friends' and your enemies' – may depend on a flaw being noticed. That is the supreme test of jungle lore. Oh I know there are umpteen tricks of the trade to help you and hinder the other fellow – walking up streams, planting living camouflage in the wake of your tracks, brushing where you've been walking to name but three. To my mind, however, the test of what I sometimes call a Maestro is more than that. I am going to give you five short examples of what I mean, five fateful flaws, you could say . . .'

I. One Leaf

'It was the time of the Indonesian incursion into Sarawak in 1966 which came to be known as the 'Sumbi Saga'. Many rumours had reached the authorities about this Indonesian Lieutenant Sumbi who was believed to be about to undertake a dangerous mission for his country. Apart from any other training he might have had, he had learnt to parachute in Abingdon in England, so it was said, and had been taught his basic jungle tactics at the Jungle Warfare School in Malaya. It was thought that the plot was for Sumbi to lead a band of some fifty soldiers from Kalimantan Utara, as Indonesian Borneo was known, infiltrating through Sarawak to Brunei and then to sabotage the Shell oil installations while the Malaysia-Indonesia Peace Talks were being held in Bangkok – trying to patch up the latter's 'Confrontation' of the former – so lulling people into a feeling of false security with their eyes turned towards mainland Asia instead of keeping watch and ward at home.

'When the incursion eventually started it came from across the border in the mountainous area of the Fourth Division of Sarawak. It was Sumbi's bad luck that the border crossing was made through a sector patrolled by the Gurkha Independent Parachute Company. A couple of ace operators, Sergeant Jitbahadur Rai, then 1/7 GR, and Rifleman Dharmalal Rai, 1/10 GR, were patrolling when Dharmé noticed a tiny glint, unnaturally bright, among the leaves on the jungle floor. He examined it and found it was a piece of tinfoil which smelt of coffee. Gurkhas didn't have coffee in their rations and there were no British troops in the area so, he reasoned, it had to be Indons, yet there were no obvious traces of them.

'The two soldiers then remade contact with their three other patrol members and, casting around, eventually met and tracked what they could dimly discern as jungle boot prints for three men and some suspicious signs where a branch, used as a brush, had swept at the foliage. Why suspicious? Two reasons: one was because some of the vegetation was lying unnaturally and, secondly, since the patrol knew it was not they who had made those tracks, trying to hide only three men's tracks was the sign of trespassing.

'The patrol, working under command of 1/7 GR, followed this vague trail for the rest of the day and the next, neither cooking nor making camp that night. This, in the cold Borneo Uplands, was a feat of discipline in itself. They then discovered a pile of strips of sacking with which Sumbi's other forty-seven men had wrapped their feet, thus leaving no footprints, and the three pairs of British pattern jungle boots that had been worn by the last men, now discarded; there were also other signs that confirmed numbers in the group, direction taken and how long ago they had moved off. The patrol then handed over their quest to 1/7 GR and back-tracked the incursors to the border, thereby allaying Higher Command's fears of a wrong interpretation being made of the findings so far: superbly good jungle craft.

'During the next month or so all hell was let loose, as far as Sumbi and his men were concerned. Some were captured, some died of starvation and some were killed. Certain inquisitors even flew over from Singapore so that the captives could tell their story while it was still fresh in their minds and they were more receptive to treatment. Did I say 'inquisitors'? I meant to say 'interrogators'.

Sumbi himself was eventually captured by a small group amongst whom were a British major, later awarded an MC, and a Queen's Gurkha Officer, who became riled when he learnt that Sumbi had earned a 'B' grading on the jungle warfare course whereas his had only been a 'C'.

'Eventually the whole group of would-be saboteurs had been accounted for less four. As a political sop or as a friendly gesture operations in Malaysia were then suspended while the Peace Talks were conducted. That didn't prevent patrols of the Gurkha Para Company from being committed just inside Brunei even though, in the thousands of square miles of jungle available for hiding in, the chances of contacting four men were almost impossible. It was by no means sure that they had got anywhere near, let alone reached, Brunei. One of the patrols near the border was led by Corporal Chandrabahadur Rai, 1/7 GR, and one of his men, Jamansing Rai, had to be evacuated by helicopter. A reinforcement was needed and Rifleman Purandhoj Limbu, 2/10 GR, flew in and Jamansing flew out. The very next day, walking along a ridge a mile or so from the Brunei-Sarawak border, Purandhoj was travelling end man, the last of five. None of the others saw it and he nearly missed it – a leaf, lying on the ground, amongst the other thousands of millions of leaves, but it had a straight crease across it. Only a man could have folded it in half. Purandhoj was not looking for it but he noticed it because the pattern of nature had been disturbed. It was common knowledge that none of the Security Forces had been in the area for a long time so who else could it be but for one of the four men the patrol was looking for? It had rained the night before and, by then, the four men were superb at covering their tracks so the leaf was the only clue there was. The search in the area was intensified and, a few days later, a patrol of the Royal Brunei Malay Regiment captured them. During the subsequent and exhaustive interrogation carried out, it transpired that one of them was a compulsive finger-twiddler, a doodler one might say who, for much of the time, had a twig or a leaf in his hand. Every time a man disturbs something, the pattern of nature is broken. So that was the end of the 'Sumbi Saga' and the end of the threat to the Brunei oil installations.

'Decorations? No, it was all reckoned to be part of the day's work. But the Major General sahib did fly across from Labuan to the Para Company camp in the 'Haunted House' so that he could personally congratulate Jitbahadur and Dharmalal. The *Times* newspaper of Wednesday, 7 December, 1966, observed that what those two had done was 'one of the most brilliant actions in the history of Gurkhas'. This is the first time the story of the leaf has been told. It's strange to think that such a bold adventure should have been thwarted, initially, by a piece of tinfoil and that just one leaf should have ended it.'

II. Two Bird Calls

'A long time ago, before jungle boots were invented and water bottles still had corks in them, operations were taking place near Sepang, on the borders of Negri Sembilan and Selangor, in Malaya. The method of operating, devised against the Japanese in Burma, was, looking back on it, crude when compared with what was achieved later on but luckily the terrorists were also learning. In a way lessons were learnt from each other, so to speak.

'As I was saying before,' the Teacher told his audience, 'only nature can improve on nature. It's a break in the pattern that gives away secrets but, of course, you've got to know the pattern before you can tell if it's been broken. Let me explain . . .

'The good people of Sepang had been victimised by a group of terrorists who lived near the jungle edge at the back of the remoter squatter areas. Their training included range practice and drill – they even blew bugle calls from time to time as the Japs had taught them. A platoon of 1/7 GR moved down to Sepang from Seremban. Once there they were briefed by the local police and they were asked if they would go and investigate the situation. Accordingly a patrol moved into the area and worked its way behind the rubber estate labour lines before dawn. It was slow going. Between them and the jungle, five miles away, was a maze of tracks criss-crossing a multitude of small rubber holdings and tapioca patches, with scattered wooden huts dotted around. The inhabitants were Chinese and each hut boasted a noisy dog or two. The aim of the one-day patrol was an aggressive reconnaissance, ready to deal with any trouble should it be found. It had to be back in Sepang by 3 o'clock the same afternoon, so there was not a lot of time to do the job in hand.

'The patrol's attention was first alerted by a dawn bugle call, away in the west, in the direction of the jungle edge but as the soldiers were going that way in any case, it did not tell them anything new, only confirmed their suspicions and made them realise they had something positive to search for. Three hours later they stopped and ate the meal they were carrying and then the patrol commander decided to split his men up into two groups, both heading west. Luckily they had two compasses. One group had a man who could make piercing whistles and the other group someone who could make cuckoo noises, so they could keep contact. It was a better way of calling to each other than by shouting. Radio? You must be joking!

'At noon, near the edge of the jungle, the patrol commander was on the point of returning as nothing positive had been found, when they came across a hut, the first they had met for some time and seemingly deserted. As a routine precaution while it was being investigated, the leading scout took up a fire position behind a tree and, as he knelt down, his foot hit a tin that was wrapped up in a sack. This turned out to be a collection of Communist training pamphlets and other documents. It was serious enough for the patrol to join forces so the man who could imitate the bird cuckooed loudly several times. The rest of the patrol then joined up. The house revealed nothing so they continued up the track that split soon after, one branch leading into the jungle and the other, which they followed, jinking up to a knoll overlooking the immediate area. At the top was a crude hob outside, an alarm system of a can with a stone in it activated from a look-out in a nearby tree and inside a couple of sleeping platforms, some army blankets and a bugle – fashioned from burnt wood. Clearly the terrorists, for it could be no one else, had been surprised so suddenly that they had not even bothered to move the simmering kettle. It was also obvious when the patrol commander went and had a look from their observation post that they had not seen the soldiers.

'Searching around for more clues, the patrol heard, from the jungle that stretched away to the west below, a jungle bird call its mate, and, from a flank, the answer. It sounded very much like the "koirala" bird at home. You must all know it, it hardly ever calls and when it does there's always a death on the opposite side of the valley.'

His audience nodded their heads, remembering other fatal omens, such as hearing a jackal's call by day or a hen crowing. The Teacher, having paused, continued:

'Again, a little later, the same call, farther away this time with the reply closer to it, as though converging on one another. And then, after another pause, derisively, a third and very faint time. It was the terrorists who had left the observation position by separate routes joining up again. They weren't followed up as the patrol wasn't geared for it and, anyway, it was late. But they had to be terrorists. Why? Because the call they happened to use at around noon belonged to a bird that only ever calls at dawn and dusk.

'What's that? What alerted them in the first place if they hadn't see the patrol? That, too, is quite simple. You see, there are no cuckoos in Malaya and you can't improve on nature without some penalty, as both parties found out . . .'

III. Three Pieces of Furniture

'Nesiot: I don't expect that means any more to you than it did to me. It's a head-shrinker's term for anybody of the south-east Asian rain forest dwellers who have always been based on the "bamboo" culture. Head-shrinkers? All right then, anthropologists, if you think it's politer.'

The Teacher's audience wondered what he was leading up to as he continued talking. 'The nearer the soil the person it, the more natural he is and by that I mean the more predictable are his patterns of behaviour. I'm talking of the aborigines.

'During the early 1950s efforts were made to wean these people from living a nomadic life in deep jungle where, it was said, they were being used as a screen for terrorist movement; so they were herded out from the high forests and brought down into resettlement camps in the open plains where many, far too many, died. The rest were let out after that and hardly a soul was seen for maybe five years, so afraid were they of another dose of Government medicine. The Communists made great capital out of the "oppressors" and their methods and this made the abos more than ever determined not to become involved with "Government" again. Interestingly enough, the "hill tribesmen" of Thailand and Laos, as well as the "Montagnards" of central Vietnam, all had the same mistakes made against them, apparently, by everyone who tried to organise them. Did I say everyone? Well, I believe the Chinese were the best in handling them and even then they made their mistakes too, but of a different sort.

'By the time of the early 1960s more efforts had to be made to wean the aborigines from the Chinese terrorists. This was not as easy as it sounded as the "Emergency" in Malaya was over. Which emergency did someone ask? Now that's a good question which needs a fuller answer another time. Someone high up in the Government ordained that Gurkha troops be committed in that area and it fell to the lot of the battalion in Ipoh to send a couple of companies at a time. They were based on a small town called Grik. It was about then that Chin Peng, the terrorist veteran, ordered his three lieutenants to step up their campaign of pro-Communist influence among the aborigines so this meant that Ah Soo Chai, who had a sore leg and couldn't squat naturally on his hunkers, Tek Myau and Lo See went stomping the ulu, as the hinterland jungle was known. It was one hell of a game of hide-and-seek which involved many abo settlements being visited by both sides, our men always arriving too late to be effective. However, Security Forces were, to an extent, able to curtail terrorist movement.

'Now I should try and explain what sort of houses these folk lived in. Raised off the ground and made of bamboo, the short answer is. Split bamboo for the floors, bamboo for the uprights and main beams, bamboo foliage for the roof and slivers of bamboo to tie all the bits and pieces together – along with notched bamboo as steps up to the sleeping platforms and living quarters. Cooking, such as it was, took place in a rudimentary fashion at one end of the house. Underneath curs, pigs and hens picked and scratched, while round about the settlement, or "ladang" as it was known in the vernacular, tapioca, caladium or Polynesian taro if you prefer it, chillies and cucumber grew haphazardly. Within the radius of a mile or two the jungle would have been felled for dry paddy and more tapioca.

'These abos, timorous, evasive and only wishing to be left alone, spoke their own language which consisted of glottal burps and sawn-off grunts. Only a few had a smattering of Malay but any conversation with them was almost impossible. What can you do with people with a thumb and four fingers on each hand who can still only count up to three?

'One particular settlement was suspect – that belonged to a certain Kerinching who had been a terrorist supporter but had recently recanted such loyalty. He lived on the banks of the River Temenggor in Perak. Special Branch had only just let any military unit into the area where this Kerinching held considerable sway and they were instructed not to go into his house unless invited. They made camp close to and he would come and watch them with grave suspicion. There was a Chinese Civilian Liaison Officer with the platoon, one Goh Ah Hok, who had the rare distinction of having the BEM and bar. Goh and Kerinching got friendly and one evening Kerinching came to the platoon camp and mentioned to Goh that one of the inmates had just died and so the whole of the settlement would have to be burnt according to custom. To save him trouble would the soldiers go and start the blaze for him? So the platoon commander said they would. They went inside Kerinching's house to check that there was no movable property left. There, besides the rudimentary furniture, were a higher than usual single sleeping platform, a stool and a little table, made from the inevitable bamboo. It seemed a shame to burn it all but that was the custom so burn it they did. But the point was that it had to be Ah Soo Chai's base for operations. You see he could not easily squat due to his bad leg so had been provided with stool, table and higher bed. Such pieces of furniture are unnatural for the Nesiot population so it had to be a "foreigner". As it wasn't our men who else could it have been? Suspicions that the terrorists still had such a base in an area that Special Branch thought was clear of them and that Kerinching and they were still so close to one another were confirmed because the natural, Nesiot, pattern had been broken . . .'

IV. Four Poles

'My fourth example,' continued the Teacher, 'happened somewhere near the Sabah-Indonesia border, during Confrontation. The Indonesian units opposite the Gurkha Para Company were, I think, Commandos and Parachutists. I seem to remember people talking about the KKO, which seems to have stood for some kind of Commando, and the RPKAD, of which the P seems to denote Para – not that it matters.

'The area of operations was thick, matted jungle, ranging between 2,000 and 4,000 feet high, with swift mountain streams and deep rivers, beetling precipices and steep hills. It often rained and was rudimentarily uncomfortable. The five-man patrols with which the Gurkha Para Company operated were, numerically, vastly inferior to the opposition ahead of them, somewhere in the region of being outnumbered by at least one hundred to one. When a small group of men is cold, wet, hungry, tired, afraid, far from base and heavily outnumbered is the time that high morale plays its decisive part. High morale? By that I mean a man giving of his best when the audience, on his side, is of the smallest.

'One day a patrol was bound for an area in Indonesian territory where 1/2 GR had had a battle not long beforehand. Its mission was to establish whether there were any Indons farther to the south. They were due to be away from base for ten days. They were to be choppered in as far as possible and then were to hoof it for three days, nose around for four, leaving three days to get back to the heli zone.

'They were well into the area, moving down a narrow ridge which, unusually, was almost bare of foliage, except, at the limit of vision, where four thin saplings were growing on a piece of ground slightly flatter than the rest of the slope. It was then that they stopped for a breather, sheltering in a small rocky outcrop, a feature not uncommon in those high hills. Quite why he never said but, since dawn that day, the patrol commander, Corporal Lachhimparsad Rai, 2/7 GR, had been uneasy. That made him ultra-cautious. He moved cautiously to the edge of the outcrop, not exposing himself and, slowly raising his head, had a good look around. There was nothing untoward between him and where the ridge dipped again the other side of the four saplings. All was peaceful, nothing was amiss. And yet, although he couldn't put his finger on it, he sensed danger. So, respecting his hunch, the patrol continued on its journey south but deviated from the ridge itself. Well, they arrived in their target area a little later than planned but safely. The map was inaccurate and they went farther south than they had intended. On a track they were crossing they came face to face with a civilian who talked a garbled brand of Malay and was obviously petrified of them. The news he gave them was not reassuring and they had to act quickly, decisively and boldly if they were to fulfil their mission and withdraw without too much fuss. A nearby longhouse was said to be harbouring some Indon soldiers and a quick attack and away was called for. In the event there were no soldiers, only some surprised inmates, chiefly old people, who offered the men bananas and groundnuts. The Corporal told them the patrol was moving east and left in that direction but jinked back up a small stream west soon afterwards.

'By that evening they had completed three of the four days and had planned to lie up near a large river to observe the traffic but next morning, early, they heard what was called a Hook helicopter, a Russian-made giant, with a fighter escort away to the east where the patrol might reasonably be expected to have reached. The Hook made a tremendous din, like a couple of steamrollers dancing. So it was decided to withdraw completely and their route led them up the same ridge where Lachhimparsad had sensed danger. They moved with the utmost caution and near where he had seen those four thin saplings they came across an Indon ambush position, freshly abandoned. Searching around they found one tree where an Indon had carved his regiment's name and the date on the bark: RPKAD and the date was only the previous day's! Their tracks moved east so it was presumed they had been sent in search of the patrol, whose action in contacting the inmates in the longhouse had been reported to the Indon HQ in Wailaya quicker than anticipated. The Corporal had a look round and came across those four saplings which had strangely withered. He tugged them one by one, and they came out of the ground. You see, they were bivouac poles for the Indon ambush who had wanted to sleep on the flatter ground. At night, when the ambush was lifted, they could have a covering draped between them and, by day, even when they had grown enough roots to regain their normal appearance, they constituted no impediment to the field of fire or vision. When first seen they were recently cut, so looked fresh and natural. But, and this was only realised later, they were in a rectangle and, as the Patrol Commander had not seen them exactly face on, they didn't immediately appear as such. Even so, nature's pattern had been disturbed with, under the circumstances, was a lucky break for the patrol ...'

V. Five Limes

'I seem to remember,' said the Teacher, 'telling you how our men traced the main Chinese contact, Kerinching, on the west of the Main Divide, as the range of mountains running like a spine down central Malaya was sometimes called. But I don't think I've ever told anyone how they found the corresponding eastern contact, a man called Bongsu Helwood, across the Divide, in Kelantan. This was a settlement on the River Blaur, consisting of four main families where, for some years, the Government and the terrorists had vied for influence, playing one family off against the other. As far as the Government was concerned, the military felt that they were unduly optimistic in thinking that Ah Soo Chai and his gang had lost all sway with Bongsu Helwood but it was important that this should be checked to make sure it was the case. Accordingly D Company, 1/7 GR, spent time in the area but noticed nothing amiss. It was richer than many other "ladangs", boasting a number of fruit trees, limes, durians and rambutans as well as extensive tapioca and dry paddy resources.

'Apart from that aspect troubling the authorities, there was another – for a number of years the Security Forces, military, the Police Field Force and Special Branch had been unsuccessful in finding the main axis of movement between the terrorist sanctuary in the Yala district of southern Thailand and their remaining rump in northern Malaya, whose aim was to maintain their influence over the many different Nesiot tribes dotted to east and west of the Divide. Did I say rump? That was how some big-wigs in Kuala Lumpur saw them: they saw themselves as the advance guard of the next thrust south. As it was, the terrorists made their visits at three-monthly intervals to all these tribes in order to keep a modicum of influence over them.

'It was D Company's turn next for a spell of duty up there and they motored from Ipoh to Grik, ninety-nine and a half miles away. After one night staging in a temporary camp they moved off up the Sungei Perak in a fleet of boats fitted with outboard engines. That journey had its moments, especially up the rapids and, what with engines breaking down and the sheer-pins often having to be changed, it was haphazard as a military movement, at times more hazard than hap, if you'll excuse the pun.

'The first boat took thirty-six hours to arrive at Tebuan, its destination, and the last boat got there another day and a half later. The early arrivals had ample opportunity to observe some interesting and unusual facets of nature, which in that region was bountiful with fauna and flora, although I prefer calling flora "roots, fruits and shoots" – sorry again! The first morning they had a wonderful view of a dozen or so monkeys crossing the Perak by using the current round a bend, clutching on to the tail of the monkey in front. They came across otters, elephants, porcupines and a bear. Wildlife was more prolific and less disturbed than farther south as that particular area had never been bombed. Bird life abounded as did wild fruit trees; prickly breadfruit, sweet bananas, smelly durians, delicious mangosteens and some nameless nuts. There were no signs of the large limes that had been a feature of Helwood's "lading".

'The route lay north to the Thai border and they found fresh footprints for four or five terrorists, unhappily soon lost, and a temporary sleeping platform by a small stream. It was thought that this movement was nothing more than routine terrorist patrolling south from Thailand. It was two days after the last find of any evidence that Corporal Arjun Rai was on a patrol in a particularly rugged piece of mountainous terrain and it was a relief when they found themselves in an easier patch. They sat down to rest when Arjun's attention was attracted to a pile of five limes that were lying under a tree. They were all rotten but he supposed they were about three months old. He thought no more about it until he came across another little lot of five limes under another tree half an hour later. This time they were fresh. Could they have been dropped at the same time as those prints had been made? When the patrol got back to Company HQ a radio message was sent to Battalion HQ asking an incredulous Intelligence Officer to find out how many patches of lime trees similar to the ones at Helwood's settlement near the Blaur there were to the north-west up to the company's jungle location. Two weeks later, back in Ipoh, it was learnt that the Forestry Office and Special Branch had got together and established that there were probably none. So, the likelihood was that those limes had come from Helwood's area and were being used as a code telling others who knew it when a party of terrorists had used that route up from the Blaur. The age of the first lot of limes and the three-monthly visits fitted into the theory without forcing it. What put Arjun on to asking the question in the first place? Yes, I was coming to that. You see, not only were the trees under which the limes were lying not lime trees but also there weren't any lime trees at all thereabouts – someone just had to have put them there. You really can't interfere with nature and not be found out . . .'

❧   ❧

Later that day the Teacher sat musing on all he had told his audience. His eyes had that faraway look that bespeaks deep concentration. And then he smiled to himself and his eyes lit up, as he remembered what an Englishman had once taught him:

> And should you ask, where do they live,
> These men with skill superlative
> Who showed superb initiative

Enhanced their name, achieved success
And gave the 'baddies' no redress?
The jungle is their home address.

[1979]

18

How History Happens

Thirty years is a long time. Much government material becomes open to scrutiny after thirty years and so, since more than thirty years have elapsed since the CIGS, Field Marshal Montgomery, held a conference in London in early 1948 about the future of the army, I feel free to tell this story. At the conference was Major General Sir Charles Boucher, Major General of the Gurkha Brigade, as we thought of ourselves still, although we were officially named the Gurkha Regiment. Soon after the conference Montgomery handed over to a soldier we knew much better, Bill Slim. Sadly these three giants are now dead and enough time has passed to ensure that what happened then is of academic interest only. Even so . . .

Boucher came to 1/7 GR and stayed for a Mess Night shortly after his return from England. At that time I was an irreverent subaltern, virtually unnoticed by my seniors who made up most of the rest of the officers of the battalion. It has to be remembered that the first Second Lieutenants to appear on the scene after the Second World War did not show their pimply faces until late 1951. Anyway, the General was first invited to the King's Gurkha Officers' Club – Messes came much later – and had enough to keep out the cold of the Malayan night, which was warm enough, if you understand me. Back in the Officers' Mess he waxed violently about the Great Field Marshal this, that and the other, giving us detail he might never have otherwise given had he not been warmed up beforehand. The crux of the matter was that the Great Field Marshal had told the Major General that no permanent commissions could be offered in a Gurkha Regiment to anybody who was commissioned after 31 December 1939. Until the Sandhurst Gurkha was ready to take up permanent commissions in the army all officers post-1939 would be seconded. The thought was that Gurkha units would be completely officered by Gurkhas by about 1975.

But that night in Seremban, listening to the General talking about the problems that we were experiencing, held no thoughts for us that were so long-term. We were virtually pioneers still, with Gurkhas in the British Army as a strange innovation to the staff which greeted us in Malaya. The conversation then drifted into other channels and the burning questions of our future remained unanswered. You must also remember we were about to be Gunners, with 10 GR just having escaped being made into Sappers, and there were many new problems involving gun-drill, aiming point directors and goodness-only-knows what else facing limber-gunner Limbus and wheel-wright Rais that bedevilled our working days.

Some months later I went on my first leave.

I went to say my farewells to the CO, James Hepper, who told me I was expected to pay my respects to the Colonel of the Regiment, who was also Number 2 of the British Railways, ex-General Sir William Slim. On the boat going home we heard that the new CIGS was Slim and, before we docked, that he had been promoted to Field Marshal. Nothing ventured . . . I contacted his staff in the War Office and arranged to go and see him. I wore battledress as the wearing of the Sovereign's uniform in the Sovereign's country was not then frowned upon.

Looking back on the occasion the point that still is vividly in my memory is the difficulty in finding, even then, anywhere to park even the smallest of cars. I had driven a 1937 'Baby' Austin 7 up to town and had thought I could park it outside the War Office building (after I had found it – the building, not the car) because I was going to see the CIGS. Not a bit of it. I was chased away. I eventually found a sanctuary in a cul-de-sac and got out of the car and was just locking up prior to walking back to the War Office when the large hand of an even larger policeman came down on my shoulder and an incredulous voice asked me if I knew where I was. London, as an answer, was insufficient for him as, it quickly transpired, I was parked exactly in front of No 10, Downing Street. I soon gathered that Clem Attlee would not have been pleased to see me. I wondered if the PM knew how I'd have voted had the vote been allowed for one of such tender years as I when he came to be Head of Government. That wasn't the problem, apparently.

Anyway, I took the hint and eventually I found a place outside an old building, a long way from the War Office that I afterwards learnt was the pre-war German embassy. It was lucky I had allowed myself more than an hour's spare time. Exactly at the appointed hour, 3.30 p.m., was I ushered into the presence of Greatness. After desultory chat, during which the CIGS called for the latest situation report and learnt that his old battalion had suffered a lot of casualties in North Malaya when they were caught with their pants down, literally, by the terrorists when a bathing party had no sentries out. The CIGS shook his head sadly and then asked me how the morale of the men was when I left them. I explained that I thought it would be a problem in any future war to find enough specialists for such esoteric units as we Gunners (1/7 GR was 101 Field Artillery RA, 2/7 GR was 102; 103, 104 and 105 were said to be other sorts of artillery with 105 being coastal gunners stationed at Port Dixon). 'It's not so much the men who are worried,' I chirruped, 'but the officers.'

A growl greeted that remark. 'What's wrong with the officers?'

'Well, sir, it's like this. In 1/7 GR there are hardly any original officers left. Most of us are ex-1/1 GR. The men don't know us and we don't know them. We have had an influx of officers from the Gunners who know even less about the men than do we. If we go to our British Regiments we leave behind a most difficult situation. If we don't go to our units soon we can hardly be welcomed with open arms when we do eventually get there.'

'Why can't you serve in 7 GR like you can in, say, the West Yorkshires?'

Why indeed but who was I to say so? Emboldened I said, 'I'm given to understand that the reason why we cannot is because we are looked on as such colonial forces as the East Africans, sir.' The Great Man looked daggers at me as though I had suggested something that verged on the indecent. 'Who said that?'

My mind flew back to that evening in Seremban with the General and the 'Great Field Marshal' tirade. 'I'm far too junior to say, sir, but in fact I have it on the best authority that it was your predecessor.' Awful visions of retribution came into my mind as I sat there, playing one Field Marshal off against another.

'When will they learn that Gurkhas are not East Africans?' The question was not aimed at me so I kept quiet. 'Never mind.' He suddenly sounded tired. 'I have not got round to that yet,' and I was dismissed.

When I got back from leave in early 1949 I found that 101 and 102 Field Regiments along with P, Q and R Batteries, with S and T batteries in 7 GRTW in Paroi, were all busy, enmeshed in the low-level war or training for it. But, by 1950, the concept of the long-term manning of the Brigade of Gurkhas, which by then we had come, had been switched to allow serving in its Permanent

Cadre for British Officers. It would have probably turned out that way, even if I had not been so brash or the Major General so warmed, yet it is tempting to speculate on what very 'slim' threads is history written.

[1980]

19

In Job's Shadow

From time to time representatives of the Brigade of Gurkhas have been called upon to perform unusual tasks. One of these was in the wild, mountainous and almost uninhabited area of Peninsular Malaysia where aboriginal tribes live. Members of 22 Special Air Service Regiment had parachuted into it, Commonwealth forces had operated in it, as had elements of the Police Field Force and an aborigine-oriented unit called the 'Senoi Pra'aq' (Temiar for 'Fighting Men') and indeed anthropologists and doctors had descended on it: none of them with any lasting degree of success. The pro-Chinese and anti-Malay feelings of the aborigines were firmly rooted in past history and politics.

It fell to the battalion based in Ipoh to commit two rifle companies into a vast area for a month or so at a time. Their aim was to try and make contact with a handful of terrorists, supposedly based in Thailand, who maintained spasmodic relations with the aboriginal population. Their tasks included patrolling, ambushing and making efforts to win over the hearts and minds of the locals. Code-named 'Operation Bamboo', it hardly merited a mention in anything so august as the Regimental History; it did, nevertheless, have unusual aspects. Bare statistics are normally misleading but, leaving aside forays lasting only one month, D Company, 1/7 Gurkha Rifles, spent just under seven months on just over six ounces of food a day with loads that averaged over a hundredweight – or at least ten of them did at any one time.

The microscopic incident I portray depicts what happens when cross-examination is undertaken in a language that admits of only three digits, nothing more definite than two days in the future or the past, no specific word for tree or animal – individual names are required, use the same word for high of hills, distant of journeys, deep of rivers and long of fingernails, to say nothing of having a system of third-person pronouns that have to include a stream between the speaker and the object spoken of even if it does not actually exist: is that upstream, downstream, on the far or near bank or so near to the speaker that the stream, mythical or otherwise, is unnecessary for the conversation? All this happened when frantically tired – so tired that at one time strength to put one leg in front of the other was not forthcoming – and when through reasons not germane to the story, the small group had to spend several weeks based on an aboriginal graveyard.

Picture the scene: a large river flowing strongly down a valley. On either side steep jungle-clad mountains, the lower slopes of which had suffered 'slash and burn' cultivation for dry paddy, maize and tapioca. Every few miles a settlement, called Sakai ladang on the map, containing a rural slum of small, dark, timorous people whose only wish in life was to be left in peace both by the Administration and by the terrorists, the former based in Kuala Lumpur and the latter in Yala province, Thailand.

Information, under any guise or in any fashion, was well-nigh impossible to obtain about mundane matters let alone of terrorist movements. Imagine our excitement when, on New Year's Day 1964, a man called Mudak came to tell me that the day before he had overheard one of the men of the local leader, Penghulu Bongsu Helwood, telling Helwood that tapioca was being dug up from nearby. The rumours in the ladang were many; was it by a mad aborigine or by terrorists? Or was it by a sane aborigine for hungry terrorists?

I called the senior Temiars up into my camp for a talk. I would not let on who had told me, so when I broached the conversation they all started speculating how I had heard about it. We started talking at 4 o'clock and went on for two and a half hours. The talk went round and round and round. My head swam by the end of it and I did not know what to think. After I had sat them down I opened the conversation with one or other of the Temiar answering:

'With what news?'

'With no news.'

'I hear, I hear strong, I hear wind, tapioca it steals.'

'How you hear?'

'I hear wind. True or not?'

'Hear woman talk. Talk tapioca it steal.'

'I hear,' I continued after that part of the conversation had been repeated and had taken five minutes, 'I hear mad Temiar, he from that side of the river, he steal tapioca, true or not?'

'Tata, Old Man,' a very respectful term of address to me, 'I say, and if I say good luck luck good and if I say bad luck not good, if you are angry, what am I to do? But I say yes.'

'Yes what?'

Came the devastating answer, 'Yes, no.'

So I started again. 'Is there a mad man?'

'Yes.'

'Tell me about him.'

'He lives in the jungle. Sometimes he comes. He has long hair and we are afraid. He has no knife. He has no fire. He cannot eat.'

'Where is he now?'

'Dead.'

'When did he die?'

'One day in the past.'

'So he does not steal tapioca?'

'No.'

'Who does?'

'The mad man.'

'But he is dead you say.'

'No, he is not dead.'

This point, try hard though I might, was never more satisfactorily resolved, despite twenty minutes solid cross-examination. So I switched tack.

'If the mad dead man does not eat, does not steal tapioca, then Temiar steals?'

'No.'

'But tapioca it steals, mad dead man not, Temiar not, who?'

'It steals.'

'The bad men China, that Ah Soo, that Lo See. They steal?'

'They are in the high hills. What am I to do?'

'What do they eat?'

'Food.'

'If no food?'

'No food.'

'If no food they die?'

'Long.'

'Dead now?'

'Yes.'

'Dead now?'

'No.'

I gradually brought them around to thinking the Chinese might be living off the land, lying up, stealing tapioca and here the use of 'the river' as an integral part of any pronoun came into its own.

'Ah Soo is near?' I asked.

'No.'

'Ah Soo is far?'

'No.'

'Where is Ah Soo?'

'If near, near, if far, far, if this side of the stream, this side, if that side, that side, if upstream, upstream, if downstream, downstream. If you are angry what am I to do? I hope strongly.'

'What do you hope?'

'Yes.'

'Yes, what?'

'Yes, no.'

'Ah Soo is upstream?' I asked.

'Ah Soo is upstream.'

'Ah Soo is downstream?'

'Ah Soo is downstream.'

'How is he upstream and downstream?'

'Yes.'

'Yes what?'

'Yes, no.'

'Where is Ah Soo?'

'In the high hills.'

'Is Ah Soo in the high hills?'

'No.'

'What is no?'

'Yes.'

'Yes what?'

'Yes, in the high hills.'

'If he is hungry?'

'He gets food.'

'What does he eat?'

'What he can get.'

'What does he get?'

'Tapioca.'

'From here?'

'Yes.'

'Now, new of it?'

'Yes.'

'Who, new of it, it steals?'

'The mad man.'

'But the mad man is dead?'

'No.'

'Not dead?'

'Yes.'

'Yes what?'

'Dead.'

This went on for two and a half hours. It remains in my memory, typifying Temiar conversation. Most of it was in this vein, as hard to pin down as quicksilver, mercurial in its inconsistency, vague, ephemeral and often meaningless. At the end of the session I felt an acute sympathy for Job and wondered how he managed. My Gurkhas shook their heads in bafflement.

There is no punch line to this. How can there be? No quip or jape or weak pun about 'Cross examination': all I can say is that it taught me patience.

[1981]

✦ 20 ✦

The 'Sinner Elf' in the Inner Self, or, An Altered State of Consciousness

The reputation of the Brigade of Gurkhas in the British Army – and the Gorkha Brigade in the Indian Army – is formidable. Men of both have something special compared with most other military men in other armies. Both are almost entirely made up of 'epicanthically eye-lidded Mongoloid men, originally in trans-Himalaya, where Bön shamanism practised by *jhañkri*s reigned supreme, and who then settled into a Cis-Himalayan society, where Hindu *jogi*s also have significant influence': the Nepali hill men we know by the English word 'Gurkha' and who have been our comrades-in-arms since 1815.

I maintain that our men's 'something special' is their 'putting more into what they do for longer than do most other troops', certainly before they are passed over for promotion, and to such an extent that their high standard has brought its own penalties of expectation. Gurkhas are a mystery to many and it is fair to ask if our men give substance to that mystery or mystery to the substance? Whichever way, there is an untapped residue of resilience that manifests itself in ways unusual and often unexpected.

Trans-Himalayan life was indeed the survival of the fittest when 'something extra' was needed. Cis-Himalayan life, coming into contact with the Laws of Manu, the 2,500-year-old 'bible' for caste that slowly moved north from India, put men born in the foothills of the Himalayas, the men we mostly enlist in the Brigade, as of the lowest caste whose touch does not contaminate water. (This classification was slightly elevated by a 'durbar' edict some 120 years ago.) Our men are much nearer the *jhankri* than they are to the *jogi* – but both impinge on them. Hindu 'inferiority' of caste now vies with Bön, and Buddhist, shamanic influence. The latter gives them inner strength while the former means they have to do more than others for their potential to be recognised, certainly in Nepal, thus creating a subcutaneous 'dis-ease'. Consequently the 'inner self' often needs added inner fortitude to compete with their *soi-disant* superiors to redress the outer imbalance. Life in a street-wise, part-secular, part-Christian army among many non-believers of another nation gives previously unexperienced challenges and brings this impetus for 'something extra' even more to the fore: an ever-present triangular paradigm. And how well have our men managed!

Quite how have they managed? Expressed differently, I believe it is because our men – and other Asians – have retained a strong 'Mystical Dimension' or 'Magic of the Inner Self', where 'mystical' describes an altered state of consciousness and 'magic' means 'the energy of the unseen'. Neither of which phenomenon will our men find indigenously during their service in Britain where both are normally met with undisguised scepticism if not disbelief but both phenomena can cure, curse or even curb one's activities – God's Law and Dame Luck or Sod's Law and Lame Duck?

Thinking about such matters has lent credence for a hypothesis, not original but strangely comforting, that both *jhankri* and *jogi*, whose ability to assume an altered state of consciousness plays such a potent part in our men's cultural upbringing, 'their collective unconscious' almost, are an influence upon our men to an extent that probably they, and assuredly we, do not fully realise, and result in a greater initial culture shock of life in England than many may have supposed.

To develop this hypothesis: only a small handful of people can enter an altered state of consciousness, a self-trance, with time-honoured herbal drugs, where 'normal' matters are subsumed by 'abnormal' ones and such a person's soul becomes untethered. This process is at least 30,000 years old and is shown in upper palæolithic cave paintings, which, according to those who have studied them, are the start of religion and art. Similarly African Bushmen, Australian aborigines, the Mayan and Aztec civilisations in South America are included in similar practices. Such 'out of consciousness' is also said to explain ghosts, angels and djinn and, in mediæval Europe, a belief in fairies, witches, elves (the 'sinner elf'), pixies and changelings to say nothing of countless equivalents in every other society the world over.

The modern phenomena are unidentified flying objects, UFOs – but for our men the *jhañkri* and *jogi* remain all pervasive.

If this hypothesis is accepted it can explain New Testament miracles, healing, 'raising from the dead', the epiphany and other activities not up to normal mortals. Likewise other seemingly implausible activities include 'chariots of fire ascending into heaven' and the Muslim belief that ten animals have been admitted into paradise.

Besides modern drugs that get people 'stoned', a heightened awareness caused by fear, when adrenaline rushes into the blood, falling in love, being hypnotised, being drunk or beside oneself with rage, severe hunger and thirst, brain damage or plain madness cause molecular changes in the brain so altering the state of consciousness.

In England one merely 'gets out of the wrong side of bed': our Gurkhas' "sinner elf" 'is being troublesome'.

Let me give some examples from my own experience of what can happen when an altered state of consciousness and untethered souls impinge, not only on our men but others in Asia:

Case A: A retired Gurkha officer, let us call him Himan, had three sons. His eldest son was still unmarried at forty and lived and worked in England as a film director. He contracted bone cancer but did not tell his father and step-mother and died soon after. I went to commiserate with the father and what I was told was surprising. His wife had died twenty years previously, his middle son ten years after that: a pilot in Royal Nepal Airlines, he had been ordered to fly an overweight aircraft and had had a fatal accident. Now, another ten years on his eldest son had died. Though a Buddhist, so not believing in Hinduism, Himan was inveigled by the man who would have been the dead pilot's father-in-law to consult a medium, a Hindu grandmother, in Kathmandu. She and her husband were total strangers to Himan. He went. He was told to sit still while she went into a trance and her husband took notes of what the 'goddess' being invoked said through the medium. She knew his entire life history, even to his inner thoughts. Because he had never worshipped the goddess that was talking to him through the medium, she was punishing him once every ten years until he did and unless her instructions on what sacrifices he had to make to her, the goddess, were followed, in another ten years his youngest son would also die. He had to make live animal sacrifices and he was told what sort these had to be.

Himan remonstrated, saying that he had never, nor would he ever, make blood sacrifices as he was a Buddhist who does not take life, not a Hindu, who does. The answer to that was that the difference in the religion was so little that he would have to make a blood sacrifice or its equivalent, which is to cut a pumpkin in half instead. And a whole lot more. Now there is a very troubled and sad old man.

Case B: Before Dashera 1955 A and D Companies, 1/7 GR, were co-located at a small village in Negri Sembilan, named Simpang Pertang. A police jungle company had an adjacent compound. One night all the soldiers in one room were woken up when a hand pulled open the mosquito net, groped and, finding the end of the sleeper's member, pinched it. No person was seen but one man was suspected. A report next morning resulted in a sentry standing over the suspected man's bed all night.

The man never arose but every man's member was once again pinched.

Consternation and suspicion, in equal amounts, ensued.

The same thing happened the next night. The Company 2 IC then ordered kukris to be stacked in the guardroom. This was done.

The next day most of the company went the fifty miles over the mountains to Battalion HQ for the sacrificial buffalo head cutting. I went ahead in my private car and was disturbed when the convoy was late. When it arrived I was told that one vehicle had overturned squashing dead the man suspected of outraging the other soldiers' innate modesty.

I was called away to the phone to talk to an incensed British Police Lieutenant in Simpang Pertang. Last night one of my soldiers had climbed into bed with a policeman and his wife and had insisted in snuggling up between the married couple.

I apologised and told him that I could do nothing about it as the man was dead.

Case C: In 1959 a signalman on duty in the 'comcen' of 17 Gurkha Division in Rasah Camp, Seremban, left his desk, wandered out, over the camp entrance road and stepped into the 'lalang', the long grass on the other side. He urinated and felt a red-hot pain enter him. He staggered back to the 'comcen' where the sergeant in charge took one look at him, did not understand what he was trying to say so took him back to the Gurkha Signals camp, a few miles off, at Sikamat, and told him to go to bed. The sergeant told the Gurkha Major.

'Let him sleep it off and I will see him when he awakes,' was the verdict.

When the man awoke he did not understand what was said to him and only answered in Chinese, of which he had no previous knowledge.

A Chinese shaman from the bazaar was sent for. He came to the camp, talked with the Gurkha in Chinese, not the normal bazaar Malay, and was understood. He was taken to see where the stricken signalman had urinated and gave his verdict. During the Japanese occupation, inmates of a local hospital had been driven out and massacred where now the lalang grew and no obsequies had been performed. The signalman had to be exorcised. This he would do, bringing him halfway back, and that had to be followed by a Gurkha *jhaṅkri* to bring him the other half.

This was done and the man fell asleep.

Next morning he was as he had ever been, speaking his own language and not understanding any Chinese.

As a rider, the history of 4 GR notes that pre-war on the North-West Frontier, during a ten-minute halt, a rifleman had wandered off and had happened to urinate on a Muslim grave. The same had happened to him: he was 'cured' by the regimental medical officer, a Muslim.

Case D: A Gurkha lady in Pokhara had a miscarriage. Some days later in her husband's village the local *jhaṅkri*, an ex-corporal of

Gurkha Military Police, was impelled to climb a tree, sit in the lower branches and, in a trance, adopted the foetal position. A four-month aborted *wayu*, a soul that had not received the correct obsequies, was communicating with him. It described something strong and sweet that it had tasted, then something astringent and finally rapid up-and-down movements that had actually started the abortion.

About four hours later the shaman climbed down in the knowledge that there had been a miscarriage in one of the twenty-three 'bone family' houses. The heads of the relevant houses were called and all denied any knowledge. Only one suspect remained, the villager who lived in Pokhara, the husband. He was sent for.

Yes, his wife had had a miscarriage and, no, there had been no obsequies.

The *jhañkri* insisted there be one so over a three-day period the *wayu* was called down. Only on the third day did the *wayu* respond and the *jhañkri* once more went into the foetal position and translated what the *wayu* was telling him. It was the same as before.

'Tell me what happened,' commanded the *jhañkri*.

'My wife went to a friend where she was given some honey,' the story started.

In Nepal honey is eaten 'raw' so the taste is 'strong and sweet'.

'She was thirsty and was given a drink of lemonade.'

The astringent taste.

'And then?'

'I took her for a pillion ride on my motor bike after which she complained of a stomach pain.'

The rapid up-and-down movements.

The obsequies were then able to be held and the *wayu* told the *jhañkri* that he was now liberated and could depart in peace.

That it did and has not returned.

Case E: I and ten men were infiltrated near the Malay–Thai border, carrying just below or just above our body weight and living off five-and-a half ounces of food a day, the equivalent of one kilogram intake of food just short of every six days. Our mission was to track the last few remaining terrorists on the police 'wanted list'. These were based in Thailand but periodically visited the aboriginal community in Malaya.

After two weeks we were weak and our thoughts went back to childhood, all of us remembering incidents that had taken place on our mother's lap. After three weeks, when we were hiding up as our three-man aboriginal escort, local Temiars, went probing for news, it took me five days to learn the Temiar language well enough to debrief them on their return.

We walked until we could walk no longer, I not being able to bring one leg in front of the other, and camped on the only flat piece of ground near an aboriginal settlement. The rest of my company flew in and one platoon went downstream where a soldier was drowned. I was ordered to go and investigate. I went with one Temiar, did what I had to do, and, painfully slowly, returned.

'I am going to wash in the river,' I told my men.

I went down and stood on a round stone two paces in the water some twenty yards from a waterfall. I had soaped myself and was just about to scoop up some water when I heard maniacal laughter. I looked round, fearing terrorists, and was pushed hard enough to lose my balance and was swept away. I got to the edge of the river five yards from the lip of the waterfall.

I went back and continued my ablutions. Again maniacal laughter, a harder push and I got out of the water just before being swept over the waterfall.

But no terrorists.

I dried myself and angrily presumed it was my men 'having fun'.

I upbraided them on my return to be met with blank astonishment at my accusation.

We only then learnt that we were camping on an aboriginal graveyard.

We were all haunted: at night my hammock was shaken drastically; one man was pushed off a bench we had made with no one near enough to touch him; the candles we had with us were doused with no wind.

No obsequies had been performed on the dead men as normally the Temiar moved their dwellings on the death of one of their people. The government had not allowed them to move. None of them dared come to us by night, only by day.

We were relieved by men from another company and resolved not to tell them that we were living in a graveyard – but the morning after their first night, they knew although none was hungry or tired enough to be 'molested'.

Case F: Mandhoj Gurung was almost stone deaf but had a gift of prophesy. Many years ago when his friend, Birkharaj Gurung, was an illiterate boy, Mandhoj had told him that he would do well if he joined the British Gurkhas and would become a high-ranking officer. And he did achieve the highest rank possible for a Queen's Gurkha Officer, Honorary Captain, MBE, although against the odds because of late promotion at every rank.

Another friend, Singabahadur Gurung, was told he would only have trouble if he went overseas as, for him, British water was 'cloudy'. He joined the Gurkha Police Contingent but fell ill as he got on the boat in Calcutta, becoming so bad after he reached Singapore that he was boarded out and returned to Nepal. As soon as he stepped ashore once more he started to recover his health and, by the time he got back home, he was sound in wind and limb – his illness never diagnosed.

He asked Mandhoj what would happen if he were to join the Indian Army and was told he would have two great crises during his service, one in the army and one at home, and would only get half his pension. So, with trepidation for the future overlaid with the challenges of the moment, he joined the 5th Gorkha Rifles. In the early '60s he was nearly killed in action. Then he had to go home to help bury an elder brother who had died without any previous signs of illness. Just before he was due out on pension as a subedar, he was promoted to Honorary Captain but, for some reason best known to others, was only allowed an Honorary Lieutenant's pension – so it was he left the army 'with half a pension'. How did Mandhoj know all that?

A fey English lady, who claimed that in a previous incarnation she had been a Nepali and had been poisoned, visited our home in Pokhara, hinting that she had been my wife. She said that Buddhiman Gurung and I had been of the same womb in a previous incarnation, as had also been said by some hill women. That decided me to go and see Mandhoj and ask him if he knew who I had been.

I had three questions for him: was Buddhiman my son during my last incarnation? Will Buddhiman be my son in my next incarnation? Thirdly who was my last wife – the fey English woman in a previous incarnation?

Mandhoj came at dawn, the best time of day for him, carrying a bag. Inside and so out of the cold, we all sat on the floor. We were offered a drink of tea and then preparations started. A plate was produced on which rice was put and, on the rice, a small goddess (strangely a Hindu one but one of whose epithets is of the Buddha, yet Mandhoj is neither, but an animist) was placed, as was a rosary. On the left of the plate was the bag in which he had brought the goddess and rosary which now only contained some leaves, though of what plants I could not say. On the right was a receptacle on which burning embers from the fireplace were put. On this, raw and precious incense, from up in the mountains, made strong and thick smoke. We three sat together, cross-legged in front; the other two with us, the man and woman of the house, sat apart.

Incantations began, using language I started to understand but which trailed off into meaningless mumbling. A spirit was being called upon and Buddhiman and I were being introduced. After a short while Mandhoj, hands clasped tightly in front of him, started trembling violently. Mostly his hands were in front of his chest but sometimes they rose to head level. Then the spirit entered him and it started to talk through him, his voice having a clearer and different timbre than when normal or when the spirit was being invoked.

The answers came out: Buddhiman and I had been uterine brothers, not son and father, living farther to the east, as Christians, low caste sweepers, both good men. My mind raced; to the east lay Kathmandu and, up to 1768, six Capuchin monks had been there for over a century. We were separated and simply had to meet in this incarnation, but as son and father. If we are both pure in this life, not only will my only perceived task, writing, be successful but we will be uterine brothers once more in our next incarnation. It seems that we are to be reborn in Kathmandu as Christians and I, using Buddhiman's help, will become the leader of the country. If that were to happen, we will both be allowed respite from this mortal coil and can join the godhead. Interestingly, what else emerged from Mandhoj's mouth was that, at their primeval level, both Hinduism and Christianity did not contradict one another.

By the end of the second question Mandhoj was so tired and dripping with sweat that he could not sustain his trance so the third question went unasked. Out of his trance, he talked about what had been relayed through him. Surprisingly, for a brief spell he clearly heard what we were saying before his deafness re-asserted itself.

I could mention many more such instances but even these few may show that my hypotheses cannot be completely ignored and a 'sinner elf' may, in one guise of another, be just around the corner . . . and that English woman, another 'sinner elf' or my previous wife? – I still do not know, but maybe neither does she!

[2006]

~ 21 ~

Ears to the Ground

'Really, it is not what you hear but what you think you hear that makes a person react in a certain way. I could give you a sad example of a man who started imagining voices calling him and so acted strangely. These voices urged him to run away into the jungle with a loaded rifle and during the subsequent hunt for him I found him lying in a patch of long grass. I had an anxious few minutes waiting for him to decide if he was going to shoot me. Luckily he was overpowered before his mind had been made up.'

The young men listened to the Pensioner, wondering why he had decided not to go on with a story that sounded gruesome but they were ready to listen to whatever he told them. 'It is when your eyes cannot reach out very far into the undergrowth that your ears have to take over. In the jungle I can remember a patrol that surrounded what was thought to be some enemy making a camp and talking, only to find an unusual combination of a pair of woodpeckers pecking holes in a tree, a group of monkeys with sticks hitting branches not so far away and a river that gurgled over stones in such a way that the leading scout reported voices. I happened to be on that patrol,' smiled the Pensioner, 'and our senses were directed towards the terrorists making that sort of noise so naturally that is what we first thought the noises we heard meant. Rather like when there's a new-born baby in the house – even a mouse squeaking makes the mother think it is the baby needing attention, or when one is waiting for an airdrop and has to put up smoke as soon as the aeroplane is heard to start putting green leaves on the smouldering fire just because one of those noisy beetles is flying about out of sight nearby.

'Having felt a bit foolish when we realised we had been surrounding monkeys and woodpeckers we did not want to be caught out another time. One day I was out on a patrol with three others, Dhojbir, Mohansing and Phistabahadur. We were travelling light, weapons and ammunition only, without even a water bottle. We only expected to be out for the best part of four hours. Going down a slope we heard what I took to be the noise of someone hoeing. Now hoeing does not make all that much of a noise and one of the others whispered that it was a pig rubbing its back on a fallen log. It did cross my mind to ask him if it were a pig why whisper so softly but I remembered in time that we were never meant to raise our voices unless shouting out orders during an attack. We moved cautiously forward, just in case it was not a pig – and it was not! It was a terrorist cultivation, fenced in and had many fallen trees lying around and at the far end there were two men hoeing, the noise being because that patch of ground was harder than most.

'We'll creep in and take up a fire position by that fallen tree,' I ordered and led the way forward. We crossed over the fence and crawled out into the open, out of sight of the two men in the far corner. We felt dreadfully exposed, especially as we were used to the dark protection of the canopy. It was strange to be crawling because however much you learn as a recruit, the times that you have to crawl seem few and far between. By the time we had gained the fallen tree we were panting with our exertions.

'We'll catch our breath and then Mohansing and I will take on the lower of the two men and Dhojbir and Phistabahadur the other men,' I ordered. I waited what seemed an age and then gave the order to fire. I had one of those carbines, light to carry but not much stopping power.

'I must leave the story for a short while to tell you that, over the past month or so, I had been haunted by a dream – a nightmare to be accurate. I was in contact with the enemy and I fired at one man but my bullet had no effect on him as the safety catch of my weapon always managed to put itself on before I fired. Then the man would turn round and fire at me, killing me but somehow so that I did not die but only awoke in hospital. It was a monochrome dream, black at the edges and white up top. So vivid was the dream, which haunted me as I said, that I especially asked if I could test my weapon on the range – and in my excitement I did forget to release the safety catch. Any rate, I thought I'd laid the jinx. But back to the cultivation.

'Ready?' I asked the three men. Yes, they were ready. So I took careful aim and saw that, such was the angle that the man on the left – my target – was bent over, I could not aim at his head. I thought a couple of bullets in his back would suffice so I squeezed the trigger and hit him where I had aimed. He swung round with his hand behind him and, keeping the same aim, I squeezed the trigger again. And, just as it had been in my dream, nothing happened – and monochrome; dark jungle and white sky. In a flash I tried to pull back the working parts but, desperate though I was in my hurry to knock down my target, I could not move the wretched thing. I was baffled. In cold blood I know it sounds stupid now, so real was the effect of the dream that I instinctively pinched myself to see if I was awake or not. In that split second the others, not the brightest of fellows, thought I had been wounded and concentrated on me and not on their target. I saw which way things were going, and which way the two Chinese had started going also, so I ordered a charge with the traditional battle cry, "Ayo Gorkhali, Charge". We rose from behind our treetrunk, I clutching my useless weapon, just as the two Chinese disappeared from sight. So the two men escaped but one of them left his rifle behind. Thinking that someone might come and collect it, I decided to send back two of our group and to keep one man with me and we would wait all night if necessary and ambush the rifle. I thought that the platoon commander might want to come up to us that evening and continue tracking the two men if there was time. In the event he did not come until the following morning. The one man who stayed with me was the only non-smoker and he could the easier bear the smokeless night.

'It was only 4 o'clock when the other two left us alone. We decided to keep in the cover of the jungle overlooking the rifle and not risk going to find water although we were thirsty. We found an ant hill that we could take a fire position behind and, tensed, we waited until it was dark. We decided that one of us should be able to doze off for half the night and the other to keep awake and change roles around midnight. At about 8 o'clock we both heard a low grumbling sound. 'What's that, do you think,' I whispered to Mohansing.

"I think it's the man you hit laughing." he replied.

"Why on earth should he laugh?" I queried in amazement.

"Only because the Gurkhas' bullets have not been able to kill him and he's happy."

'I felt it was highly unlikely that it was a man laughing. Far rather it was the wretched fellow I had shot and what we had heard – and then again – was the death rattle in the hapless man's throat. That was my theory and I stuck to it although Mohansing preferred his version. Be that as it may. It was one of the longest nights I can remember.

'I was alert for an attempt to regain the jettisoned weapon but visibility, already limited, disappeared when it started to rain. I was also wondering what the platoon commander would have to say to me on the morrow. Before it had become fully dark I had banged my weapon heavily on the ground with my hand depressing the working parts and, at last, I had managed to open the breech. The spent cartridge had swollen to such a size on its being fired that normal force could not move it. I kept the spent cartridge as evidence.

'Around midnight, when it was my turn to doze off, I was scared out of my wits by a gentle and plaintive snickering noise that I could not identify for sure. It was castrato treble and I also heard the undergrowth being moved. I shook Mohansing who, like all our countrymen, had God's gift of being able to fall asleep under the most adverse of situations.

' "What's that?" I asked him when I'd woken him up. The noise had not been heard again since I'd shaken him so how could he know? "Mouse deer," he said, referring to the smallest animal of that kind there is.

'Ages later the dawn came. We were both hungry and thirsty but we stayed where we were until the rest of the platoon arrived around 8 o'clock. We then emerged. Recriminations were kept till later, certainly while the area was being searched. There was a maze of tracks showing that the terrorists were in strength somewhere albeit not in the immediate vicinity. I went to see if the corpse was still there. It had to be, for how could anyone have come and taken it away during the night? But it wasn't anywhere at all. If I had killed the man he certainly hadn't died there.

'Did someone ask what was the laughter or the rattle we heard? Yes, I'm coming on to that, but I still feel a bit ashamed when I think of it. No, it wasn't a man at all. We only thought we had heard one because no other noise fitted what we were expecting. It was a tiger. There were big pug marks. Its scent drifted downwind and that is why we didn't smell it. The mouse deer would come in and nibble the new produce in the terrorists' cultivation and the tiger was waiting for its supper.

'I think you'll agree, on both sides, we had a lucky escape that time. It's not that we can't hear so much as we don't know how to listen.

'Did someone say "Hear, hear"?'

[1982]

❧ 22 ❧

A Peek at the Past:
The Nepalese Army in the
Nineteenth Century

Before King Prithvi Narayan Shah of Gorkha, the founder of the Shah dynasty in Nepal, unified the kingdom in 1768, there were three Malla kingdoms in the Kathmandu valley. Their defence depended upon irregular forces and the lack of any standing army was a major cause of the conquest of the valley by the Gorkhas.

Up to that time warfare in Nepal was a hand-to-hand affair, battle-axes, swords, spears, bows and arrows, kukris and a few firearms only were used.

A Christian missionary, Father Loro, described the warfare he witnessed some time before 1740:

> Whichever side kills a man first is the ultimate victor. When this happens the other side sues for peace, sending a naked woman with dishevelled hair. Crying and beating her chest, she implores for mercy, peace and an end to the bloodshed. At this, the victors call a delegation. After negotiations, conditions are imposed on the vanquished and the war is over.

The same missionary wrote about the standard of fighting that took place in 1740:

The war is a protracted affair, but because it is a puerile type of war the major qualification of a soldier is having legs strong enough to run away. If one of the enemy has his head cut off the other side wins the fight. The soldiers are mainly armed with arrows though some of them have firearms.

By 1767 the King of Gorkha had raised five regular companies and these were instrumental in his conquest of the valley, although it is fair to say that they were seldom engaged in direct combat as might be thought from reading the histories of those times. There were also irregular troops, mostly conscripted with little, if any, remuneration.

From the end of King Prithvi Narain's rule in 1775 and the conclusion of the Anglo-Nepal war in 1816 it seems that the standing army had been increased to more than fifty companies. This is vouched for by two Englishmen, Kirkpatrick and Hamilton. The average strength of each would be around 140 muskets. Twenty-five companies were in Kathmandu, fifteen in Tansen, Palpa, and around twenty to twenty-five were with General Amarsing Chhetri Thapa in the west. After the war a number of these companies were disbanded.

Weapons that were used both against the East India Company and the Tibetans, 'guns, rifles and cannon', were manufactured in Nepal itself, as was ammunition.

After the 1814–16 war, the central government consolidated its hold over the rest of the country and the constraints imposed by the British resulted in the army losing much of its previous virility and efficiency. Jangabahadur Rana became the first hereditary prime minister and commander-in-chief on 6 August 1856, second in rank to the king. In fact, for most purposes, the chief of the army staff (also confusingly known as the commander-in-chief) ran military affairs. Military officers played an important part in the civil administration, with the army chief both the deputy premier and the home minister.

Records show that the two top men did not get a fixed salary but the amount paid to the commander-in-chief was certainly increased every year. In 1853 it is noted that he received Rs 25,000 and, in 1856, Rs 41,000. Big money then.

In those days there was no such thing as a steady career with hopes of promotion for the majority of civil and military men. They were all dismissed once a year and reappointed or not, in the same post or not, almost at random it would seem. Nevertheless, the four top-ranking officers under the commander-in-chief and his deputy were normally assured of a steady job. The agnate law of succession, elder brother to elder brother, was introduced in August 1856. The four senior brothers were commanding generals for the four points of the compass, with the western being the most important, followed by the eastern.

The western man was responsible for civil and military affairs between the rivers Trisuli and the Mahakali. The eastern commander was responsible for the whole Tarai region west of the river Mechi and east of the river Mahakali. The southern commander looked after the eastern hills and there are no details of what the northern general commanded.

There seem to have been three formations, the *kampani*, the *paltan* or regiment and the *kampu*. This last may have been larger than a regiment or may have referred to regiments stationed in the capital. By 1877 there were thirteen *kampani*, thirteen *paltan* and nineteen *kampu*.

The establishment of a regiment, in this case the Shri Nath, contained officers, enlisted men and non-combatants. To us the officer content seems top-heavy: one commanding general, one major general, one commander colonel, one colonel, four lieutenant colonels, five major captains, six captains, twelve lieutenants and two major *ajitan* (adjutants). There were two officials in charge of the ammunition, ten *subedar* and ten *jemadar*, two writers, one physician, two standard bearers and one person in charge of the key of the box containing orders from above and one horseman. There were eighty-one NCOs and 431 sepoys. The non-combatants included tent-pitchers, a time-keeper, a barber, goldsmiths, a brazier, a dhobi, a gardener, a sweeper and uniform makers.

The composition of the army was Brahmans, Thakuris, Khas, Gurungs and Magars, with Rais and Limbus drafted later. A certain Orfeur Cavenagh found mixed and separate units but he wrote that Jangabahadur seemed to prefer the latter: '. . . in the event of mutiny showing itself in any particular regiment, there would be no difficulty in bringing up other troops to overawe it.'

Recruiting was done by written orders emanating from the capital to district governors, then down to village headmen requiring them to produce so many men within a given period of time. Aged between twenty and fifty, only able-bodied men were required to prevent their having to return home once they had reached the capital. Newly-enlisted soldiers had their details recorded: names, addresses and the names of father and grandfather were required. There does not seem to be any fixed term of engagement and it is probable that many were dismissed not to be reinstated at the end of the year. Such men were known as *dhakré* (a word still commonly used, but now for one who does not join the army but lives by non-agrarian tasks such as portering) and they were the backbone for any speedy reinforcement requirement by doubling or trebling the strength of those currently serving.

Training does not merit many references in archives and writings of those times. However there was a manual prepared in 1883 for drilling and manoeuvring. Words of command were in English and bugle calls the same as those in India. Dress and accoutrements were also copied from India. There was some range work but so scarce was the supply of ammunition that many infantry units were poorly trained. When there was enough the soldiers were good. One Englishman of the time, Campbell, wrote as far back in 1835 that: 'Their firing is unquestionably the best performed part of the drill. In file as well as in volley-firing they are quick and exact. It is said that at target practice also they excel.'

By 1843, however, there seemed to be no range work at all. In 1862 Jangabahadur expressed his intention of advertising for some gunnery instructors in the *Banares Gazette*. The resident, Ramsey, observed that:

> The artillery, in particular, is ludicrously inefficient . . .
> The Maharajah . . . now and then orders down to the
> neighbourhood of his Palace 2 or 3 guns and mortars,
> which are fired at a mark, but this is nearly all the practice
> of the Artillery during the year; even Infantry field days . . .
> firing . . . unknown here, as the Durbar does not choose to
> incur the expense of the powder.

Discipline was strict, both in war and peace. A document prepared on the eve of the Nepal-Tibet War of 1854–56 gives these details:

1 If a colonel questioned the authority or command of a general he was to be fined Rs 100.
2 Such disobedience for a senior captain was Rs 50, a captain Rs 30, a lieutenant Rs 20, down to a soldier Rs 2.
3 if any officer or soldier returned home after deserting his position in the front line he was to be shot.
4 If any above the rank of havildar sent to the war front did not report on time he was deprived of his position and re-enrolled

as a private soldier. For havildar and below the punishment was to be reduced to the status of a *pipa* or coolie.

5 Once the order to go to the front was given all, from general to coolie, would be hanged if he went absent from duty.

6 Anyone who attempted to loot the belongings of a fallen enemy was to be shot dead.

7 If a soldier deserted in peace time, discarded his uniform and fled to a foreign country, he was liable to be punished by the confiscation of his share of his family's property.

As examples of strict discipline, on 7 July 1857, a deserter from a regiment detailed to go to India (to help the British during the Mutiny) was executed on the Tundikhel parade ground.

> . . . his head fastened to a tree, a board stating his offence erected below it, and the parade of all the troops ordered, to show them what would be the fate of any man who showed himself a coward.

When deserters could not be apprehended civilian murderers, dressed in military uniform, were hanged instead.

There are no reliable Nepalese sources of what uniforms were worn. Kirkpatrick, at the end of the eighteenth century found:

> The regular troops . . . are clothed somewhat in the slovenly manner of the Purgunnah Sepoys, formerly in the Company's service, with the difference that none of the corps would appear to have any general uniform of appropriate colour; some among the company of guards which escorted me appearing, for example, in red, some in blue, and others in green coats.

By the early 1840s all regiments wore loose red jackets, less one which was dressed in blue. Troops used to receive their uniforms every seventh or eighth year and expenses incurred were recovered from them.

Despite strict caste rules in Nepalese society, the troops in the field seem to have dispensed with them. This did not seem to worry any of them. They performed only a simple ceremony before their meals, high caste soldiers having a little ghee in the cooking put before the food was cooked. Soldiers were not allowed to remove leather items – boots and belt – before eating. Compared with the East India Company's troops, who took three hours to feed, Nepalese army meals were over in half an hour.

[1988]

23

Bhakti Thapa and his Place in the Gurkha Connection

Those who saw Michael Begg's documentary film on Gurkhas (shown on BBC 2 on 26 December 1995) may have noticed a momentary shot of two paintings when the Anglo-Nepal War of 1814-16 was being touched on. One shows Major General Ochterlony of the East India Company. It is an oil painting done by one of the most talented artists in Nepal, Alok Gurung of Pokhara. The other is of Bhakti Thapa, the Company's finest adversary during the war. It is a watercolour done by the same artist. Both paintings were commissioned by Buddhiman Gurung and hang in the sitting room in our house in Pokhara.

The reason why we have these two great men's pictures is because they sowed the seed which grew into the deep-rooted and time-proven relationship between Nepal and the United Kingdom that has allowed me to become a paradoxically real fictitious grandfather and father of an extended family of twenty. For the British, Ochterlony was the only commander in that war able to beat the Gorkhali army in fair combat, and Bhakti Thapa was one of the greatest Gurkha commanders in the field ever, leaving his mark on Nepalese history as few others have.

Captain Jimmy Coleman, late 1 Gurkha Rifles, in a seminal work on the roots of the Gurkha Connection, almost miraculously found Ochterlony's sole surviving direct descendant, Ean

219

Ramsay, a great-great-greatgrandson, living in the same village of Beaminster. Buddhiman's relationship to Bhakti Thapa could well be 'great-great-great-grandnephew'. Prior to Buddhiman's visit to England in 1994, he commissioned oil paintings of both great men to give to Ean Ramsey. So, six generations after their forebears were adversaries, their descendants met in perfect harmony.

Buddhiman's village is Thuloswara, two days' walk east-north-east from Pokhara and it was there, in 1493, that the Dura people made Kalu Shah, the second son of Kulamandan Shah of [Syangja] Nawakot, raja of Lamjung. About six months afterwards Kalu was murdered by people to the north and Kulamandan's sixth and youngest son, Yasobam, aged seven, was fetched from Nawakot and made raja as his brother's replacement. Nine direct generations later it was Prithvi Narayan Shah of Gorkha who unified Nepal, having expanded east. In other words, Buddhiman's family was instrumental in setting up the Shah dynasty.

In a parchment I have seen, written nearly 400 years ago, the people of Buddhiman's area of Lamjung, Gurungs and Duras, called themselves Gurung Thapa or Dura Thapa. As the suffix 'Thapa' is a shortened form of the word prasTHAPAna which, with its verb, means 'to establish', it was added after they had done just that to the new royal family. When, in the middle of the eighteenth century, they found themselves the target of Shah expansion towards the west, they dropped the suffix. It was during one of these probes from the east that captured Bhakti Thapa in 1782 when he was taken away as a prisoner to the Valley.

A word or two about the Duras: in the main there is no difference between Dura and Gurung but Duras are unusual in that they sacrifice a pig twice a year. Until late in 1995 I thought that only happened in Turlung, not far from Thuloswara, where the village elders have documents of authority dating back to sometime around 1520. No Gurung would think of having anything to do with pigs so it was with intense interest that I found out that this sacrifice was not unique to Turlung. Above the village of Tandrang – a morning's walk from the present Lamjung-Kaski border and a shorter distance to Thuloswara and Turlung – is a shrine where fourteen of Bhakti Thapa's weapons (seven scimitars and seven swords) are still kept and worshipped twice a year at the spring and autumn Dashera when the same pig sacrifice is made by the high-caste Gurung village headman. This man uses a language called 'Tandrang' which, in fact, is the almost extinct Dura language. The village has an extensive Gurung population with only six Dura households.

In 1995 a Brahman gained his Master's degree having researched the Dura language for over fifteen years and he confirms that the 'Tandrang' language is exactly the same as that of the Duras. During his research he found that about 2,000 Dura households now call themselves Gurung and an unspecified number now call themselves Magar Thapa. He estimated that there are 13,000 Dura households.

There is controversy on Bhakti Thapa's caste, his provenance one might say. Chhetris, who also have Thapas, say he is theirs; Magars likewise. In fact, there is almost no doubt that he is neither but a Dura Thapa. While there are some Chhetris in the area of his birth, none of them Chhetri Thapas, there are no Magars for many, many miles around. One likely reason why he was most likely not a Chhetri, apart from what old pictures of him that show a Mongoloid face with epicanthic eyelids, is that none of his forbears' names are given in any document so far unearthed. This more than unusual lapse of Chhetri custom can best be explained by his not being of that caste. Later on I do not doubt that he was made into an 'honorary' Chhetri. (Incidentally, Buddhiman is also a Dura. Furthermore, there are some Shrestha Thapas to be found at Thimi in the Valley.)

To me most, if not all, 'caste' names, not merely Thapa, are more labels or nicknames than, say, are those more intimate 'clan' (*gotra*) names less frequently used. For instance, Sen comes from Sena, an army; Khan means leader (the original Jenghis Khan was a title signifying 'Supreme Leader' and its renowned holder, Temujin, was neither Moslem nor Hindu but an animist); Malla a wrestler; Subba a rank of authority; and Gurung, GURUko aNG, follower of a teacher.

Bhakti Thapa was born in Tandrang in about 1743, of a rich and powerful family. Legend still has it that he inherited thirty yoke of ploughing oxen, had a fiery temper, was strong and a natural leader. Not long after he was captured he entered the service of the Gorkhali government.

Seven years later in 1789, Farther Nepal was established when Doti, Achham and Jumla were absorbed into the Gorkhali empire. Bhakti Thapa was promoted to Subba in that region and, as expansion of the empire was made farther west still, towards Kumaoñ, Almora, Sirmur, Srinagar and Dehra Dun, he played a commanding part in the military occupation and the administration of those places.

He was the main lieutenant of the commander, Kaji Amarsing Chhetri Thapa, who faced General Ochterlony in 1815. The part Bhakti Thapa played in the battle of Deuthal, near Malauñ (the First Gorkha Rifles are still The Malauñ Regiment), was crucial to the Gurkha Connection as, indeed, was Ochterlony's.

The following description of this battle is taken from *Nepalko Sainik Itihas*, pages 414 and 415. The whole work was commissioned by the Royal Nepal Army in 1992. My translation is 'unpolished':

> About four miles to the south of Malauñ fort was a strong fort named Surgarh and the defence of that was the responsibility of the junior Gorkhali officer, Bhakti Thapa.

Between Malauṅ and Surajgarh the English found two similar places where they wanted to establish a camp from where they could observe both forts. One and a half miles north of Suraj is a place called Raila and a mile south of Malauṅ is a place called Deuthal. Ochterlony set up camps in both places. From the night of 15 April 1815, the English army reached both places and started making their camps. The English were also successful in getting two small artillery pieces to Deuthal. On learning about this, Bhakti Thapa, thinking that it was more important to join his commander Amarsingh Thapa than to stay and defend his own fort, left Surajgarh fort that night and, making his way carefully through his enemy, was successful in reaching the inside of Malauṅ fort. Realising that until he could clear the English Colonel Thomson from his camp in Deuthal to the south of Malauṅ fort, he would be unable to defend Malauṅ fort, Amarsingh Thapa gave the responsibility of this operation to the recently-arrived Bhakti Thapa and his troops. Bhakti Thapa gladly accepted the authority for this request by his superior. The plan was to go with 2,000 chosen Gorkhalis with him from Malauṅ fort. They prepared for this attack all night long.

In the Nepal-English war, from the morning of 16 April 1815, near the fort of Malauṅ in the far west, the Gorkhalis gave a demonstration of such bravery that a new chapter of bravery was written in the history of bravery. The commander-in-chief of the Gorkhali forces, brave 73-year-old Bhakti Thapa gave such a demonstration of such formidable courage that his name reached letters of gold in history.

Before 0400 hours on 16 April Bhakti Thapa's Gorkhalis had gone downhill in the direction of Deuthal. After going downhill from Malauñ fort, Deuthal was reached after moving uphill. After the Gorkhalis had reached the top of Deuthal, they hoped to attack from three directions, east, north and west. Immediately on receiving their orders for attack, uttering shrill battle cries of victory, the Gorkhalis attacked the English camp with naked kukris in their right hands and shotguns in their left hands. First of all, Bhakti Thapa, having decided to capture the two English artillery pieces, launched his main attack on the artillery. The attacking Gorkhalis could not reach the guns, which opened ruinous fire on them. Bhakti Thapa again led a charge against the guns with the rest of his men. Again the artillery mowed the Gorkhalis down like a litter of straw. At that time six out of seven English gunners had been wounded by the Gorkhalis' bullets. Bhakti Thapa withdrew his remaining men and ordered them all to charge the artillery all together in one wave. This time the Gorkhalis got so near to the artillery pieces that it really seemed as if they had taken them but a few seconds later the guns fired and caused the Gorkhalis so many casualties that they were forced to retire. After three tireless but unsuccessful attempts to capture the guns, Bhakti Thapa took his remaining men and made a frontal attack on the English camp from the east. There was a great struggle for about two hours. During the fight eventually the aged Bhakti Thapa was wounded in the chest and fell dead on the battlefield. When they saw their leader dead, the Gorkhalis started to leave the scene of the battle and withdraw. In this way the Gorkhalis were unsuccessful in their great attempt to capture the auxiliary fort of Deuthal from the English but in this battle of Deuthal the story of a brave people's bravery has been safely put in the pages of history for all time. The fearless Gorkhali attack on the artillery and their resolute demonstration to fulfil their aim made the entire English force amazed. The English [sic] General Ochterlony freely gave praise to such Gorkhali bravery. Amarsingh watched that horrific struggle for Deuthal from Malauñ fort from where he had a clear view. Amarsingh Thapa was most upset at Bhakti Thapa's death. That day he lost his most trusted and very brave warrior. Bhakti Thapa's death was also greatly mourned by the Gorkhali troops with fervour.

In the battle many brave Gorkhali soldiers died. Around 150 bodies were recovered from the battlefield and altogether 500 men were wounded. Among 253 English casualties, twenty were killed. As a mark of respect, the English General Ochterlony sent Bhakti Thapa's body, wrapped in a shawl [of expensive cloth], with a detachment of troops to Amarsingh Thapa. Bhakti Thapa's two wives went with the body. From near Deuthal the English officers and men watched with overwhelming emotion the full compassionate sight of the flame from Bhakti Thapa's funeral pyre. After Bhakti Thapa's death in the battle of Deuthal one after another affliction mounted on Amarsingh Thapa. His rations were short and those escaping from a probable English attack left him and started mingling with the English. His force dwindled daily. On one day alone 1,600 men left him and went to mix with the English. On the day of 10 May 1815, the English moved from Deuthal with their big guns and started shelling. Now he saw no way out so he sent his son Ramdas to General Ochterlony to talk about an agreement to leave the fort. Eventually, on 15 May 1815, Kaji Amarsingh Thapa and General Ochterlony agreed on a treaty, according to which the Gorkhalis would evacuate all forts from Jaithak to the west of the river

Jumna, all those Gorkhalis who so wished, to take their belongings into Nepal and Amarsingh Thapa, his relations and officers with their weapons and possessions to go into Nepal in safety etc., were respected. General Ochterlony was full of wisdom with this treaty. 'Let the snake die but also let the stick not break', was what he fully understood. He was pleased with the Gorkhalis who left the forts empty. But he tried to win them over with property and fully friendly treatment. In fact, having regard for Amarsingh Thapa and Ramjor Singh's honour and respect, he made arrangements for his friends, their belongings and their weapons, also with respect, with English army help to get back to Nepal. In making this kind of high-minded treaty, if they had maintained Amarsingh Thapa's old friendship, the English would have had no need to appraise such a long and stressful enmity or have had reason to scrutinise and experience the Nepalis' bravery from so close in this war. Now even the English started to be firm in making great endeavours concerning friendship with Nepal.

Seldom, if ever, before can the victors have raised a second memorial to the vanquished as was the case here.

[1996]

❧ 24 ❧

A General Remembers:
Major General Sir Ksatra Bikram Rana
KCVO CIE, Commanding Officer
The Mahindra Dal Nath Nepalese
Contingent: 1943–45

I was the CO of The Famous Mahindra Battalion from 1942 to 1945 AD. Its name was originally Mahindra Dal but was changed after Lord Louis Mountbatten, the Supreme Allied Commander of South East Asia Command, first orally then in writing referred to us as The Famous Mahindra Battalion as a result of the excellent work we had done. Its name, starting with THE, is still retained in the Royal Nepal Army.

All my early army knowledge had been gleaned from training with the Indian Army, chiefly with Gurkha battalions and their British officers. It stood me in good stead all my life, as general, as ambassador to China, as secretary and chief secretary. The way the British taught me how to make Appreciations was the best thing that ever happened to me. Much later, as a Secretary in the Government and an ambassador in China, people thought I had been possessed by inner sight, so logical and clear was my thinking and the correctness of my prognostications.

I will give you two examples, the first from when I was a Secretary in the Government; when everyone else in the Government feared

Indian intervention in Nepal during one particularly difficult and tense period, my appreciation of the situation led me to believe firmly that there would not be an invasion. And I was right.

The second was when I was ambassador in China at the time of Mao's death. I was the only ambassador who did not write any condolences to his wife, Chin Cheng, as I knew she wouldn't last. I got a reprimand from the Durbar and a request for an immediate explanation. It was based in the form of an Appreciation and accepted. Later I was the only diplomatic representative who foresaw her downfall. This was also based on a correct Appreciation.

I give full credit for everything to my military training under the British. I did not go to the Staff College at Quetta but attended countless periods of study and training at battalion/brigade/divisional level. Some were at Rawalpindi others at Bombay, where I learnt enough of Indian tactics for the Quit India movement to be of the greatest value when I was Home Secretary. Apart from tactics I learnt about logistics. I asked advice from British officers and read military literature in my quest for learning.

I went to the war fully trained and understanding it all. I took over from Lieutenant Colonel (later General and Commander-in-Chief) Kiran Shamsher JB Rana.

The battalion had been in upper Assam on airfield protection for nine months when I got there to command it. It was spread over a wide area, based on four places. Battalion HQ was at Dinjan, not far from Dibrugarh, near the Digboi oil field. These airfields were used chiefly by supply 'planes, Dakotas, for resupplying the Chinese armies based in Chungking, over the 'Hump'. There were also fighters and bombers to be guarded. I remember seeing thousands of flights daily, taking off from first light until after dusk. The Japs were a long way to the south, at Imphal.

According to the Agreement signed by the Governments of Nepal and India – by which we were only to be deployed in India

– we were established as were all other infantry battalions of the Indian Army. Our strength was around 900 and that included First Line Reinforcements, in the shape of a Training Company. Our weapons included assault rifles, Tommy Guns, LMGs, Vickers Bertha MMGs and PIATs.* Our rations were supplied exactly as for other Hindu battalions.

I found that most of the soldiers took to these conditions without any difficulty although there were isolated cases of some men finding the life strange to an extent that it bothered them and their performance was not up to standard. In the main nobody outside the battalion realised we were not a Gurkha battalion of the Indian Army.

We were in 268 Independent Brigade and sometimes came under command of 2 British and 19 Indian Divisions. When the Japs made a push west, in 1943, my battalion was ordered 'with white-hot priority' to advance south to Silchar but we had no idea why. We went about 100 miles and the track was very difficult. We went along a range of hills to one that looked like Shiva Puri in Nepal at a place called Sansad near Ukhral, where the Kali Bahadurs had fought. It had a number of suspension bridges that, at first sight, seemed impossible to bear our weight or that of Jeeps. After being there for several days 43 Assault Brigade arrived, a Special Service brigade composed of Commandos and Marines, designed for combined and amphibious work. 'They are specimens of humanity' who moved at 6 to 7 mph. Even so, we moved in front of them.

We were still thirty to forty miles from any action and we still had no idea of our task. Then, would you credit the idea, higher formation gave us a lot of fireworks!! Our job was to get close to the Japs surrounding Imphal and let these fireworks off. Some sounded

---

* Projector, Infantry, Anti-Tank.

like rifle fire, some like machine guns and 2in mortars, while others looked like flares. We would fire away at twenty minutes a time. All we could do was frighten anybody in that area. The aim was to give the Japs the impression that the spearhead of the attack was coming from that direction. Who would believe that?

2 British Division was about to attack, as were other divisions. Our patrols occasionally met the enemy but there was no organised patrol or ambush programme. There was nothing on a large scale.

One of my havildars earned an MM taking a message to another HQ across the Jap lines.

We did not take part in any action at Imphal. We got the chance to do some training and once Imphal was cleared we advanced from Imphal and entered Burma. I saw two novel and useful aspects of war during our time on that track. One was the use of fireworks and the other of carrier pigeons for messages.

Until then we had not had all that action, everything was slow, with low level contacts through small patrols and ambushes. We learnt as we went along. Later, when we made large attacks, morale shot up and we found all happening as taught us in the manuals, which proved to be of the greatest value.

We advanced along the axis of the track that the Indian army had retired down in 1942, sending out fighting patrols and laying ambushes. We moved across country through the jungle until we came to the valley of Kabaw, which means the Valley of Death and is as unhealthy as Surkhet once was.

We reached the approaches to Mandalay where the Japs were forming 'withdrawal protection' and we started large-scale operations. We had to make extensive preparations to cross the River Irrawaddy and play a deception role while the bridgehead was being established on the far side by moving a company upstream ten miles and creating a diversion.

One night we changed with a British battalion, the Norfolks, whose MMG platoon stayed behind. They told us that the Japs would fire from a certain hill at 1600 hours, which they did, but all their rounds overshot our forward positions and our cookhouse to the rear. They knew a new unit had arrived. They saw movement around our cooking area to the rear. The BOR returned fire for a few minutes and then there was 'pin-drop silence'. Before dawn the next morning the Japs opened fire again.

Our position was in a naturally defendable place, a three-sided square into which the Japs came. We slaughtered them for fifteen to twenty minutes. Those that escaped went back to their previous positions which were less than 300 yards away.

Brigadier (later DQMG*) Moti Dayar sent a message for us to leave the corpses until he could come up and see them for himself the next day which he did with a few reinforcements, at 1100 hours. I was ordered to send a strong fighting patrol to assess the Jap strength but it did not get very far. The Japs were estimated to be a battalion less a company. The enemy opened fire from 150 yards. The brigadier said there were no tanks, no APCs,† no support at all but that he would get them all for the next morning so a counter attack could be launched.

There was much heavy firing that took off the top of the prickly cactus that was on top of the bunker behind which the Brigadier Major (who was new and wanted to make a good impression) and I were sheltering, having been caught by the enemy fire. The Brigadier saw us stuck and good-naturedly teased us for being there. Firing stopped and we managed to get to the rear and behind cover.

At 1600 hours that day Jap artillery fire opened and the brigade commander sent us some reinforcements as we were thin on the ground. Over the next three days one of my drivers was killed

---

* Deputy Quartermaster General.

† Armoured Personnel Carrier.

by splinters from artillery piercing his head. Nothing happened during the night so, after we had got our reinforcements and attacked the Japs, we withdrew. Two days later we got four tanks and one section of APCs to help us attack the Japs.

Soon afterwards General Slim came there and wanted to visit us. He said he could stand the shelling but we had to clear a Jap road block on a track to the front before he would come. This we did the next day and it was a new experience for me and I was afraid. The road block defended a Jap assembly area and at night it was most dangerous. Firing was intense as we cleared it. One of my soldiers killed a Japanese officer with his bayonet. We had been afraid of the Japanese when we started the campaign but not by this time. We telephoned back to brigade that the block was clear and brought the corpse back to show Slim. We got a big shabash and Slim said that he would send a copy of his thanks to our HQ in Delhi.

We then had a build-up period during which major unit commanders had to attend a meeting. There we were lined up with mugs in our hands and given rum. I could not get out of it: join it and it would be too much; not join it and be different. I had too much and left tipsy and was in great fear as to any consequences as had any of my superiors known about it I would have been replaced.

Lord Mountbatten visited the battalion. He was very pleased with all he saw and said he would write a letter to Nepal and tell them all about us. A copy went to Delhi and I got a rocket for taking my unit into Burma against the Agreement. The Sher Dal had not done too well and had already lost its name and it was incumbent on me to restore the name of our army. With all the martial spirit shown by my men our morale would suffer severely if we were withdrawn. Despite Delhi's anger, PM Joodha was so pleased that he abrogated that part of the Agreement as far as we were concerned.

But back to crossing the Irrawaddy: it was our turn to cross a couple of days after the main assault, using a number of boats including DUKWs.* The Japs were retiring with their 7 Div moving back down Burma from Tidim and Kabaw. We moved forward to the end of the Arakan Yomas, not far from the foot of Mount Popa, an extinct volcano over 5,000 feet high. It was mostly rocks with no cover and the Japs had posts in many places. They also started withdrawing.

There was an interesting incident when we were there: with us in 268 Bde were a battalion each of the Madras and the Kamaoñ Regiments, plus gunners and other ancillaries. The brigade was ordered forward, the Madrasis in the lead, followed by the gunners, then us, Brigade HQ and the Kamaonis. The objective was a small hill, marked on the map as a spot height, at the top of the Mount Popa feature.

The Japs started firing on the Madrasis and we only managed to advance with difficulty, chiefly by crawling. One of my soldiers, a Bren gunner, stood up and, despite everything that his platoon commander ordered to the contrary, tried to open fire on the Japanese but was straightway killed.

The brigade was given a bearing to move on. A little later a message was dropped by air to tell us that the spot height we had been told to reach was wrong so therefore the bearing we were on was wrong and we had to move on another one and to wait on the main North–South (Mandalay–Rangoon) road that night. At that juncture a most violent storm broke making it as dark as night and, such was the static interference, none of our wireless sets worked. No message was able to be sent to the Madrasis who did not find their way back and join up with us for three days.

We reached the road, which was dead straight, but found out we were about two miles farther to the north, and so much nearer Mount Popa, than we should have been. We stayed in that area that

* D = model; U = amphibian; K = all-wheel drive; W = dual rear axles.

night, with no food and in the pouring rain. We were very hungry. We made a perimeter to the west of the road with one company on the road side. By then it was dark and we were surprised when 225 JIF* soldiers, mostly Sikhs, commanded by a pre-war regular captain, came into our area. They did not know we were there but they surrendered to us. They told us to keep quiet as there were some Japanese not so far away and it was dangerous. We took the weapons from those who had them and they all huddled to one side, silent and demoralised.

The Japanese came along and, using the company alongside the road as a linear ambush, we killed most of them. We had no casualties ourselves and counted it as a minor action.

Next morning around 1100 hours Brigade HQ, the signallers, the gunners, our LOB† men and bulldozers came into the area, expanding our perimeter. Everybody was very pleased with us. They brought us rations but by that time we had managed to ease our hunger by eating many of the biscuits the Japanese had been carrying. Our position was enlarged and consolidated as we were nicely near Mount Popa. The Marathas joined us a day later.

A couple or so nights later three of us were sitting down having a chat and a drink. It was about 1930 hours. With me were a Colonel Irvine, a British signals officer and an Indian officer, called Tika Khan, famous as the Commander-in-Chief of the Pakistan Army later. We were attacked by a Japanese patrol from Mount Popa with grenades and the three who were sitting with me were hit, luckily none in any vital area. A very lucky escape.

Next morning the Brigade Commander told us how lucky we had been. None of the wounded men agreed to go to hospital.

---

* Japanese-Indian Forces, the name used for the so-called Indian National Army (INA).
† Left Out Of Battle.

Two days after that my battalion was ordered to attack Mount Popa, with all the 2in mortars in the brigade concentrated and the Madrasis acting as porters for our rations, ammunition and other stores. I ordered 3-up (D, A, B companies) with C Company in reserve. We reached a feature fairly near the top but even with considerable air support, fighters and bombers, we could not take our objective. I recall one of the metal caps of an artillery shell landing on the head of one of my soldiers. The Japs were to our left, clustered around a Buddhist temple. In the gap of 200 to 300 yards between us and the Japs were a whole lot of wild pig, some of which we managed to shoot and collect before we were ordered to withdraw at 1500 hours.

I seem to remember the code names for the features to our front were CLOWN HAT and SUGAR BLOCK or LOAF, but I can't be sure.

Now there was an officer in 1 GR, a Captain Don Collard who had an American wife. He was so clever he was nicknamed the Fox. He suggested to me that he and I walk in sight of the Japs over to the Madras battalion, hoping that the Japs would then attack them. This they did in great strength during which the Fox and I escaped unscathed. On our return to my battalion he turned to me and said how successful we had been. How I laughed! He was always of great use to us. The Madrasis took more casualties than necessary as they disregarded the brigade commander's orders for their own protection.

For two days we dug in then the Japs attacked us. Twelve of our bunkers were destroyed. We asked for counter-fire but nothing happened. Later Brigadier Moti Dayer said that he had given our gunners a day off but I believe they were too frightened to fire. However, we were out-gunned by the Japs and took casualties.

Three or four days later we heard the Japs withdrawing, at night, very close to the Madrasis, but the Madrasis said they heard nothing. Next morning the Jap positions had been vacated. B Company of my battalion, under Captain Guptabahadur Gurung, was ordered to cut the Japs off. A staff major from brigade brought him rations but night fell and so the victualling party had to stay there the night. B Company fought the Japs all night and inflicted heavy casualties on them. The staff major reported to me that 'that night Captain Dayabahadur Gurung was not a man but a superman' and I used that phrase in the recommendation that won him an MC.

We continued south down Burma, fighting most of the way. We crossed the Irrawaddy north of Tharawaddy and moved west, ahead of Jap 7 Div, with orders to delay them and let the rest of our forces catch up. We ambushed many of them one night and OC B Company won an MC. Three to four days later a big concentration of Japs, amongst whom was said to be the Division Commander, moved to the river. They crossed it silently and started fighting to our rear.

We ended up in Rangoon, made out twelve copies of embarkation nominal rolls and embarked on HMT *Dunera* and sailed away. On the high seas we heard that the atomic bomb had been dropped and that was the end of the Japanese.

Since those days I have received many honours and awards, Nepalese and foreign. But, of them all, the ones I am the most proud of and which mean the most to me are the two Mention-in-Dispatches I was awarded during the Burma Campaign. Why? Because they reflected what I did, not who I was nor where I was. And, as a postscript, I have to put on record that, when I was asked to go to Britain and march in front of Her Majesty, Queen Elizabeth II, for the fiftieth anniversary of Victory over Japan Day, it was the nearest I could get to heaven and still be alive.

[1998]

25

Profiles for Perpetuity

In May 1998 I was asked by Lionel Leventhal, the owner of Greenhill Books, if I would try and fill a gap in his forty-year-long stint as a military publisher: to produce an English version of what the Gurkhas themselves have to say about their war service. The working title of the book is *Gurkhas At War: An Oral History*. Gurkhas' actions have always cast a long, collective shadow rather than a medley of individual ones. This book will, I hope, remedy this lacuna. As one who falls, just, into the same bracket as World War II veterans, with none of us having all that mileage left, it seemed apposite that I undertook the task. It involved talking to well over 400 people, travelling from one end of the country to the other and walking a long way.

Recording the stories of the 'Old and Bold' was not easy with many wartime men, apart from suffering from 'selective amnesia', now deaf, toothless, sometimes almost voiceless or even suffering from a stroke – or all four – so are difficult to understand. For some, storytelling is essentially a 'liquid' affair with friends, not a 'dry' performance into a microphone. Even the recorded talk of the non-afflicted was sometimes too hard for Buddhiman to understand, so mauled, muted and muttered were the words.

When young the army had beckoned them beguilingly. Many men had no idea a war was in progress and some had no idea of what country they found themselves in nor, at times, who were their adversaries. One man claimed that his Japanese captors had sent him on Nepal leave.

Recruits came from the underprivileged sector of society with no hope of any other enhancement and little intellectual curiosity, yet all had considerable superstitious prudence, an infinite capacity to learn and a marvellous ability for improvisation. Many of them could not even speak 'that rustic dialect of Nepali called Khaskura'. The attractions of service were being in an honourable employment and a good marriage on first leave, seeing new places, the chance to win a bravery award and, in due course, promotion, possibly to officer rank, and finally to have a pension and be of status in retirement. Such details as food, education, and medical facilities were never mentioned, except to say that they were nearly always hungry when a recruit.

Most were illiterate and innumerate, certainly functionally, when they joined up. This, in fact, is a bonus for recording their stories as the power of recall of the illiterate is, of necessity, better than that of those who can refer to the printed page to refresh their memories. As to the language used, the Nepali as spoken in the Hills when many 'Old and Bold' joined, had a limited vocabulary and, while being very good for onomatopoeic ululations, is not so satisfactory for 'grades' of description. Many have a wonderful memory for the actual details of battle; evocative descriptions are rare. Names, of officers and places, especially in Italy and Burma, are infernally hard to reconcile as are the difficulties of trying to render such portmanteau generalities as 'going, going, going, going, going here, there, hither thither, up down, what what how, what what how, utter distraction', into acceptable or even definitive English.

One facet of their talk was that they did not complain of any British inefficiency – thoughtlessness, yes – but not at bad tactics or such events as blowing up the Sittang Bridge when so many men were on the far side of the river, nor at lack of rations, ammunition and stores as such. Sure, it was *dukha* but it was not seen as anyone's fault. Having taken of the Government's salt and their oath ('never complaining, never explaining') they showed a pathological dislike of making adverse comments. As young men they were (and as old men still are) so used to incompetence and inefficiency that any deviation from normal army arrangements were either seldom as bad as had happened at home or accepted with the fortitude of a fundamental fatalism. At least, that is the way I have come to explain this phenomenon.

One common plaint was the *dukha* of and in service. *Dukha* stretches from 'pain' and 'grief' to 'trouble', 'distress' and 'suffering' to 'a hard time'. Active service conditions, let alone in battle, or when wounded or hungry, thirsty, cold, wet, outnumbered, far from base or far from home as a prisoner of war are natural candidates for *dukha*. I also wondered if it was a reaction to a deprivation of female company, discomfort and boredom as well as the fretful, nagging constant of inescapable duties of line sentry, inlying piquets, fatigues, broken sleep for one reason or another alike in the line and out of it. Whatever the reason it seemed pervasive then – and, with senescence sucking strength from once-lively limbs and the depression caused by 'life not being what it was', is pervasive now.

That the name and fame of the Gurkhas is worldwide is beyond dispute. The Gurkhas themselves are mostly reticent about their achievements and they told their stories dispassionately and, for the most part, modestly. Fear before an action was understandable but I believe that 'stage fright' would be more apt. After shot and shell started to fly and the enemy charged at them, 'We had nothing to lose by risking our lives as we had lost them already,' with the unsaid rider that they gave their all to master the situation. Strangely most men did not talk about the more horrendous events until, at the end, one of us asked them if there was anything else they'd like to add. Then came personal details, from the more prosaic 'I had my hat shot off my head twice'; 'I was wounded', to the unbelievable 'As a prisoner of war in Singapore I refused to join the Indian National Army (INA) so, to try and force me to, I was made to strip in front of a parade and had the whole of the nightsoil bucket poured over my body and not allowed to wash'; 'We were fallen in and threatened with being killed if we did not join the INA. We refused and three men were taken out and shot in front of us. We still refused.'

One Indian Pioneer Corps company was held by the Japanese in the Arakan for three or so months. 'Was there nothing else?' I asked him after a banal story. Yes, there was: 'We were rescued by Habsis [Africans] who crucified six Japanese, cut off their member and stuffed it in their mouth, castrated them and put the testicles into their by-then empty eye sockets, pierced their eardrums, hacked pieces of flesh off their bodies, rubbed salt into the wounds and left them to die which took about two hours. The Habsis cut off their thigh meat and cooked it. They invited us to join them but we refused.' When pressed for more details as to why this macabre event had happened, he only then explained that, when they had been captured and used as forced labour in the first place, the Japanese had done exactly that to five of their number, except eat their flesh. Apart from telling his wife, he said that that was the first time he had spoken about it. He wept as he told his story.

I have found that my interviews acted in a therapeutic and cathartic way: one was a 1/9 GR rifleman whose one ambition since 1945 when he jumped into enemy-occupied Malaya with Force 136 had been to 'chew the military cud' with a British officer. Now aged 80, he had thought it would never happen and his eyes glinted with gladness and his smile was genuine and broad when he left us to tell the welfare staff he could now die happily as he had no more major wishes to fulfill; some spoke almost as at confession and later appeared similarly shriven: 'Sahib, I ignored the advice given to me by my company commander in 1944 and I am sorry. I was wrong. I can't tell him but I am telling you as I have wanted to tell someone all this time'; a naik from 1/9 GR who won the IDSM (Indian Distinguished Conduct Medal, equivalent to the Military Medal) in Italy so wanted to show his appreciation that he gave me the ceremonial salute from an inferior to a superior by kneeling down and putting his forehead on my feet. Most embarrassing. And a 1/2 GR man who was reliving his times on operations in 1951 told me: 'I saved the lives of most of my section by eliminating an enemy group the others had not seen. I was told I was bound to get an award. When I came back from leave a man who had not been on any jungle operations, although the oldest riflemen in the platoon, was the one who was decorated. I have to tell someone about this so I am telling you. This opportunity is heaven-sent.'

In the same vein, one man walked two days to be interviewed, wearing one of his wartime shirts he kept for special occasions. He also wore his medals, including the MM. Decorations for glory play an unusually big part in a Gurkha's psyche. The temptation to 'steal' a junior man's work for an award to be written up in a senior's name, regarded as scurrilous by British officers, is not so seen. The British give awards for 'collective action' or 'sustained effort over a period'. What really upsets Gurkhas is not getting an award for something achieved when others were rewarded for seemingly, in the mind of him unawarded, doing far less or even nothing at all. The Gurkha soldier's holy grails are based on effort being rewarded, whether by promotion or a bravery award. For such not to happen is seen as a negation of trust: not for nothing did Napoleon say something to the effect of 'give me enough ribbon and I will conquer the world'. Many are the times that disappointment in not being recognised by not having a medal is a recurring theme in the soldiers' stories, resulting in non-return from leave post-1948 and not staying in a unit designated for the British Army pre-1947. And I could have added that, as a bravery award seems to uplift a recipient for a military lifetime, the reverse is true for a court-martial: a wrong paid for once is a dishonour with a permanent penalty.

But even if memories of awards are inaccurate, lesser matters are even more so. 'I know that Field Marshal Auchinleck's wife was Queen Alexandra,' from a 3 GR man; 'I tell you, Sahib, the Irrawaddy does not flow into the sea in Burma as you said but it comes out at Tokyo;' 'How can you say that "planes damaged in Italy did not have to go to Calcutta for repair?"' Um, er, well . . .

Apart from everything else, gathering the data from almost all the Welfare Centres was a wonderful time to meet old friends. As I put in an essay written in 1988 when I trekked in the east of the country to let the Old and Bold know that the eastern depot was to close:

> The glamour and vainglory of regimental soldiering over the years of four decades had long faded but the magic of camaraderie then formed, dormant for so long, instantly and without hesitation rose to the surface everywhere I went. At eight welfare centres, in villages or on the way, names and numbers, in the main, sprang to the mind and almost everybody had his own anecdote about the times we had spent together – some true and flattering, some untrue and flattering, others neither! Looking at the men's animated faces and shining eyes was like looking into a mirror in reverse: smooth-faced, clean-limbed, upright lads that had been were sometimes scarcely recognised now that they had become shriveled, wrinkled, toothless and grey-haired or bald. I, too, after so much time, was one of that large army of 'those who fade away'.

One irony of World War II as far as Gurkhas were concerned was that they were on the side of those who were fighting for democracy but had none of that misunderstood commodity in the land of their birth. The vast majority stood rock-solid firm before and during the war before and after the war and despite decades of accusations of 'divide and rule', the Indian Army in fact showed how to 'unite and rule'; ironically giving the lie to the supreme and crowning irony of British rule in India, the fact that the Indians themselves could only settle for 'divide and rule'.

For some soldiers, the wartime ethos quickly crumbled once the war had ended. The change in attitude to the British Army Gurkhas in 1947 – 'do you really want to eat cow meat and "double roti" over the "black water"? If you do you'll not be allowed to sleep in our barrack room'– and the perceived and inexplicable British weakness shown by five years of sacrifice for Burma and India to be saved from Japanese rule only to give both away, exacerbated by unending, wounding and virulent anti-British propaganda, especially between 1945 and 1947, resulted in our eight regiments coming over in greatly reduced strength.

Regimental officers work at a lower level than do our Lords and Masters in Whitehall but the regimental officer is the one who has his fingers on the pulse. It was Winston Churchill who wrote that 'the further backward you look, the further forward you can see.' Now, I believe current regimental officers need to heed that maxim more than ever before. Let the next edition of *Gurkhas At War* be just as interesting a read!

[2002]

26

Truth is Strange Indeed: Five Small Nuggets

Nugget 1

During Confrontation, Gurkhas in the Second Division of Sarawak had to deal with Ibans, the head–hunters of fame; flamboyant, mercurial, sulky and the world's most colourful exponents of fiction that fits their facts. An Iban could sulk for up to three days when he had been shown to be wrong in front of other Ibans. On one occasion the whole of one Iban Border Scout section, under command of a rifle company of 1/10 Gurkha Rifles, surrounded their Gurkha section commander. They told him that they would not take any more orders from him and that they were going to cut off his head. The Gurkha, canny as ever, told them that they would have to get the local military commander's permission. They agreed to this, so they were fallen in and marched to the military camp a short distance away, having left one men in their own camp to act as sentry. On reaching the company office the Gurkha left the men outside and went in to report to the British major, who happened to be his company commander in more normal times.

The whole business was carried out smartly. The Ibans were marched in, 'right dressed', being told off when their drill was faulty, then stood to attention while the Gurkha saluted the Major and reported what the trouble was, in Nepali, which the Ibans did

244

not understand. The Major spoke about as much Malay as did the Ibans and told them that they had to obey orders and his order was that they were not to decapitate their section commander but to do what he told them. They were then dismissed and the Gurkha marched them back to their camp, all much happier than before; the Gurkha because he had shown that military discipline prevailed; and the Ibans because they had impressed the Gurkha so much with their threat that he had had to take them in front of the 'Tuan Besai' – the Great Man.

The only man who was unhappy at not having 'proved his manhood' was the Iban sentry left behind who, perversely, was told by his comrades that as he had not joined in the mass censuring of the Gurkha, it would have to be his head instead. Once it was dark this man stole away from his camp and went to the main camp where he asked for sanctuary as his head was to be chopped off. He was suitably comforted and sent back to his section post where he was given a rocket by the Gurkha for being absent without leave. 'Oh,' came the answer, 'I had to go and tell the "Tuan Besai" that I thought you ought to be beheaded.'

Thus, in its convoluted Asian way, was one tiny problem defused.

Nugget 2

When I was commanding the Border Scouts I had to cover the whole of the border, mostly on foot. In one longhouse I visited I caught sight of the coloured cover of a magazine produced by the Shell Company of Brunei. It was a photograph of a traditional and typical Kelabit: red feather in his hair, worn in the old style of fringe in front and pig-tail behind; strong face with high cheek bones and epicanthic eyelids; elongated ear lobes with an embroidered ivory hornbill cope hanging from each ear; 'bare buff', showing a strong body used to hard work; and the whole having a quality of robustness that asked to be noticed.

I looked at it for some time, then turned my attention to a man who was pottering about. Tall as the man in the picture, bespectacled and wearing a shabby T-shirt and trousers, his ear lobes had been sewn up and his hair given a 'short back and sides' cut. He had a hangdog look, almost shifty, and I felt here was someone, unlike that man in the photograph, who had been tainted by 'civilisation' to an extent that the tribal traits were severely weakened but, however hard he might try, he was far back in the race for status or a non-agricultural job. He was, in fact, a member of the Hygiene Department. He took off his T-shirt and his strong body belied my first impression. He looked up and saw me staring at him, with the magazine in my hand.

'Do you know who this is?' I asked, pointing to the photograph. He mumbled something I did not catch. I asked him again and I saw him look embarrassed. I could not believe it when he answered. It was he, taken when he had gone down to the coast to look for a job. He had since been shorn of all his glory, made to feel ashamed of it and had been reduced to non-tribal anonymity. It saddened me to see the hangdog and lacklustre person in place of the vital and dynamic man of the photograph but who could judge whether he was loser or gainer from the change? A passing thought: had the Indian and British armies treated the Gurkha hill men so cavalierly, would our soldiers have their world-wide reputation they so proudly have now?

Nugget 3

In 1957, the Sultan of Johore did not want the British to hand over the reins of power to Malaya. He told the other rulers and politicians that the Malays would still be collecting coconuts had the British not come when they did. However, he too had had his disagreements with the British: it was pre-war and a new hospital was to be opened by the sultan in the Kluang district in the north of his state. The young British District Officer had arranged lunch in his bungalow for the Sultan and Sultana before the ceremony. He took them to the coolest room and offered the Sultana a long bamboo-slatted chair. She sat down and, no longer being sylph-like, immediately went through it. It was unfortunate that the broken pieces of bamboo acted as a fish trap to the extent that each time the exasperated lady tried to wriggle her way out she merely made matters worse – and more painful.

Eventually she was rescued but the Sultan was so angry that he ordered the District Officer out of the state within twenty-four hours, never to return and forbade him to go to the hospital.

The Englishman had the last word: 'Yes, Your Highness.'

Shortly after the end of World War II the erstwhile District Officer was Governor of Singapore and the Sultan of Johore, who had made a trip to Britain, flew back to regain his state. He had to get there through Singapore as there was then no international airport in Malaya. Protocol demanded that he get the Governor's permission. 'I still called him "Your Highness" but this time he had to call me "Your Excellency", the Great Man told me at a cocktail party the battalion threw for the Good and the Great of Hong Kong on our arrival in the Colony – after ten years' service in Malaya – where he was then Governor.

Nugget 4

1/7 Gurkha Rifles had its first posting to Hong Kong in 1959, after nine years of Emergency in Malaya: we were the last battalion to

247

have our turn there. We were stationed away from the island to the north of Kowloon in the New Territories. One night I arranged a company patrol exercise which featured about six patrols half a mile apart and at various points of the compass. Their task was to move to a central point, a long expanse of sandy waste where I waited, then on to where the patrol opposite them had started without letting the other side know of their presence.

As I waited there was no wind or moonlight. Quicker than expected I heard one lot, then another, move across the sand, their tread muffled. I wanted to know which patrols they were but even though I called out loudly I got no answer. I noted the time. Later I saw patrols pass and, once we were all together at the end of the exercise, I asked which patrols had passed by at such-and such a time. None had. It was only much later that I learnt that that place was shunned by locals, especially at night, as it was said to be haunted. In 1949 when Mao Tse-tung's men crossed the border in pursuit of Nationalists, scores of soldiers had been killed around that spot.

Nugget 5

Chinese place names fascinated me: a battalion camp was at Fook Heng Lai which means 'Happily, Religiously Joyful, Chinese Straight Mile'; the frontier hillock at Lok Ma Chau means 'Get Off Your Horse Island' because, even though it is not an island and there are no horses, had you a horse you'd have to get off it before you got up it; Kowloon, 'the Nine Dragons', for the eight tallest peaks. In ancient times a Big Man from another province came with an escort to see about taking the place over for himself. He was a stranger and he asked a local what the name of the place was. 'Kau Lung,' came the reply. 'Point them out to me,' was the order and the local pointed out eight peaks. 'Eight? Only eight? Where is the ninth?' 'You, oh Mighty One,' was the answer and legend would have us know that the visitor was so pleased with the reply that he departed whence he had come and the locals were left in peace.

[2007]

❧ 27 ❧

Gurkha Motto

'Better to die than be a coward' has become the motto of all Gurkha soldiers to this day. In fact, the originator of the quotation was not a 'traditional martial class' hill man but an Aryan Nepali, Kaji Amarsing Thapa, who at the age of sixty-four was made a General with hardly any active military background, if any at all, at the beginning of the Anglo-Nepal War in 1814. He was a relation of Bhimsen Chhetri Thapa, the prime minister, who started the war and also lost it. Amarsing was just not interested in fighting the East India company but, not wanting to appear against the most powerful man in Kathmandu, echoed, but did not originate, similar sentiments as expressed by the Sikh, Mokhan Chand, in 1809 when Ochterlony moved from Delhi to compel the Sikh durbar to give up its recent conquests, 'It is better to die in honour than to live in shame' and later by the Afghan Muzaffar Khan, defender of Multan in 1818, 'It is more honourable to die fighting than to capitulate without firing a shot.'

[2007]

❧ 28 ❧

Journeys of the Mind

I. Thinks

The valley runs from north to south, its fields giving a rude living to a scattered and pastoral few. Remote from its administrative base in Hanoi, for many years the area was secluded and peaceful, which is what its name – Dien (district) Bien Phu – means. (The nearest to this in Nepali is 'Dharan'.) By the early 1950s, when Communism fought Democracy – or was it Capitalism? – an airstrip nestled between a road and the river, Nam Yum. On 7 May 1954 Dien Bien Phu became notorious worldwide as the largest and worst French military defeat in Asia.

The battle between the North Vietnamese Army and the French, earth-shattering as it was at the time, has now entered into the limbo of memory of a few, completely forgotten by most or never been heard of. But it has seared itself onto the psyche of everyone who took part in it – and remains alive in just the same way the disaster at the Sittang river in late February 1942, is etched for ever in the minds of those who suffered there. To this day those aged Gurkha warriors who managed to escape from that catastrophe still refer to it with dismay and disbelief at the slightest provocation.

And yet . . . the Frenchman's voice was dully insistent and his eyes were unresponsive, staring ahead at nothing . . . or was it at something others could not see? He sat on a stone resting place at

251

the edge of the airstrip, his wife by his side, a look of anxiety on her face as she bent forward the better to pick up what he was saying. I was just near enough to catch his words.

He pointed to one of the hills. 'Isabelle. We held out as long as we could before withdrawing north to the main position by Claudine and Eliane,' and he jerked his head to show his wife where he meant. The French forces had given the ten main hill features female names.

He was mesmerised by the tree-covered hills in front of us; he could still hear the sounds of battle, the Vietnamese artillery and mortar fire, the French returning what they could, the rattle of musketry, the curses and oaths of the sweating, dirty soldiers, the groans and cries of the wounded; could still see the muck and rubble and debris of a battlefield; could still smell the stench of enemy corpses stuck on the wire, and their own unwashed bodies, rank clothing and fear.

His wife's gaze left her husband's troubled face and looked up at the hills, uncomprehendingly, bothered that she could not join him in his flight back to a past which had so cruelly come back to haunt his present.

'Where?' she asked.

He pointed up at the high ground and mumbled something I could not catch. He stared around him, jerking a bit and looking bemused. His wife looked bewildered and I, in my turn, turned my gaze to where he had pointed but, of course, all I saw was what there was to be seen in fact, not in fancy.

He continued talking, oblivious of anyone else. By then a number of other passengers had settled nearby, waiting for their plane and his wife had stopped paying her distraught husband any attention. The place, with its friendly people, its peaceful valley and tree-covered hills, held no fear for her. She glanced at her watch and looked around her impatiently. Not much longer to have to wait. I had inched closer, not very polite of me I know, but I wanted to hear all I could and, to tell the truth, my own French was rustier than it had been when I too was in Indo-China.

The siren hooted to warn us that the plane would land in a few minutes but the Frenchman did not seem to notice. Then the plane landed and his wife nudged him, waking him out of his daydream. He started in surprise, looked around him, saw where he really was and, shaking his head at how he had made such a mistake with the terrain, got up and joined the queue to board the Royal Nepal Airlines scheduled flight from the valley of Pokhara to the valley of Kathmandu.

I, waiting to meet one coming off the flight, also wandered away.

II. Kinks

Unusually there had been thieving in our lines. Not only had the soldiers been affected but one of the British officers also. Cases such as this are always troublesome: call in the local or military police and the unit is almost bound to get a poor reputation – ours as the Gurkha Independent Parachute Company was particularly sensitive on this point; don't call in any outside help and drifting until a break is made is not good for morale, discipline nor, necessarily, for success.

Malaya, as it was then, is a fay place. I have come across cases where people have been convinced that the paranormal was at work, ghosts were at play and fickle man was at the mercy of something he could not control.

One day the company senior Queen's Gurkha Officer, Dhanman Gurung, told me that the soldiers were getting so restless that 'something had to be done' and it was obvious that I, the boss, would have to do it. But what? That was on the Friday. I'd tell him on the Monday.

The Mess where we British officers lived was staffed by Chinese and Tamils. Gurkhas were responsible for normal batman duties and I did not like to think that any one of them was guilty. If only some of the civilian staff were implicated, that would mean two thieves, one operating in the soldiers' barracks and one in the Mess. The senior Tamil waiter was distressed to think that, after so many years' loyal service, even he was under suspicion.

That evening he sidled up to me after my meal and asked if he could speak about the most recent theft that had occurred the day before. He felt that one man and not a gang was responsible in both the barracks and the Mess. He told me 'normal' methods could not catch the thief but he knew of an 'abnormal' way to help us find out who the miscreant was.

He knew a Tamil boy who could tell us by writing down where the stolen stuff was. 'Write?' 'Yes, write, not speak.' All we then needed to do was to go and get it from where we had been told to.

The idea was certainly a novel one and was worth a try. It would be interesting to see the boy in action. Against my inner conviction I agreed.

On Sunday evening the waiter led the Tamil boy into the Mess, with an elder man in train. The boy was nervous as if unsure of himself – I could not blame him – and sat cross-legged on the floor with a writing pad on his lap and a pencil in his hand. His companion sat in front of him and, crooning softly, put him into a trance. We three Para Company officers understood not a word but we looked on with great interest and not a little skepticism.

Motionless to start with, a while later the boy's hand went to the writing pad and he started making meaningless lines. I was too far away to see anything in detail but near enough to know that there was no inspired writing there. But had I really expected there to be? The boy's hand started kinking, making patterns. By the time he had reached the bottom of the page he was in stress, weaving backwards and forwards, sweating and moaning softly. His mentor then took him out of his trance and led him away for a cold drink before taking him back to wherever he had come from.

The Mess waiter showed me the piece of paper but I could make nothing out of it. I was disappointed even though I had expected nothing. But the waiter was excitedly telling me that, among the kinks and squiggles, there indeed was a message, written in Tamil. 'Under the bed, in the room.'

We three officers went back to our rooms, looked under the mattress and felt under the bottom sheet. Nothing. How could there be?

As I told Dhanman about this next morning his eyes lit up. 'Sahib, let's have a kit check. Maybe it will be under a soldier's bed in his kit box.'

And, just as the Tamil boy had told us, the wooden box under the bed of one of the batmen contained all the officer's stolen kit and all that he had lifted from the soldiers.

I asked him to explain himself. His answer still intrigues me: 'My father was a thief. Do you expect his son to be any different?'

Kinky!

III. Links

During the war my parents decided to give a pair of gold cuff-links to my elder brother who was killed before they were ready. Accordingly it was decided that one link of each pair would have his initials engraved and, the other, with mine – a twenty-first birthday present.

Four years later, on my first leave, I was given them with due solemnity and told not to lose them. I went back to Malaya and, a year later, decided to buy a shirt that needed links, not buttons. The first time I wore the links there was a power failure and I had to get undressed in the dark. I took them out of the cuffs, carefully put them on the chest-of-drawers and wondered to myself – but why? – what I'd do if, on the morrow, one was not there. Telling myself not to be stupid, I got into bed, went to sleep and, next morning, one of the pair was not there. I cursed myself for ever wondering that one might be missing. I had the room completely searched and found nothing so, in case I was killed and my heavy kit went back home without them, I went to Singapore and had another made to match. Now I had a pair.

A year later I dared to wear them again. By then I was in Singapore and I felt any Malayan jinx (I had been living in a one-time lunatic asylum whose inmates the Japanese had either let loose or killed off) would have been left behind. I took them off, in the light, put them on the top of the chest-of-drawers, turned the light out and, knowing they were safe and willing them to be there in the morning, got into bed . . . but next morning only one was there. I had the room completely searched with no result. I went back to the same Chinese goldsmith for a replica lest these links be missing from my heavy kit were the worst to happen to me. I had another one made to have a pair.

Another year elapsed before I dared wear them again. On taking off my shirt I hung it up, having felt and seen the two pairs of links still in the cuffs. I got into bed, turned off the light and, some time later I got up in the dark and felt if both links were there. Yes. Third time lucky? I mused as I went to sleep. But no. Come the morning, one was missing.

When I asked the goldsmith for yet another singleton he looked at me enquiringly but said nothing. Had he been an Englishman rather than a Chinese I could have expected a crack about 'the missing link'. I vowed never to wear them again.

A year or so later I went on home leave. 'Shall I tell you something about those cuff-links you gave me as a present?' I asked my mother, father having died by then. 'What cuff-links?' she answered, having forgotten all about them.

Over fifty years later I still have them, still unused

[1998]

↫ 29 ↬

How Children Happen to Help

'There is always one moment in childhood when the door opens and lets the future in.'

The Power and the Glory, Graham Greene (1940),

Part 1, Chapter 1.

Three times I have come across currents in history, whose headwaters rose in the dark and convoluted past, unexpectedly and irrevocably changed by chance reactions of children.

The first happened in Rangoon, of all unlikely places: in 1951 I was OC Troops, taking a leave party to Calcutta.

On the third day there I was sent for by the Purser. Three Nepalis, one man, somewhere in his thirties, chubby-cheeked with an incipient pot belly, and two ladies had come to see me. The man gave me a long, lingering, quizzical look as I gave him a namasté. 'Welcome on board, Hajur. I am the Officer Commanding the Gurkha troops and their families going on leave to Nepal. What can I do for you?' I asked.

'Oh, you speak our language,' he replied, looking pleasantly surprised as the ladies also cooed their appreciation. 'We had heard about the Nepalese citizens on board and would like to meet them.'

'Please may I know who you are?'

'I am the Nepalese Vice Consul in Burma and the two ladies are my wife and the Consul's wife.'

258

'I will lead you first around the deck so that you can meet the single men then go to the cabins and meet the families. Before that I must make an announcement to that effect.' I turned to the Purser. 'Please let me use your broadcast system.'

Off we went. I had expected some conversational initiative to be shown by the Vice Consul but no, he only spoke to a few men in general terms, not specifics, as if he were trying to make his mind up about something. Mostly he stared speculatively at them: for their part, the soldiers looked away after making initial eye contact. I felt something was unusual, if not wrong.

Down a deck in the cabins the two lady visitors tried to make conversation with the wives and embrace the children. The wives showed deference but no interest and the two ladies were astonished to see some of the little ones run to me and grab me round a knee, looking up and smiling, obviously happier with me than with them.

Long before every cabin had been visited, the Vice Consul glanced at this wrist watch and said, 'Captain sahib. That's enough, thank you. I have seen all I need to. Will you please come back with us to the Consulate?'

I went with him. I saw a metal archway with a notice '66 Transit Camp' hanging from it and, under that another smaller notice hung, 'Nepal Consulate'. I recognised the place from the end of the war.

The car drew up outside what had been the Officers' Mess. I stood in the hot sun while the car was locked up. The ladies disappeared. I was led into a room where there were rattan chairs and a small rattan table beside each one. He left me to myself and returned with an elder, puffier man, wearing thick glasses, who proffered his hand. 'I am the Consul. You are welcome.'

The Consul gave me the same sort of look that his underling had given the men on board. 'Sit down and I will give you a drink.'

259

A bottle of whisky was produced and my glass was filled half full before some soda water was added. I intuited that the two Nepalis were out to learn something and the looser my tongue, the more forthcoming would I be. 'Cheers!'

Boring small talk ensued. I steadfastly refused to alter the pace or the amount of what I drank.

'Captain sahib,' the Consul said. 'What you said on arrival here surprised me and, I fear, disturbed me.'

'Oh? Consul sahib. I am sorry if I said the wrong thing. You are the first Consul I have spoken to.'

The two Nepalis glanced at one another and the junior gave a slight nod.

'You said "leave party".'

'I did.'

'From one battalion?'

'No, from all eight battalions plus from the Engineers, Signals and Military Police.'

'Are you sure?'

'Yes, Consul sahib. I am as sure of that as I am sure I am sitting here, drinking and talking to you, in Rangoon, Burma and nowhere else.'

'What you told us is not what we have been told.'

Not knowing what they had been told and not knowing how to reply, I said nothing.

'We have had a letter from Kathmandu, secret I'll have you know, telling us that this boatload of Nepalese soldiers, Gurkhas from the British Army, were a battalion that mutinied so was immediately disbanded and sent back to Nepal as civilians.'

'Utter and unadulterated nonsense, Consul sahib, I can assure you of that. Which battalion were you told had mutinied?'

The Consul went to get the message. 'A rifle company of 1/7 Gurkha Rifles, at Kota Bharu.'

'No Gurkha troops have ever been sent to the north-eastern corner of Malaya, Hajur. Only Malay Regiment battalions ever operate there. That I know as a fact.'

The Consul gave me a beady look. 'My information says that the unit was A Company, 1/7 Gurkha Rifles mutinied and the whole battalion was instantly disbanded on orders from the British Government.'

'Yes, sorry, last month A Company was unexpectedly ordered to go to Kota Bharu to oversee a three-week operation and had come back just before I embarked. Nothing was out of place.'

'The Captain sahib must be correct, Consul-ji,' interpolated his subordinate. 'Going round the men on deck and meeting the families in the cabins there was no disrespect whatever shown to Cross sahib here, just the opposite. The few people I did make a remark to in no way showed anything but normality. There was no look of mutiny on any soldier's face. The women, who might have unwittingly said something to the ladies to give them a clue that the battalion was in disgrace and that they were going home before they were due, were also quite normal. In other words, everything seemed to be perfectly natural.'

The Consul turned to me. 'That is a relief to me. I don't like the idea of Nepalis misbehaving in foreign countries where they should be our unofficial ambassadors and blackening our country's name. In fact, we were ordered not to go to visit you, not to make any contact at all.'

'May I make a suggestion?'

'Indeed. Let's hear it.'

'When I get back to Singapore I'll ask the producers of our Gurkhas' newspaper, *Parbaté*, to include you on their distribution list. In that way you will know what is happening and will not be disturbed by such appalling rumours.'

And that is what happened. The central plot of trying to defame Gurkhas coincided with the terrorists being defeated in Malaya. Troops were also spuriously required in Sarawak and jute mill coolies tried to coerce leave men, when in Barrackpore transit camp from returning from leave

None of that would ever have come to light but for those little children.

❧   ❧

The second time children were concerned was when I was living nearby an aboriginal ladang on the Kelantan side of the main 'divide' of Peninsular Malaysia, in 1963, where I realised that getting through to recalcitrant, fearful and primitive adults was by getting their inquisitive children fascinated with 'tricks'. As my face grew tired by contortions with trying to win them over, I mentally dismissed sniggering and sneering peers' reactions were they to witness what I was trying to do and likewise exorcised the souls of Commanding Officers past and present as I tried to see myself as they would have seen me. But successful I was: only after I found myself asked to live in the aborigines' houses as their children had asked their parents did I get firm and accurate reports of guerrilla movements. The Temiar aborigines held the keys to the whereabouts of the last of the rump of terrorists who would come down to visit them from the Thai border – and had been looked up to ever since Spencer Chapman's time avoiding the Japanese some score of years previously I had succeeded in winning them over for firm and accurate information.

❧   ❧

The third time occurred in Borneo when I was Commandant of the Border Scouts (which involved my simultaneously being a lieutenant colonel in two armies and a superintendent in three police forces with each entity thinking one of the others was paying me when, for ten months, none did), in 1964. The Border Scouts had disintegrated after a savage Indonesian attack at Long Jawi and the Resident of the Third Division, a pompous man allergic to common sense, had told me that he, not I, would publicise the requirement for thirty new recruits and that his putting it out over Radio Sarawak and by word of mouth would produce the desired results. I travelled to Belaga with two junior officers of the local administration as representatives of the Resident to welcome and recruit them. In the event no one turned up.

I suggested going upstream to Long Linau, where the headman, an influential person, might help us in our quest. Certainly we could achieve nothing by staying where we were. Two and a half hours after starting out, we arrived. It was mid-afternoon. We met the headman and the local councillor, who made us comfortable. That meant we were given a mat to sit on, which was just as hard as was the wooden floor. They retired to one end of the longhouse and left us at the other end, in splendid isolation. The two administrators decided to go fishing and left me on my own. On looking around I felt that there was a glass curtain between me and the inmates, distorting, clouding and colouring what they saw, so making normal contact difficult, if not impossible. Our quest seemed even more remote and as useless as the Resident's efforts.

To pass the time I went to the river for a wash, but the water was muddy, so I didn't bother and returned, feeling stale. I went back to my mat and sat down, completely ignored. I glanced up and saw the children, who had also been gathered with the others at the other end of the longhouse so that they should have nothing to do with men representing Government and unhappiness, who had so unexpectedly arrived to spoil their peace yet again. I wobbled my eyebrows independently of each other and was seen by one youngster. For the next hour I carried on a one-man cabaret show, by which time, face aching, I was festooned with children and the womenfolk were halfway between me and their menfolk, still unconvinced and glowering balefully at me from the other end of the longhouse. I could see how the women tattoo their arms so that they look like lace gloves, as indeed do they also from the knees upwards towards their thighs but, from that range, exactly how far up I could not be sure.

Another half hour passed. By then it was dark outside and the men had moved up and joined the women who, by then, were all around me. Serious talk started after that: what, exactly, did I want? Thirty men, I said. Before long I was promised thirty men and, in the event, twenty-nine did turn up.

⟤ 30 ⟤

VC, GC and PVC Reunion

On 5 February 1994 there was a grand reunion – a Felicitation Ceremony, as it was billed – for all holders of the Victoria Cross (VC) and the Indian Army equivalent, Param Vir Chakra (PVC), in the Royal Nepal Academy. This may not sound much but it was the very first time that such an event had been staged on Nepalese soil. It will also be the last of its kind. It was organised by the ex-servicemen of both armies, chiefly the British.

I was asked to be a Special Adviser. Initially I was not particularly interested in the scheme as, when it was announced, it had a marked ethnic bias pro the Mongoloid hill men – who are Gurkhas? was to be publicly debated and would have been quashed – as well as the absurd question of Palace pays Palace 'hidden royalties'. I had to put the record straight on both points, especially the latter. Here I requoted authentic denials that I had had published in Kathmandu in a university journal the previous year as well tell the organisers that the origin of the 'royalty' rumour must only have come from the fact that the currency crisis at the end of the war resulted in a grave loss of personal savings for returning soldiers. This I had learnt from my visit to Kathmandu in 1947.

It must have been my initial disquiet about the whole exercise that prevented my asking about the one remaining holder of the George Cross (GC), Nandalal Thapa of 2/8 GR, who was awarded the Empire Gallantry Medal after the Quetta Earthquake of 1934.

I had produced him for the Prince of Wales on 10 December 1980 when the latter visited us at Pokhara – as Colonel-in-Chief of 2 GR – explaining how EGM holders were given the option of keeping the EGM or changing it into a GC. I further explained that Nandalal had rescued ten survivors. The old man, chair bound, then told the Prince that he had, in fact, rescued twelve but that the company commander had only put ten in the citation.

The Prince turned to me and said, 'Poor old man, still worrying about it nearly fifty years later.'

I rang up the committee and told them that, as there had been no mention of the two Gurkha GCs to date, they simply had to be included in the souvenir brochure when that was produced. I was told that both were dead, relatives had not been traced but, yes, mention would be made of them.

There were more holders present this time than there were for the Queen and the Duke on 20 February 1986 in the British embassy. Then there were five, now there were seven, with Lachhuman Gurung and Gaje Ghale were also present. The one holder of the PVC was Lt Col Dhansing Thapa, 1/8 GR. It was during the 1962 Chinese war and he personally took the brunt of the first Chinese attack at Srijap 1 post, on the north bank of Panggong Lake, Aksai Chin, on 21 October 1962, and was the only one of that post who remained alive. He was taken by the Chinese and, reported dead, spent six months in Sinkiang. His widow was presented with her late husband's posthumous award [I can't remember hearing of any Gorkha (Indian Army spelling) being awarded the honour non-posthumously although there may be some] and when the Chinese let him go back to India, he did come back, they had to remarry.

There was also the oldest surviving soldier, Rfm Dhané Thapa, 2/3 GR – when Sir Ralph Turner was adjutant – now 108 years old. He would have been 28 years old in 1914. Three dead holders, Lalbahadur Thapa, Netrabahadur Thapa and Karnabahadur Rana (who won his award in April 1918) had relations there to represent them and they were on stage with the others. Subedar Lalbahadur's grandson, an ex-sergeant of 2 or 6 GR, was also on stage. He wore Western dress and a civilian jungle hat that he kept on his head at all times. I somehow thought he would have allowed himself to 'look more the part', so to speak.

No trace could be found of the families of the remaining three holders of the award who thereby remained unrepresented. A mischievous thought did strike me: those being 'felicitated' were all billed as Nepalis of Nepal, so the casual observer would have surmised but, in fact, this was not the case as Ganju Lama is a Sikkimese national and, so I gather, always has been, while Gaje Ghale has become an Indian national. On the other hand, no one could think of leaving either out.

In 1986 we had all thought that that was the last time we would ever see such a show as five VC holders together in one place. Never seldom happens and, when it does, it lasts a long time! Then I described it as a heart-throbbing, blood-tingling and tear-jerking occasion. Apart from Portugal, England's oldest ally, Nepal is the only non-Commonwealth country to be visited twice by a reigning British monarch. As the royal couple drove through the town, some of the elder women on the pavement wept with emotion, while two young Limbus walked all the way from the east as they had heard that the Queen herself had come to do the recruiting as more than the usual amount of men were needed, so who better to carry out the task?

This time the chief guest was the Prime Minister and Defence Minister, Girijaprasad Koirala. After the welcome address we stood for a minute's silence as homage to known and unknown Gurkha dead. There were messages from HM the Queen and HM the Queen Mother (in connection with the VC and GC Association), the President of India, the King of Nepal, the heads of the British,

Indian and Nepal Armies, the Inspector-General of Police and others such as the Gurkha Reserve Unit in Brunei. These were read out by one of Ganju Lama's daughters. The Prime Minister played his part with considerable aplomb and earned bonus points. His speech was a good one and it was relayed on Nepal TV.

It was a most moving ceremony and I had tears in my eyes and a lump in my throat more than once. After the Felicitation Ceremony was over and gifts of money had been made, notice was given about a memorial to the holders of the VC and PVC to be established in Nepal. I believe it will be in the nature of a museum based on a bravery theme.

When it was over there was a break. The VIPs left before a well-executed cultural show was presented, hosted by the two most popular male singers in the kingdom, with the youngest dancer 100 years younger than the oldest guest! What a time span. At the end of that all those holders of the VC who could stand unaided went onto the stage and 'danced'. Buddhiman and I did not go to the evening meal as it was late by then and in the opposite direction from where we have our digs. Evening transport is not easy to get hold of. On the morrow, the Sunday, there was a full-blown meal midday to which I had been invited. I would have liked to have gone to meet so many of my old friends – the previous day was too crowded and concentrated for a 'good old' gup – but I called it off as on the Monday there was a by-election in Kathmandu. During such times there is no telling what will happen and we feared that the roads would be blocked so preventing our timely return to Pokhara.

. . . And Finally

So, My Best Beloved, as the best of all authors on matters Indian had it, how to finish off a book such as this? After much thought, I have decided to tell you about a visit to my first ever Gurkha unit, to celebrate its 175th anniversary of the raising in 1990:

Early that year I had been asked to go to Puné (Poona) for the 175th raising of the First Battalion, 1st Gorkha Rifles (1/1 GR), by the Commanding Officer, Lt Col N M Daniels, from 22 to 25 April 1990. We had become friendly when he was in charge of the Indian Embassy Pension Paying Office in Pokhara, Nepal, where I live. The battalion made the rail bookings for us and a reception party was at Gorakhpur railway station to arrange the onward journey of those travelling from west Nepal. Even before that I had received a message of welcome from Major General R P Singh, the Colonel of the Regiment, and from the Subedar Major, Bijay Bahadur Thapa.

Buddhiman and I travelled down from Pokhara to Gorakhpur by bus with a group of ex-Junior Commissioned Officers (Viceroy's Commissioned Officers when I joined the regiment in 1944) and their families. Two and a half days later we arrived in Puné, later than scheduled by thirteen hours because the train had been stopped on the way up and the engine driver killed. A reception committee of smartly dressed Gorkhas was on the platform to welcome us and a large banner told the world and his wife (had they been interested) that this was the 175th anniversary welcoming committee for 1/1 GR. It was a blessing to be in the capable hands of an organised body of dedicated men. Cold water in glasses on a napkinned salver was offered to us by a smiling soldier and I knew I had arrived back in the battalion I had as a first military love. I was given a chair (the last thing I wanted) and invited to sit down, asked how the journey was and had sympathetic tutting at our lateness and the uncomfortably hot conditions we had had to experience. Puné is well over 1,000 feet above sea level and it was not quite so hot there as it had been for the past three days.

Buddhiman and I were then given a jeep to ourselves and driven to the battalion, a few miles outside the town. I had been told that guests would be put up in a hotel but I was delighted to see we had a double room in the Officers' Mess. It was 1947 all over again: the same uneven floor, the same lumpy mattress, the same cups and teapots, the same basin with the water going down the plug hole onto the floor and splashing onto the feet of the user, the same noisy fan, the same brown mosquito nets, the same off-white ceiling and the same smiling face of a Gorkha batman who welcomed us warmly yet shyly, showing us clean towels and new cake of soap and suggesting we have a shower and put on clean clothes while he would take our dirty stuff to be laundered there and then. Only the thunderbox was not there; instead was a flush toilet that had more off moments than on! Neither of us needed any second invitation and bathed while tea was brought.

I was still in my underpants when the Commanding Officer and the Subedar Major came to see if we were all right. He apologised for the sparse accommodation but I told him, with complete sincerity, that I really could not be happier. The CO told me that no one was coming from Britain and that he had had very nice letters from two who had been invited but could not attend, both of which were much appreciated. That meant I was the only Briton there.

That afternoon, after lunch in the Mess, we went for a walk around the lines (built in the early 1900s and last occupied some years ago so everywhere there is a dilapidated atmosphere). We soon met some Old and Bold from my time and the joy of reunion was wonderful. I remembered the numbers of men I had not seen for thirty-one years since I went to Dharamsala in 1959 on a fleeting leave and some since I left the battalion in 1947. I learnt who had died, who were ill and who were fit but could not attend. News of British officers I could tell them about was of great interest.

Monday 23rd April at 8 o'clock, dressed in thin black suits and I wearing miniatures, saw Buddhiman and me at the temple for a Hindu service for the auspicious occasion. My presence and my dress were of interest to the soldiers gathered there to pray and the man I sat next to, a retired battalion pundit, was the nephew of the civil schoolmaster man who had taught me how to read and write Nepali up in Razmak, now in Pakistan, in 1946. That over we traipsed across to the sports field where the CO gave a short speech of welcome and the Colonel of the Regiment was invited to inspect a Guard of Honour which was followed by a march past of that and the pipes and drums. Turn out and drill were immaculate.

That evening saw the final of the inter-company football competition, a band display and retreat. As I listened to the band, which had a horn-type instrument playing an echo to a flank, I was transported back to Razmak where I had last heard such a rendering; a specialty in those far-off days. I also remembered that the Brass band of 1 GR was the first one ever to play on All India Radio. In the fading gloom of evening, the strong young men dressed so smartly seemed no different from then and I asked myself was I the only one who had grown old as the bitter-sweet mixture of memory and magic gripped me. It was all very moving.

Their drill was slightly changed but, although it might have offended a purist, I liked it. Later I got the chance to tell them all how much I appreciated their performance.

An anniversary Mess Night for serving officers, visiting ex-officers, wives and children followed. We assembled on the Mess lawn, some sitting and others making the rounds, hospitality and friendship ever to the fore. Some time afterwards we were called inside to witness the unveiling of something special. A most handsome and expensive silver centre piece had been wrapped up and placed on a table with some dark cloth hiding it until it was cut open by the Colonel of the Regiment. Set on a wooden plinth, the piece consisted of a pair of Gorkha hands holding a globe with the figure of a Gorkha soldier, brandishing a kukri, atop. The significance of the globe was that its safety had been and still was in Gorkha hands as they had fought and served virtually everywhere in their 175 years' history. On one side of the plinth were the names of the officers who had subscribed to the piece, on the second a map of where the battalion had served, on the third a short history and outline map of the Sri Lankan campaign along with the Roll of Honour and those awarded gallantry awards and on the fourth a display of the regiment's battle honours. Those of us who had come from afar were, one by one, called forward and given a present: a small plaque on which the centre piece was outlined and a box with something inside, which turned to be a bowl to put food in and that had the regimental badge and an inscription; '1/1 GR – 175th anniversary of raising'. Major Mehta, the battalion Second-in-Command, made an excellent master of ceremonies as he wittily called us forward one by one. I had had to fill in a tedious form to get permission to visit a military unit. In it I was asked to say if I was married or not. My answer was that I had nearly been married four or five times but I was not really sure how many. This was wittily and gently mentioned, to much laughter, when my turn came for my present.

Day 2 started at 9 am, with a 'durbar'. There was a raised platform on which were easy chairs. In front of the platform were serried ranks of serving soldiers squatting on the floor and, on chairs behind them, the ex-servicemen who had come from Nepal and India, chiefly from Dharmsala. On one side were many ex-Indian officer guests. I suppose there were 300 or more souls there. I was told to sit up on the platform and chatted with ex-brigadiers and ex-colonels till the Colonel of the Regiment arrived with the Commanding Officer. An air of expectancy was obvious when the Colonel of the Regiment went to the rostrum and addressed the audience. He went out of his way to laud the battalion for its performance in Sri Lanka and, from all reports, I gather that not only was 1/1 GR the best battalion in that campaign but is thought by the top brass to be about the best battalion in the Indian Army. The oldest representative present, Brigadier Inder Sethi, enlisted in 1 GR in 1943 and who was a Havildar clerk when I joined, followed and talked of how well the battalion had done in previous campaigns.

It was then my turn and I detected an added expectancy. I later learnt that some of the audience did not know that I spoke Nepali and thought I would talk in English. I started off by thanking the battalion for the invitation and how proud I was to be there, then said I represented those British officers who could not be with us that day and I made a special point of giving them the name of the last English Commanding Officer, a well-loved person. My theme was the family aspect of the battalion and quoted an ex-1/1 GR soldier in Pokhara who had come up to me the previous year to tell me that we had served together over forty years before, how I asked him his number and got his name correctly but that he had not shown any surprise at my remembering it as we were all part of the family and therefore names should be known. I went on to talk about the two men who had been in Dharmsala when I got there in 1944 and who wore the Tirah campaign medal of 1897; one had enlisted in 1892 and the other in 1891. Now it was 1990 and I was the link of ninety-nine years of battalion history. I told a story of how the British officers and men were at the time I got to Dharmsala and a few more aspects of life before finishing off with an old Nepalese prayer for the enhancement of the battalion and all those in it. The last speaker was the previous Subedar Major.

I had been warned that the press wanted to interview me at some juncture and it was during this session that I was hauled in front of eight reporters and interviewed, but I was a bit taken aback when one of them asked me to sing a Nepali song. This I did, adding to the cacophony of other songs and musical instruments around the place. In the railway compartment on the way back I borrowed a newspaper and found an account of the anniversary celebrations, a bit about my connection with Nepal and the battalion, including my photo! The last time an Indian newspaper made any mention of me was back in 1946, at Nagpur, when I played football 'like a tiger'!

Day 3 was a quieter day, starting off with a welfare-type meeting with the ex-servicemen. A sewing-machine was presented to two widows of men killed in Sri Lanka, each of the wounded received a plaque (with the motif of the new presentation piece thereon) and blankets were distributed. I was honoured to be asked to help in this. The oldest ex-service soldier there had joined in 1943, had been an ace footballer but now could hardly move: the burden of old age only too apparent. It was then the turn of what was billed as 'Fun and Frolic' and some very nice articles, mostly with the 175th anniversary motif on them, were for sale. It was during this that I was able to talk to many soldiers, many of whom asked questions about Nepal, and who also told me where they lived, whom we knew in common and if we had met before.

The last engagement was another regimental party in the Mess, this time with guests including all the brass from the many military units in Puné. Once again I was forcibly struck by the friendliness of all and the younger officers made sure that I was introduced to those I did not know. Mess etiquette and good manners were ever-present and, dare I say it? of a higher standard than in the modern British Army. We bade a most fond farewell to Colonel Daniels as we left for yet another midnight bedtime with most of the guests still dancing.

To finish off I quote part of my letter of thanks to Colonel Daniels:

> It is thirty-seven years since I served with the battalion and thirty-one since I last visited it. After I left in 1947 I vowed that I would never again become so involved with any group of people that it made me weep when I had to pull my roots up, so proud and happy was I in the battalion – I have never been able to keep that vow! On my visit to the battalion in Bhagsu [Dharmsala] in 1959 I was back where I had belonged and where I had started. Now, many years later, the three and a half days during which I was privileged to be amongst you were the highlight of a lifetime and a return home once more. Most humbly, most sincerely and most happily do I thank you, all your officers, all your soldiers and all the many visitors (ex-service and otherwise) for spreading their kindness and fellowship in a most wonderful way. To say that Buddhiman and I were overwhelmed with kindness is neither an understatement nor an exaggeration, but the simple truth.
>
> All the arrangements were perfect and it must have taken many months' hard work and planning to achieve such excellence. It would be wrong to single out any particular

aspect of the whole but it would be equally wrong not to mention the help that Subedar Purna Bahadur and his team gave us from Gorakhpur onwards. What wonderfully safe hands to be in. I must congratulate you all and I can truthfully say that I have NEVER seen better anywhere; it would also surprise me if any other unit in any other army could have done as well. The hospitality and kindnesses shown by high and humble to Buddhiman and me were constant, overwhelming and everywhere. The light emanating from the soldiers' faces, the sparkle in their eyes, their meticulous turnout, their very Gorkha-ness were all something that I, an outsider yet part of the family, was most struck by; you, as Commanding Officer, must not only be very pleased and proud of such men but also very glad to have them as a superb military machine in which you can have complete trust – and who are on your side!

Buddhiman and I were wondering how we could, in some small way, show our appreciation and express our thanks to you all for such a wonderful time. We have come to the conclusion that our answer is that our doors will be ever open for whomsoever of the battalion if he or his family were to visit us here in Pokhara.

The Old and Bold of yesteryear would be very proud to have had the same wonderful privilege as was vouchsafed to me. Such an experience seldom falls more than once a lifetime.

Bless you all and Jay Hari.

Other Books by J. P. Cross

English for Gurkha Soldiers (1955, 1957, 1962)
Gurkha - The Legendary Soldier (1966), text only, in English and Roman Nepali.
Gurkhas (1985), text only.
In Gurkha Company, The British Army Gurkhas, 1948 to the Present [31.12.82] (1986).
Jungle Warfare, Experiences and Encounters (1986 1992, 2007, 2009)
Gurkhas at War: The Gurkha Experience in their Own Words: World War II to the Present (2002, 2007).
Whatabouts and Whereabouts in Asia (2002).

Autobiographical Trilogy

First In, Last Out, An Unconventional British Officer in Indo-China (1945–46 and 1972–76) (1992, 2007).
The Call of Nepal, A Personal Nepalese Odyssey in a Different Dimension (1996, 1998, 2009).
'A Face Like A Chicken's Backside': An Unconventional Soldier in South-East Asia, 1948-1971 (1996, 2003).

Historical Novels

The Throne of Stone 1479–1559 (2000).
The Restless Quest: Britain and Nepal on Collision Course and The Start of the British–Gurkha Connection 1746–1815 (2004, 2010).

The Crown of Renown: Gurkhas in Nepal and the East India Company, 1819–1857/8 (2009 and 2010).
The Fame of the Name: Gurkhas Civil and in the Indian Army, 1857–1947 (2011).
The Age of Rage: Gurkha, Gorkhas, Nepal and Communism: Cure or Curse? 1947–2008 (awaiting publication).